Praise for *Cloud Native DevOps with Kubernetes*

Cloud Native DevOps is an essential guide to operating today's distributed systems. A super clear and informative read, covering all the details without compromising readability. I learned a lot, and definitely have some action points to take away!

—*Will Thames, Platform Engineer, Skedulo*

The most encompassing, definitive, and practical text about the care and feeding of Kubernetes infrastructure. An absolute must-have.

—*Jeremy Yates, SRE Team, The Home Depot QuoteCenter*

I wish I'd had this book when I started! This is a must-read for everyone developing and running applications in Kubernetes.

—*Paul van der Linden, Lead Developer,
vdL Software Consultancy*

This book got me really excited. It's a goldmine of information for anyone looking to use Kubernetes, and I feel like I've levelled up!

—*Adam McPartlan (@mcparty), Senior Systems Engineer,
NYnet*

I really enjoyed reading this book. It's very informal in style, but authoritative at the same time. It contains lots of great practical advice. Exactly the sort of information that everybody wants to know, but doesn't know how to get, other than through first-hand experience.

—*Nigel Brown, cloud native trainer and course author*

Cloud Native DevOps with Kubernetes

Building, Deploying, and Scaling
Modern Applications in the Cloud

John Arundel and Justin Domingus

Beijing · Boston · Farnham · Sebastopol · Tokyo

Cloud Native DevOps with Kubernetes

by John Arundel and Justin Domingus

Printed in the United States of America.

Published by O'Reilly Media, Inc., 1005 Gravenstein Highway North, Sebastopol, CA 95472.

O'Reilly books may be purchased for educational, business, or sales promotional use. Online editions are also available for most titles (*http://oreilly.com*). For more information, contact our corporate/institutional sales department: 800-998-9938 or *corporate@oreilly.com*.

Acquisitions Editor: Rachel Roumeliotis   **Developmental Editors:** Virginia Wilson and Nikki McDonald
Production Editor: Nan Barber   **Copyeditor:** Kim Cofer
Proofreader: Amanda Kersey   **Indexer:** Judith McConville
Interior Designer: David Futato   **Cover Designer:** Karen Montgomery
Illustrator: Rebecca Demarest

February 2019:   First Edition

Revision History for the First Edition
2019-01-24:   First Release
2019-03-08:   Second Release
2020-07-31:   Third Release

See *http://oreilly.com/catalog/errata.csp?isbn=9781492040767* for release details.

This work is part of a collaboration between O'Reilly and NGINX. See our statement of editorial independence (*http://www.oreilly.com/about/editorial_independence.html*).

978-1-492-04076-7

[LSI]

Table of Contents

Foreword

Welcome to *Cloud Native DevOps with Kubernetes*.

Kubernetes is a real industry revolution. Just a brief look at the Cloud Native Computing Foundation's Landscape (*https://landscape.cncf.io/*), which contains data about more than 600 projects that exist in the cloud native world today, highlights the importance of Kubernetes these days. Not all these tools were developed for Kubernetes, not all of them can even be used with Kubernetes, but all of them are part of the huge ecosystem where Kubernetes is one of the flagship technologies.

Kubernetes changed the way applications are developed and operated. It's a core component in the DevOps world today. Kubernetes brings flexibility to developers and freedom to operations. Today you can use Kubernetes on any major cloud provider, on bare-metal on-premises environments, as well as on a local developer's machine. Stability, flexibility, a powerful API, open code, and an open developer community are a few reasons why Kubernetes became an industry standard, just as Linux is a standard in the world of operating systems.

Cloud Native DevOps with Kubernetes is a great handbook for people who are performing their day-to-day activities with Kubernetes or are just starting their Kubernetes journey. John and Justin cover all the major aspects of deploying, configuring, and operating Kubernetes and the best practices for developing and running applications on it. They also give a great overview of the related technologies, including Prometheus, Helm, and continuous deployment. This is a must-read book for everyone in the DevOps world.

Kubernetes is not just yet another exciting tool; it is an industry standard and the foundation for next-generation technologies including serverless (OpenFaaS, Knative) and machine learning (Kubeflow) tools. The entire IT industry is changing because of the cloud native revolution, and it's hugely exciting to be living through it.

— Ihor Dvoretskyi
Developer Advocate, Cloud Native
Computing Foundation
December 2018

Preface

In the world of IT operations, the key principles of DevOps have become well understood and widely adopted, but now the landscape is changing. A new application platform called Kubernetes has become rapidly adopted by companies all over the world and in all kinds of different industries. As more and more applications and businesses move from traditional servers to the Kubernetes environment, people are asking how to do DevOps in this new world.

This book explains what DevOps means in a cloud native world where Kubernetes is the standard platform. It will help you select the best tools and frameworks from the Kubernetes ecosystem. It will also present a coherent way to use those tools and frameworks, offering battle-tested solutions that are running right now, in production, for real.

What Will I Learn?

You'll learn what Kubernetes is, where it comes from, and what it means for the future of software development and operations. You'll learn how containers work, how to build and manage them, and how to design cloud native services and infrastructure.

You'll understand the trade-offs between building and hosting Kubernetes clusters yourself, and using managed services. You'll learn the capabilities, limitations, and pros and cons of popular Kubernetes installation tools such as kops, kubeadm, and Kubespray. You'll get an informed overview of the major managed Kubernetes offerings from the likes of Amazon, Google, and Microsoft.

You'll get hands-on practical experience of writing and deploying Kubernetes applications, configuring and operating Kubernetes clusters, and automating cloud infrastructure and deployments with tools such as Helm. You'll learn about Kubernetes support for security, authentication, and permissions, including Role-Based Access

Control (RBAC), and best practices for securing containers and Kubernetes in production.

You'll learn how to set up continuous integration and deployment with Kubernetes, how to back up and restore data, how to test your cluster for conformance and reliability, how to monitor, trace, log, and aggregate metrics, and how to make your Kubernetes infrastructure scalable, resilient, and cost-effective.

To illustrate all the things we talk about, we apply them to a very simple demo application. You can follow along with all our examples using the code from our Git repo.

Who Is This Book For?

This book is most directly relevant to IT operations staff responsible for servers, applications, and services, and developers responsible for either building new cloud native services, or migrating existing applications to Kubernetes and cloud. We assume no prior knowledge of Kubernetes or containers—don't worry, we'll walk you through all that.

Experienced Kubernetes users should still find much valuable material in the book: it covers advanced topics such as RBAC, continuous deployment, secrets management, and observability. Whatever your level of expertise, we hope you'll find something useful in these pages.

What Questions Does This Book Answer?

In planning and writing this book, we spoke to hundreds of people about cloud native and Kubernetes, ranging from industry leaders and experts to complete beginners. Here are some of the questions they said they wanted a book like this to answer:

- "I'd like to learn why I should invest my time in this technology. What problems will it help to solve for me and my team?"

- "Kubernetes seems great, but it's quite a steep learning curve. Setting up a quick demo is easy, but operating and troubleshooting it seems daunting. We'd like some solid guidance on how people are running Kubernetes clusters in the real world, and what problems we're likely to encounter."

- "Opinionated advice would be useful. The Kubernetes ecosystem has too many options for beginning teams to choose between. When there are multiple ways of doing the same thing, which one is best? How do we choose?"

And perhaps the most important question of all:

- "How do I use Kubernetes without breaking my company?"

We kept these questions, and many others, firmly in mind while writing this book, and we've done our level best to answer them. How did we do? Turn the page to find out.

Conventions Used in This Book

The following typographical conventions are used in this book:

Italic

> Indicates new terms, URLs, email addresses, filenames, and file extensions.

`Constant width`

> Used for program listings, as well as within paragraphs to refer to program elements such as variable or function names, databases, data types, environment variables, statements, and keywords.

`Constant width bold`

> Shows commands or other text that should be typed literally by the user.

`Constant width italic`

> Shows text that should be replaced with user-supplied values or by values determined by context.

This element signifies a tip or suggestion.

This element signifies a general note.

This element indicates a warning or caution.

Using Code Examples

Supplemental material (code examples, exercises, etc.) is available for download at *https://github.com/cloudnativedevops/demo*.

This book is here to help you get your job done. In general, if example code is offered with this book, you may use it in your programs and documentation. You do not need to contact us for permission unless you're reproducing a significant portion of the code. For example, writing a program that uses several chunks of code from this book does not require permission. Selling or distributing a CD-ROM of examples from O'Reilly books does require permission. Answering a question by citing this book and quoting example code does not require permission. Incorporating a significant amount of example code from this book into your product's documentation does require permission.

We appreciate, but do not require, attribution. An attribution usually includes the title, author, publisher, and ISBN. For example: "*Cloud Native DevOps with Kubernetes* by John Arundel and Justin Domingus (O'Reilly). Copyright 2019 John Arundel and Justin Domingus, 978-1-492-04076-7."

If you feel your use of code examples falls outside fair use or the permission given above, feel free to contact us at *permissions@oreilly.com*.

O'Reilly Online Learning Platform

 For almost 40 years, *O'Reilly Media* has provided technology and business training, knowledge, and insight to help companies succeed.

Our unique network of experts and innovators share their knowledge and expertise through books, articles, and our online learning platform. O'Reilly's online learning platform gives you on-demand access to live training courses, in-depth learning paths, interactive coding environments, and a vast collection of text and video from O'Reilly and 200+ other publishers. For more information, please visit *http:// oreilly.com*.

How to Contact Us

Please address comments and questions concerning this book to the publisher:

O'Reilly Media, Inc.
1005 Gravenstein Highway North
Sebastopol, CA 95472
800-998-9938 (in the United States or Canada)
707-829-0515 (international or local)
707-829-0104 (fax)

We have a web page for this book, where we list errata, examples, and any additional information. You can access this page at *http://bit.ly/cloud-nat-dev-ops*.

To comment or ask technical questions about this book, send email to *bookquestions@oreilly.com*.

For news and more information about our books and courses, see our website at *http://www.oreilly.com*.

Find us on Facebook: *http://facebook.com/oreilly*

Follow us on Twitter: *http://twitter.com/oreillymedia*

Watch us on YouTube: *http://www.youtube.com/oreillymedia*

Acknowledgments

Our grateful thanks are due to the many people who read early drafts of this book and gave us invaluable feedback and advice, or assisted us in other ways, including (but not limited to) Abby Bangser, Adam J. McPartlan, Adrienne Domingus, Alexis Richardson, Aron Trauring, Camilla Montonen, Gabriell Nascimento, Hannah Klemme, Hans Findel, Ian Crosby, Ian Shaw, Ihor Dvoretskyi, Ike Devolder, Jeremy Yates, Jérôme Petazzoni, Jessica Deen, John Harris, Jon Barber, Kitty Karate, Marco Lancini, Mark Ellens, Matt North, Michel Blanc, Mitchell Kent, Nicolas Steinmetz, Nigel Brown, Patrik Dudits, Paul van der Linden, Philippe Ensarguet, Pietro Mamberti, Richard Harper, Rick Highness, Sathyajith Bhat, Suresh Vishnoi, Thomas Liakos, Tim McGinnis, Toby Sullivan, Tom Hall, Vincent De Smet, and Will Thames.

CHAPTER 1

Revolution in the Cloud

> There was never a time when the world began, because it goes round and round like a circle, and there is no place on a circle where it begins.
>
> —Alan Watts

There's a revolution going on. Actually, three revolutions.

The first revolution is the creation of the cloud, and we'll explain what that is and why it's important. The second is the dawn of DevOps, and you'll find out what that involves and how it's changing operations. The third revolution is the coming of containers. Together, these three waves of change are creating a new software world: the *cloud native* world. The operating system for this world is called Kubernetes.

In this chapter, we'll briefly recount the history and significance of these revolutions, and explore how the changes are affecting the way we all deploy and operate software. We'll outline what *cloud native* means, and what changes you can expect to see in this new world if you work in software development, operations, deployment, engineering, networking, or security.

Thanks to the effects of these interlinked revolutions, we think the future of computing lies in cloud-based, containerized, distributed systems, dynamically managed by automation, on the Kubernetes platform (or something very like it). The art of developing and running these applications—*cloud native DevOps*—is what we'll explore in the rest of this book.

If you're already familiar with all of this background material, and you just want to start having fun with Kubernetes, feel free to skip ahead to Chapter 2. If not, settle down comfortably, with a cup of your favorite beverage, and we'll begin.

The Creation of the Cloud

In the beginning (well, the 1960s, anyway), computers filled rack after rack in vast, remote, air-conditioned data centers, and users would never see them or interact with them directly. Instead, developers submitted their jobs to the machine remotely and waited for the results. Many hundreds or thousands of users would all share the same computing infrastructure, and each would simply receive a bill for the amount of processor time or resources she used.

It wasn't cost-effective for each company or organization to buy and maintain its own computing hardware, so a business model emerged where users would share the computing power of remote machines, owned and run by a third party.

If that sounds like right now, instead of last century, that's no coincidence. The word *revolution* means "circular movement," and computing has, in a way, come back to where it began. While computers have gotten a lot more powerful over the years— today's Apple Watch is the equivalent of about three of the mainframe computers shown in Figure 1-1—shared, pay-per-use access to computing resources is a very old idea. Now we call it *the cloud*, and the revolution that began with timesharing mainframes has come full circle.

Figure 1-1. Early cloud computer: the IBM System/360 Model 91, at NASA's Goddard Space Flight Center

Buying Time

The central idea of the cloud is this: instead of buying a *computer*, you buy *compute*. That is, instead of sinking large amounts of capital into physical machinery, which is hard to scale, breaks down mechanically, and rapidly becomes obsolete, you simply buy time on someone else's computer, and let them take care of the scaling, maintenance, and upgrading. In the days of bare-metal machines—the "Iron Age", if you like —computing power was a capital expense. Now it's an operating expense, and that has made all the difference.

The cloud is not just about remote, rented computing power. It is also about distributed systems. You may buy raw compute resource (such as a Google Compute instance, or an AWS Lambda function) and use it to run your own software, but increasingly you also rent *cloud services*: essentially, the use of someone else's software. For example, if you use PagerDuty to monitor your systems and alert you when something is down, you're using a cloud service (sometimes called *software as a service*, or SaaS).

Infrastructure as a Service

When you use cloud infrastructure to run your own services, what you're buying is *infrastructure as a service* (IaaS). You don't have to expend capital to purchase it, you don't have to build it, and you don't have to upgrade it. It's just a commodity, like electricity or water. Cloud computing is a revolution in the relationship between businesses and their IT infrastructure.

Outsourcing the hardware is only part of the story; the cloud also allows you to outsource the *software* that you don't write: operating systems, databases, clustering, replication, networking, monitoring, high availability, queue and stream processing, and all the myriad layers of software and configuration that span the gap between your code and the CPU. Managed services can take care of almost all of this *undifferentiated heavy lifting* for you (you'll find out more about the benefits of managed services in Chapter 3).

The revolution in the cloud has also triggered another revolution in the people who use it: the DevOps movement.

The Dawn of DevOps

Before DevOps, developing and operating software were essentially two separate jobs, performed by two different groups of people. *Developers* wrote software, and they passed it on to *operations* staff, who ran and maintained the software *in production* (that is to say, serving real users, instead of merely running under test conditions). Like computers that need their own floor of the building, this separation has its roots in the middle of the last century. Software development was a very specialist job, and so was computer operation, and there was very little overlap between the two.

Indeed, the two departments had quite different goals and incentives, which often conflicted with each other (Figure 1-2). Developers tend to be focused on shipping new features quickly, while operations teams care about making services stable and reliable over the long term.

Figure 1-2. Separate teams can lead to conflicting incentives (photo by Dave Roth)

When the cloud came on the horizon, things changed. Distributed systems are complex, and the internet is very big. The technicalities of operating the system—recovering from failures, handling timeouts, smoothly upgrading versions—are not so easy to separate from the design, architecture, and implementation of the system.

Further, "the system" is no longer just your software: it comprises in-house software, cloud services, network resources, load balancers, monitoring, content distribution networks, firewalls, DNS, and so on. All these things are intimately interconnected and interdependent. The people who write the software have to understand how it relates to the rest of the system, and the people who operate the system have to understand how the software works—or fails.

The origins of the DevOps movement lie in attempts to bring these two groups together: to collaborate, to share understanding, to share responsibility for systems reliability and software correctness, and to improve the scalability of both the software systems and the teams of people who build them.

Nobody Understands DevOps

DevOps has occasionally been a controversial idea, both with people who insist it's nothing more than a modern label for existing good practice in software development, and with those who reject the need for greater collaboration between development and operations.

There is also widespread misunderstanding about what DevOps actually is: A job title? A team? A methodology? A skill set? The influential DevOps writer John Willis has identified four key pillars of DevOps, which he calls culture, automation, measurement, and sharing (CAMS). Another way to break it down is what Brian Dawson has called the DevOps trinity: people and culture, process and practice, and tools and technology.

Some people think that cloud and containers mean that we no longer need DevOps—a point of view sometimes called *NoOps*. The idea is that since all IT operations are outsourced to a cloud provider or another third-party service, businesses don't need full-time operations staff.

The NoOps fallacy is based on a misapprehension of what DevOps work actually involves:

> With DevOps, much of the traditional IT operations work happens before code reaches production. Every release includes monitoring, logging, and A/B testing. CI/CD pipelines automatically run unit tests, security scanners, and policy checks on every commit. Deployments are automatic. Controls, tasks, and non-functional requirements are now implemented before release instead of during the frenzy and aftermath of a critical outage.
>
> —Jordan Bach (AppDynamics (*https://blog.appdynamics.com/engineering/is-noops-the-end-of-devops-think-again/*))

The most important thing to understand about DevOps is that it is primarily an organizational, human issue, not a technical one. This accords with Jerry Weinberg's *Second Law of Consulting*:

> No matter how it looks at first, it's always a people problem.
>
> —Gerald M. Weinberg, *Secrets of Consulting*

The Business Advantage

From a business point of view, DevOps has been described as "improving the quality of your software by speeding up release cycles with cloud automation and practices, with the added benefit of software that actually stays up in production" (The Register (*https://www.theregister.co.uk/2018/03/06/what_does_devops_do_to_decades_old_planning_processes_and_assumptions*)).

Adopting DevOps requires a profound cultural transformation for businesses, which needs to start at the executive, strategic level, and propagate gradually to every part of the organization. Speed, agility, collaboration, automation, and software quality are key goals of DevOps, and for many companies that means a major shift in mindset.

But DevOps works, and studies regularly suggest that companies that adopt DevOps principles release better software faster, react better and faster to failures and problems, are more agile in the marketplace, and dramatically improve the quality of their products:

> DevOps is not a fad; rather it is the way successful organizations are industrializing the delivery of quality software today and will be the new baseline tomorrow and for years to come.
>
> —Brian Dawson (Cloudbees), Computer Business Review (*https://www.cbron line.com/enterprise-it/applications/devops-fad-stay*)

Infrastructure as Code

Once upon a time, developers dealt with software, while operations teams dealt with hardware and the operating systems that run on that hardware.

Now that hardware is in the cloud, everything, in a sense, is software. The DevOps movement brings software development skills to operations: tools and workflows for rapid, agile, collaborative building of complex systems. Inextricably entwined with DevOps is the notion of *infrastructure as code*.

Instead of physically racking and cabling computers and switches, cloud infrastructure can be automatically provisioned by software. Instead of manually deploying and upgrading hardware, operations engineers have become the people who write the software that automates the cloud.

The traffic isn't just one-way. Developers are learning from operations teams how to anticipate the failures and problems inherent in distributed, cloud-based systems, how to mitigate their consequences, and how to design software that degrades gracefully and fails safe.

Learning Together

Both development teams and operations teams are also learning how to work together. They're learning how to design and build systems, how to monitor and get feedback on systems in production, and how to use that information to improve the systems. Even more importantly, they're learning to improve the experience for their users, and to deliver better value for the business that funds them.

The massive scale of the cloud and the collaborative, code-centric nature of the DevOps movement have turned operations into a software problem. At the same time, they have also turned software into an operations problem, all of which raises these questions:

- How do you deploy and upgrade software across large, diverse networks of different server architectures and operating systems?
- How do you deploy to distributed environments, in a reliable and reproducible way, using largely standardized components?

Enter the third revolution: the container.

The Coming of Containers

To deploy a piece of software, you need not only the software itself, but its *dependencies*. That means libraries, interpreters, subpackages, compilers, extensions, and so on.

You also need its *configuration*. Settings, site-specific details, license keys, database passwords: everything that turns raw software into a usable service.

The State of the Art

Earlier attempts to solve this problem include using *configuration management* systems, such as Puppet or Ansible, which consist of code to install, run, configure, and update the shipping software.

Alternatively, some languages provide their own packaging mechanism, like Java's JAR files, or Python's eggs, or Ruby's gems. However, these are language-specific, and don't entirely solve the dependency problem: you still need a Java runtime installed before you can run a JAR file, for example.

Another solution is the *omnibus package*, which, as the name suggests, attempts to cram everything the application needs inside a single file. An omnibus package contains the software, its configuration, its dependent software components, *their* configuration, *their* dependencies, and so on. (For example, a Java omnibus package would contain the Java runtime as well as all the JAR files for the application.)

Some vendors have even gone a step further and included the entire computer system required to run it, as a *virtual machine image*, but these are large and unwieldy, time-consuming to build and maintain, fragile to operate, slow to download and deploy, and vastly inefficient in performance and resource footprint.

From an operations point of view, not only do you need to manage these various kinds of packages, but you also need to manage a fleet of servers to run them on.

Servers need to be provisioned, networked, deployed, configured, kept up to date with security patches, monitored, managed, and so on.

This all takes a significant amount of time, skill, and effort, just to provide a platform to run software on. Isn't there a better way?

Thinking Inside the Box

To solve these problems, the tech industry borrowed an idea from the shipping industry: the *container*. In the 1950s, a truck driver named Malcolm McLean (*https:// hbs.me/2Q0QCzb*) proposed that, instead of laboriously unloading goods individually from the truck trailers that brought them to the ports and loading them onto ships, trucks themselves simply be loaded onto the ship—or rather, the truck bodies.

A truck trailer is essentially a big metal box on wheels. If you can separate the box— the container—from the wheels and chassis used to transport it, you have something that is very easy to lift, load, stack, and unload, and can go right onto a ship or another truck at the other end of the voyage (Figure 1-3).

McLean's container shipping firm, Sea-Land, became very successful by using this system to ship goods far more cheaply, and containers quickly caught on (*https:// www.freightos.com/the-history-of-the-shipping-container*). Today, hundreds of millions of containers are shipped every year, carrying trillions of dollars worth of goods.

Figure 1-3. Standardized containers dramatically cut the cost of shipping bulk goods (photo by Pixabay (https://www.pexels.com/@pixabay), licensed under Creative Commons 2.0)

Putting Software in Containers

The software container is exactly the same idea: a standard packaging and distribution format that is generic and widespread, enabling greatly increased carrying capacity, lower costs, economies of scale, and ease of handling. The container format contains everything the application needs to run, baked into an *image file* that can be executed by a *container runtime*.

How is this different from a virtual machine image? That, too, contains everything the application needs to run—but a lot more besides. A typical virtual machine image is around 1 GiB.[1] A well-designed container image, on the other hand, might be a hundred times smaller.

Because the virtual machine contains lots of unrelated programs, libraries, and things that the application will never use, most of its space is wasted. Transferring VM images across the network is far slower than optimized containers.

Even worse, virtual machines are *virtual*: the underlying physical CPU effectively implements an *emulated* CPU, which the virtual machine runs on. The virtualization layer has a dramatic, negative effect on performance (*https://www.stratoscale.com/blog/containers/running-containers-on-bare-metal/*): in tests, virtualized workloads run about 30% slower than the equivalent containers.

In comparison, containers run directly on the real CPU, with no virtualization overhead, just as ordinary binary executables do.

And because containers only hold the files they need, they're much smaller than VM images. They also use a clever technique of addressable filesystem *layers*, which can be shared and reused between containers.

For example, if you have two containers, each derived from the same Debian Linux base image, the base image only needs to be downloaded once, and each container can simply reference it.

The container runtime will assemble all the necessary layers and only download a layer if it's not already cached locally. This makes very efficient use of disk space and network bandwidth.

Plug and Play Applications

Not only is the container the unit of deployment and the unit of packaging; it is also the unit of *reuse* (the same container image can be used as a component of many

---

1 The *gibibyte* (GiB) is the International Electrotechnical Commission (IEC) unit of data, defined as 1,024 *mebibytes* (MiB). We'll use IEC units (GiB, MiB, KiB) throughout this book to avoid any ambiguity.

different services), the unit of *scaling*, and the unit of *resource allocation* (a container can run anywhere sufficient resources are available for its own specific needs).

Developers no longer have to worry about maintaining different versions of the software to run on different Linux distributions, against different library and language versions, and so on. The only thing the container depends on is the operating system kernel (Linux, for example).

Simply supply your application in a container image, and it will run on any platform that supports the standard container format and has a compatible kernel.

Kubernetes developers Brendan Burns and David Oppenheimer put it this way in their paper "Design Patterns for Container-based Distributed Systems" (*https://www.usenix.org/node/196347*):

> By being hermetically sealed, carrying their dependencies with them, and providing an atomic deployment signal ("succeeded"/"failed"), [containers] dramatically improve on the previous state of the art in deploying software in the datacenter or cloud. But containers have the potential to be much more than just a better deployment vehicle—we believe they are destined to become analogous to objects in object-oriented software systems, and as such will enable the development of distributed system design patterns.

Conducting the Container Orchestra

Operations teams, too, find their workload greatly simplified by containers. Instead of having to maintain a sprawling estate of machines of various kinds, architectures, and operating systems, all they have to do is run a *container orchestrator*: a piece of software designed to join together many different machines into a *cluster*: a kind of unified compute substrate, which appears to the user as a single very powerful computer on which containers can run.

The terms *orchestration* and *scheduling* are often used loosely as synonyms. Strictly speaking, though, *orchestration* in this context means coordinating and sequencing different activities in service of a common goal (like the musicians in an orchestra). *Scheduling* means managing the resources available and assigning workloads where they can most efficiently be run. (Not to be confused with scheduling in the sense of *scheduled jobs*, which execute at preset times.)

A third important activity is *cluster management*: joining multiple physical or virtual servers into a unified, reliable, fault-tolerant, apparently seamless group.

The term *container orchestrator* usually refers to a single service that takes care of scheduling, orchestration, and cluster management.

Containerization (using containers as your standard method of deploying and running software) offered obvious advantages, and a de facto standard container format has made possible all kinds of economies of scale. But one problem still stood in the way of the widespread adoption of containers: the lack of a standard container orchestration system.

As long as several different tools for scheduling and orchestrating containers competed in the marketplace, businesses were reluctant to place expensive bets on which technology to use. But all that was about to change.

Kubernetes

Google was running containers at scale for production workloads long before anyone else. Nearly all of Google's services run in containers: Gmail, Google Search, Google Maps, Google App Engine, and so on. Because no suitable container orchestration system existed at the time, Google was compelled to invent one.

From Borg to Kubernetes

To solve the problem of running a large number of services at global scale on millions of servers, Google developed a private, internal container orchestration system it called Borg (*https://pdos.csail.mit.edu/6.824/papers/borg.pdf*).

Borg is essentially a centralized management system that allocates and schedules containers to run on a pool of servers. While very powerful, Borg is tightly coupled to Google's own internal and proprietary technologies, difficult to extend, and impossible to release to the public.

In 2014, Google founded an open source project named Kubernetes (from the Greek word κυβερνήτης, meaning "helmsman, pilot") that would develop a container orchestrator that everyone could use, based on the lessons learned from Borg and its successor, Omega (*https://ai.google/research/pubs/pub41684.pdf*).

Kubernetes's rise was meteoric. While other container orchestration systems existed before Kubernetes, they were commercial products tied to a vendor, and that was always a barrier to their widespread adoption. With the advent of a truly free and open source container orchestrator, adoption of both containers and Kubernetes grew at a phenomenal rate.

By late 2017, the orchestration wars were over, and Kubernetes had won. While other systems are still in use, from now on companies looking to move their infrastructure to containers only need to target one platform: Kubernetes.

What Makes Kubernetes So Valuable?

Kelsey Hightower, a staff developer advocate at Google, coauthor of *Kubernetes Up & Running* (O'Reilly), and all-around legend in the Kubernetes community, puts it this way:

> Kubernetes does the things that the very best system administrator would do: automation, failover, centralized logging, monitoring. It takes what we've learned in the DevOps community and makes it the default, out of the box.
>
> —Kelsey Hightower

Many of the traditional sysadmin tasks like upgrading servers, installing security patches, configuring networks, and running backups are less of a concern in the cloud native world. Kubernetes can automate these things for you so that your team can concentrate on doing its core work.

Some of these features, like load balancing and autoscaling, are built into the Kubernetes core; others are provided by add-ons, extensions, and third-party tools that use the Kubernetes API. The Kubernetes ecosystem is large, and growing all the time.

Kubernetes makes deployment easy

Ops staff love Kubernetes for these reasons, but there are also some significant advantages for developers. Kubernetes greatly reduces the time and effort it takes to deploy. Zero-downtime deployments are common, because Kubernetes does rolling updates by default (starting containers with the new version, waiting until they become healthy, and then shutting down the old ones).

Kubernetes also provides facilities to help you implement continuous deployment practices such as *canary deployments*: gradually rolling out updates one server at a time to catch problems early (see "Canary Deployments" on page 244). Another common practice is *blue-green* deployments: spinning up a new version of the system in parallel, and switching traffic over to it once it's fully up and running (see "Blue/ Green Deployments" on page 243).

Demand spikes will no longer take down your service, because Kubernetes supports autoscaling. For example, if CPU utilization by a container reaches a certain level, Kubernetes can keep adding new replicas of the container until the utilization falls below the threshold. When demand falls, Kubernetes will scale down the replicas again, freeing up cluster capacity to run other workloads.

Because Kubernetes has redundancy and failover built in, your application will be more reliable and resilient. Some managed services can even scale the Kubernetes cluster itself up and down in response to demand, so that you're never paying for a larger cluster than you need at any given moment (see "Autoscaling" on page 102).

The business will love Kubernetes too, because it cuts infrastructure costs and makes much better use of a given set of resources. Traditional servers, even cloud servers, are mostly idle most of the time. The excess capacity that you need to handle demand spikes is essentially wasted under normal conditions.

Kubernetes takes that wasted capacity and uses it to run workloads, so you can achieve much higher utilization of your machines—and you get scaling, load balancing, and failover for free too.

While some of these features, such as autoscaling, were available before Kubernetes, they were always tied to a particular cloud provider or service. Kubernetes is *provider-agnostic*: once you've defined the resources you use, you can run them on any Kubernetes cluster, regardless of the underlying cloud provider.

That doesn't mean that Kubernetes limits you to the lowest common denominator. Kubernetes maps your resources to the appropriate vendor-specific features: for example, a load-balanced Kubernetes service on Google Cloud will create a Google Cloud load balancer, on Amazon it will create an AWS load balancer. Kubernetes abstracts away the cloud-specific details, letting you focus on defining the behavior of your application.

Just as containers are a portable way of defining software, Kubernetes resources provide a portable definition of how that software should run.

Will Kubernetes Disappear?

Oddly enough, despite the current excitement around Kubernetes, we may not be talking much about it in years to come. Many things that once were new and revolutionary are now so much part of the fabric of computing that we don't really think about them: microprocessors, the mouse, the internet.

Kubernetes, too, is likely to disappear and become part of the plumbing. It's boring, in a good way: once you learn what you need to know to deploy your application to Kubernetes, you're more or less done.

The future of Kubernetes is likely to lie largely in the realm of managed services. Virtualization, which was once an exciting new technology, has now simply become a utility. Most people rent virtual machines from a cloud provider rather than run their own virtualization platform, such as vSphere or Hyper-V.

In the same way, we think Kubernetes will become so much a standard part of the plumbing that you just won't know it's there anymore.

Kubernetes Doesn't Do It All

Will the infrastructure of the future be entirely Kubernetes-based? Probably not. Firstly, some things just aren't a good fit for Kubernetes (databases, for example):

> Orchestrating software in containers involves spinning up new interchangeable instances without requiring coordination between them. But database replicas are not interchangeable; they each have a unique state, and deploying a database replica requires

coordination with other nodes to ensure things like schema changes happen everywhere at the same time:

—Sean Loiselle (*https://www.cockroachlabs.com/blog/kubernetes-state-of-stateful-apps*) (Cockroach Labs)

While it's perfectly possible to run stateful workloads like databases in Kubernetes with enterprise-grade reliability, it requires a large investment of time and engineering that it may not make sense for your company to make (see "Run Less Software" on page 46). It's usually more cost-effective to use managed services instead.

Secondly, some things don't actually need Kubernetes, and can run on what are sometimes called *serverless* platforms, better named *functions as a service*, or *FaaS* platforms.

Cloud functions and funtainers

AWS Lambda, for example, is a FaaS platform that allows you to run code written in Go, Python, Java, Node.js, C#, and other languages, without you having to compile or deploy your application at all. Amazon does all that for you.

Because you're billed for the execution time in increments of 100 milliseconds, the FaaS model is perfect for computations that only run when you need them to, instead of paying for a cloud server, which runs all the time whether you're using it or not.

These *cloud functions* are more convenient than containers in some ways (though some FaaS platforms can run containers as well). But they are best suited to short, standalone jobs (AWS Lambda limits functions to fifteen minutes of run time, for example, and around 50 MiB of deployed files), especially those that integrate with existing cloud computation services, such as Microsoft Cognitive Services or the Google Cloud Vision API.

Why don't we like to refer to this model as *serverless*? Well, it isn't: it's just somebody else's server. The point is that you don't have to provision and maintain that server; the cloud provider takes care of it for you.

Not every workload is suitable for running on FaaS platforms, by any means, but it is still likely to be a key technology for cloud native applications in the future.

Nor are cloud functions restricted to public FaaS platforms such as Lambda or Azure Functions: if you already have a Kubernetes cluster and want to run FaaS applications on it, OpenFaaS (*https://www.openfaas.com/*) and other open source projects make this possible. This hybrid of functions and containers is sometimes called *funtainers*, a name we find appealing.

A more sophisticated software delivery platform for Kubernetes that encompasses both containers and cloud functions, called Knative, is currently under active development (see "Knative" on page 240). This is a very promising project, which may mean that in the future the distinction between containers and functions may blur or disappear altogether.

Cloud Native

The term *cloud native* has become an increasingly popular shorthand way of talking about modern applications and services that take advantage of the cloud, containers, and orchestration, often based on open source software.

Indeed, the Cloud Native Computing Foundation (CNCF) (*https://www.cncf.io/*) was founded in 2015 to, in their words, "foster a community around a constellation of high-quality projects that orchestrate containers as part of a microservices architecture."

Part of the Linux Foundation, the CNCF exists to bring together developers, end-users, and vendors, including the major public cloud providers. The best-known project under the CNCF umbrella is Kubernetes itself, but the foundation also incubates and promotes other key components of the cloud native ecosystem: Prometheus, Envoy, Helm, Fluentd, gRPC, and many more.

So what exactly do we mean by *cloud native*? Like most such things, it means different things to different people, but perhaps there is some common ground.

Cloud native applications run in the cloud; that's not controversial. But just taking an existing application and running it on a cloud compute instance doesn't make it cloud native. Neither is it just about running in a container, or using cloud services such as Azure's Cosmos DB or Google's Pub/Sub, although those may well be important aspects of a cloud native application.

So let's look at a few of the characteristics of cloud native systems that most people can agree on:

Automatable
> If applications are to be deployed and managed by machines, instead of humans, they need to abide by common standards, formats, and interfaces. Kubernetes provides these standard interfaces in a way that means application developers don't even need to worry about them.

Ubiquitous and flexible
> Because they are decoupled from physical resources such as disks, or any specific knowledge about the compute node they happen to be running on, containerized microservices can easily be moved from one node to another, or even one cluster to another.

Resilient and scalable

Traditional applications tend to have single points of failure: the application stops working if its main process crashes, or if the underlying machine has a hardware failure, or if a network resource becomes congested. Cloud native applications, because they are inherently distributed, can be made highly available through redundancy and graceful degradation.

Dynamic

A container orchestrator such as Kubernetes can schedule containers to take maximum advantage of available resources. It can run many copies of them to achieve high availability, and perform rolling updates to smoothly upgrade services without ever dropping traffic.

Observable

Cloud native apps, by their nature, are harder to inspect and debug. So a key requirement of distributed systems is *observability*: monitoring, logging, tracing, and metrics all help engineers understand what their systems are doing (and what they're doing wrong).

Distributed

Cloud native is an approach to building and running applications that takes advantage of the distributed and decentralized nature of the cloud. It's about how your application works, not where it runs. Instead of deploying your code as a single entity (known as a *monolith*), cloud native applications tend to be composed of multiple, cooperating, distributed *microservices*. A microservice is simply a self-contained service that does one thing. If you put enough microservices together, you get an application.

It's not just about microservices

However, microservices are not a panacea. Monoliths are easier to understand, because everything is in one place, and you can trace the interactions of different parts. But it's hard to scale monoliths, both in terms of the code itself, and the teams of developers who maintain it. As the code grows, the interactions between its various parts grow exponentially, and the system as a whole grows beyond the capacity of a single brain to understand it all.

A well-designed cloud native application is composed of microservices, but deciding what those microservices should be, where the boundaries are, and how the different services should interact is no easy problem. Good cloud native service design consists of making wise choices about how to separate the different parts of your architecture. However, even a well-designed cloud native application is still a distributed system, which makes it inherently complex, difficult to observe and reason about, and prone to failure in surprising ways.

While cloud native systems tend to be distributed, it's still possible to run monolithic applications in the cloud, using containers, and gain considerable business value from doing so. This may be a step on the road to gradually migrating parts of the monolith outward to modern microservices, or a stopgap measure pending the redesign of the system to be fully cloud native.

The Future of Operations

Operations, infrastructure engineering, and system administration are highly skilled jobs. Are they at risk in a cloud native future? We think not.

Instead, these skills will only become more important. Designing and reasoning about distributed systems is hard. Networks and container orchestrators are complicated. Every team developing cloud native applications will need operations skills and knowledge. Automation frees up staff from boring, repetitive manual work to deal with more complex, interesting, and fun problems that computers can't yet solve for themselves.

That doesn't mean all current operations jobs are guaranteed. Sysadmins used to be able to get by without coding skills, except maybe cooking up the odd simple shell script. In the cloud, that won't fly.

In a software-defined world, the ability to write, understand, and maintain software becomes critical. If you can't or won't learn new skills, the world will leave you behind —and it's always been that way.

Distributed DevOps

Rather than being concentrated in a single operations team that services other teams, ops expertise will become distributed among many teams.

Each development team will need at least one ops specialist, responsible for the health of the systems or services the team provides. She will be a developer, too, but she will also be the domain expert on networking, Kubernetes, performance, resilience, and the tools and systems that enable the other developers to deliver their code to the cloud.

Thanks to the DevOps revolution, there will no longer be room in most organizations for devs who can't ops, or ops who don't dev. The distinction between those two disciplines is obsolete, and is rapidly being erased altogether. Developing and operating software are merely two aspects of the same thing.

Some Things Will Remain Centralized

Are there limits to DevOps? Or will the traditional central IT and operations team disappear altogether, dissolving into a group of roving internal consultants, coaching, teaching, and troubleshooting ops issues?

We think not, or at least not entirely. Some things still benefit from being centralized. It doesn't make sense for each application or service team to have its own way of detecting and communicating about production incidents, for example, or its own ticketing system, or deployment tools. There's no point in everybody reinventing their own wheel.

Developer Productivity Engineering

The point is that self-service has its limits, and the aim of DevOps is to speed up development teams, not slow them down with unnecessary and redundant work.

Yes, a large part of traditional operations can and should be devolved to other teams, primarily those that involve code deployment and responding to code-related incidents. But to enable that to happen, there needs to be a strong central team building and supporting the DevOps ecosystem in which all the other teams operate.

Instead of calling this team *operations*, we like the name *developer productivity engineering* (DPE). DPE teams do whatever's necessary to help developers do their work better and faster: operating infrastructure, building tools, busting problems.

And while developer productivity engineering remains a specialist skill set, the engineers themselves may move outward into the organization to bring that expertise where it's needed.

Lyft engineer Matt Klein has suggested that, while a pure DevOps model makes sense for startups and small firms, as an organization grows, there is a natural tendency for infrastructure and reliability experts to gravitate toward a central team. But he says that team can't be scaled indefinitely:

> By the time an engineering organization reaches ~75 people, there is almost certainly a central infrastructure team in place starting to build common substrate features required by product teams building microservices. But there comes a point at which the central infrastructure team can no longer both continue to build and operate the infrastructure critical to business success, while also maintaining the support burden of helping product teams with operational tasks.
>
> —Matt Klein (*https://medium.com/@mattklein123/the-human-scalability-of-devops-e36c37d3db6a*)

At this point, not every developer can be an infrastructure expert, just as a single team of infrastructure experts can't service an ever-growing number of developers. For larger organizations, while a central infrastructure team is still needed, there's also a case for embedding *site reliability engineers* (SREs) into each development or product team. They bring their expertise to each team as consultants, and also form a bridge between product development and infrastructure operations.

You Are the Future

If you're reading this book, it means you're going to be part of this new cloud native future. In the remaining chapters, we'll cover all the knowledge and skills you'll need as a developer or operations engineer working with cloud infrastructure, containers, and Kubernetes.

Some of these things will be familiar, and some will be new, but we hope that when you've finished the book you'll feel more confident in your own ability to acquire and master cloud native skills. Yes, there's a lot to learn, but it's nothing you can't handle. You've got this!

Now read on.

Summary

We've necessarily given you a rather quick tour of the cloud native DevOps landscape, but we hope it's enough to bring you up to speed with some of the problems that cloud, containers, and Kubernetes solve, and how they're likely to change the IT business. If you're already familiar with this, then we appreciate your patience.

A quick recap of the main points before we move on to meet Kubernetes in person in the next chapter:

- Cloud computing frees you from the expense and overhead of managing your own hardware, making it possible for you to build resilient, flexible, scalable distributed systems.

- DevOps is a recognition that modern software development doesn't stop at shipping code: it's about closing the feedback loop between those who write the code and those who use it.

- DevOps also brings a code-centric approach and good software engineering practices to the world of infrastructure and operations.

- Containers allow you to deploy and run software in small, standardized, self-contained units. This makes it easier and cheaper to build large, diverse, distributed systems, by connecting together containerized microservices.

- Orchestration systems take care of deploying your containers, scheduling, scaling, networking, and all the things that a good system administrator would do, but in an automated, programmable way.

- Kubernetes is the de facto standard container orchestration system, and it's ready for you to use in production right now, today.

- *Cloud native* is a useful shorthand for talking about cloud-based, containerized, distributed systems, made up of cooperating microservices, dynamically managed by automated infrastructure as code.

- Operations and infrastructure skills, far from being made obsolete by the cloud native revolution, are and will become more important than ever.

- It still makes sense for a central team to build and maintain the platforms and tools that make DevOps possible for all the other teams.

- What will go away is the sharp distinction between software engineers and operations engineers. It's all just software now, and we're all engineers.

CHAPTER 2

First Steps with Kubernetes

To do anything truly worth doing, I must not stand back shivering and thinking of the cold and danger, but jump in with gusto and scramble through as well as I can.

—Og Mandino

Enough with the theory; let's start working with Kubernetes and containers. In this chapter, you'll build a simple containerized application and deploy it to a local Kubernetes cluster running on your machine. In the process, you'll meet some very important cloud native technologies and concepts: Docker, Git, Go, container registries, and the kubectl tool.

 This chapter is interactive! Often, throughout this book, we'll ask you to follow along with the examples by installing things on your own computer, typing commands, and running containers. We find that's a much more effective way to learn than just having things explained in words.

Running Your First Container

As we saw in Chapter 1, the container is one of the key concepts in cloud native development. The fundamental tool for building and running containers is Docker. In this section, we'll use the Docker Desktop tool to build a simple demo application, run it locally, and push the image to a container registry.

If you're already very familiar with containers, skip straight to "Hello, Kubernetes" on page 29, where the real fun starts. If you're curious to know what containers are and how they work, and to get a little practical experience with them before you start learning about Kubernetes, read on.

Installing Docker Desktop

Docker Desktop is a complete Kubernetes development environment for Mac or Windows that runs on your laptop (or desktop). It includes a single-node Kubernetes cluster that you can use to test your applications.

Let's install Docker Desktop now and use it to run a simple containerized application. If you already have Docker installed, skip this section and go straight on to "Running a Container Image" on page 22.

Download a version of the Docker Desktop Community Edition (*https:// hub.docker.com/search/?type=edition&offering=community*) suitable for your computer, then follow the instructions for your platform to install Docker and start it up.

 Docker Desktop isn't currently available for Linux, so Linux users will need to install Docker Engine (*https://www.docker.com/prod ucts/docker-engine*) instead, and then Minikube (see "Minikube" on page 31).

Once you've done that, you should be able to open a terminal and run the following command:

```
docker version
Client:
 Version:      19.03.8
 ...
```

The exact output will be different depending on your platform, but if Docker is correctly installed and running, you'll see something like the example output shown. On Linux systems, you may need to run sudo docker version instead.

What Is Docker?

Docker (*https://docs.docker.com/*) is actually several different, but related things: a container image format, a *container runtime* library, which manages the life cycle of containers, a command-line tool for packaging and running containers, and an API for container management. The details needn't concern us here, since Kubernetes uses Docker as one of many components, though an important one.

Running a Container Image

What exactly is a container image? The technical details don't really matter for our purposes, but you can think of an image as being like a ZIP file. It's a single binary file that has a unique ID and holds everything needed to run the container.

Whether you're running the container directly with Docker, or on a Kubernetes cluster, all you need to specify is a container image ID or URL, and the system will take care of finding, downloading, unpacking, and starting the container for you.

We've written a little demo application that we'll use throughout the book to illustrate what we're talking about. You can download and run the application using a container image we prepared earlier. Run the following command to try it out:

```
docker container run -p 9999:8888 --name hello cloudnatived/demo:hello
```

Leave this command running, and point your browser to *http://localhost:9999/*.

You should see a friendly message:

```
Hello, 世界
```

Any time you make a request to this URL, our demo application will be ready and waiting to greet you.

Once you've had as much fun as you can stand, stop the container by pressing Ctrl-C in your terminal.

The Demo Application

So how does it work? Let's download the source code for the demo application that runs in this container and have a look.

You'll need Git installed for this part.[1] If you're not sure whether you already have Git, try the following command:

```
git version
git version 2.25.1
```

If you don't already have Git, follow the installation instructions (*https://git-scm.com/download*) for your platform.

Once you've installed Git, run this command:

```
git clone https://github.com/cloudnativedevops/demo.git
Cloning into demo...
...
```

Looking at the Source Code

This Git repository contains the demo application we'll be using throughout this book. To make it easier to see what's going on at each stage, the repo contains each

---

1 If you're not familiar with Git, read Scott Chacon and Ben Straub's excellent book *Pro Git* (*https://git-scm.com/book/en/v2*) (Apress).

successive version of the app in a different subdirectory. The first one is named simply *hello*. To look at the source code, run this command:

```
cd demo/hello
ls
Dockerfile  README.md
go.mod      main.go
```

Open the file *main.go* in your favorite editor (we recommend Visual Studio Code (*https://code.visualstudio.com/*) which has excellent support for Go, Docker, and Kubernetes development). You'll see this source code:

```go
package main

import (
        "fmt"
        "log"
        "net/http"
)

func handler(w http.ResponseWriter, r *http.Request) {
        fmt.Fprintln(w, "Hello, 世界")
}

func main() {
        http.HandleFunc("/", handler)
        log.Fatal(http.ListenAndServe(":8888", nil))
}
```

Introducing Go

Our demo application is written in the Go programming language.

Go is a modern programming language (developed at Google since 2009) that prioritizes simplicity, safety, and readability, and is designed for building large-scale concurrent applications, especially network services. It's also a lot of fun to program in.[2]

Kubernetes itself is written in Go, as are Docker, Terraform, and many other popular open source projects. This makes Go a good choice for developing cloud native applications.

How the Demo App Works

As you can see, the demo app is pretty simple, even though it implements an HTTP server (Go comes with a powerful standard library). The core of it is this function, called `handler`:

---

2 If you're a fairly experienced programmer, but new to Go, Alan Donovan and Brian Kernighan's *The Go Programming Language* (*https://www.gopl.io/*) (Addison-Wesley) is an invaluable guide.

```
func handler(w http.ResponseWriter, r *http.Request) {
        fmt.Fprintln(w, "Hello, 世界")
}
```

As the name suggests, it handles HTTP requests. The request is passed in as an argument to the function (though the function doesn't do anything with it, yet).

An HTTP server also needs a way to send something back to the client. The http.ResponseWriter object enables our function to send a message back to the user to display in her browser: in this case, just the string Hello, 世界.

The first example program in any language traditionally prints Hello, world. But because Go natively supports Unicode (the international standard for text representation), example Go programs often print Hello, 世界 instead, just to show off. If you don't happen to speak Chinese, that's okay: Go does!

The rest of the program takes care of registering the handler function as the handler for HTTP requests, and actually starting the HTTP server to listen and serve on port 8888.

That's the whole app! It doesn't do much yet, but we will add capabilities to it as we go on.

Building a Container

You know that a container image is a single file that contains everything the container needs to run, but how do you build an image in the first place? Well, to do that, you use the docker image build command, which takes as input a special text file called a *Dockerfile*. The Dockerfile specifies exactly what needs to go into the container image.

One of the key benefits of containers is the ability to build on existing images to create new images. For example, you could take a container image containing the complete Ubuntu operating system, add a single file to it, and the result will be a new image.

In general, a Dockerfile has instructions for taking a starting image (a so-called *base image*), transforming it in some way, and saving the result as a new image.

Understanding Dockerfiles

Let's see the Dockerfile for our demo application (it's in the *hello* subdirectory of the app repo):

```
FROM golang:1.14-alpine AS build

WORKDIR /src/
COPY main.go go.* /src/
```

```
RUN CGO_ENABLED=0 go build -o /bin/demo

FROM scratch
COPY --from=build /bin/demo /bin/demo
ENTRYPOINT ["/bin/demo"]
```

The exact details of how this works don't matter for now, but it uses a fairly standard build process for Go containers called *multi-stage builds*. The first stage starts from an official `golang` container image, which is just an operating system (in this case Alpine Linux) with the Go language environment installed. It runs the `go build` command to compile the *main.go* file we saw earlier.

The result of this is an executable binary file named *demo*. The second stage takes a completely empty container image (called a *scratch* image, as in *from scratch*) and copies the *demo* binary into it.

Minimal Container Images

Why the second build stage? Well, the Go language environment, and the rest of Alpine Linux, is really only needed in order to *build* the program. To run the program, all it takes is the *demo* binary, so the Dockerfile creates a new scratch container to put it in. The resulting image is very small (about 6 MiB)—and that's the image that can be deployed in production.

Without the second stage, you would have ended up with a container image about 350 MiB in size, 98% of which is unnecessary and will never be executed. The smaller the container image, the faster it can be uploaded and downloaded, and the faster it will be to start up.

Minimal containers also have a reduced *attack surface* for security issues. The fewer programs there are in your container, the fewer potential vulnerabilities.

Because Go is a compiled language that can produce self-contained executables, it's ideal for writing minimal (*scratch*) containers. By comparison, the official Ruby container image is 1.5 GiB; about 250 times bigger than our Go image, and that's before you've added your Ruby program!

Running docker image build

We've seen that the Dockerfile contains instructions for the `docker image build` tool to turn our Go source code into an executable container. Let's go ahead and try it. In the *hello* directory, run the following command:

```
docker image build -t myhello .
Sending build context to Docker daemon  4.096kB
Step 1/7 : FROM golang:1.14-alpine AS build
...
```

```
Successfully built eeb7d1c2e2b7
Successfully tagged myhello:latest
```

Congratulations, you just built your first container! You can see from the output that Docker performs each of the actions in the Dockerfile in sequence on the newly formed container, resulting in an image that's ready to use.

Naming Your Images

When you build an image, by default it just gets a hexadecimal ID, which you can use to refer to it later (for example, to run it). These IDs aren't particularly memorable or easy to type, so Docker allows you to give the image a human-readable name, using the -t switch to docker image build. In the previous example you named the image myhello, so you should be able to use that name to run the image now.

Let's see if it works:

```
docker container run -p 9999:8888 myhello
```

You're now running your own copy of the demo application, and you can check it by browsing to the same URL as before (*http://localhost:9999/*).

You should see Hello, 世界. When you're done running this image, press Ctrl-C to stop the docker container run command.

Exercise

If you're feeling adventurous, modify the *main.go* file in the demo application and change the greeting so that it says "Hello, world" in your favorite language (or change it to say whatever you like). Rebuild the container and run it to check that it works.

Congratulations, you're now a Go programmer! But don't stop there: take the interactive Tour of Go (*https://tour.golang.org/welcome/1*) to learn more.

Port Forwarding

Programs running in a container are isolated from other programs running on the same machine, which means they can't have direct access to resources like network ports.

The demo application listens for connections on port 8888, but this is the *container's* own private port 8888, not a port on your computer. In order to connect to the container's port 8888, you need to *forward* a port on your local machine to that port on the container. It could be any port, including 8888, but we'll use 9999 instead, to make it clear which is your port, and which is the container's.

To tell Docker to forward a port, you can use the `-p` switch, just as you did earlier in "Running a Container Image" on page 22:

```
docker container run -p HOST_PORT:CONTAINER_PORT ...
```

Once the container is running, any requests to `HOST_PORT` on the local computer will be forwarded automatically to `CONTAINER_PORT` on the container, which is how you're able to connect to the app with your browser.

Container Registries

In "Running a Container Image" on page 22, you were able to run an image just by giving its name, and Docker downloaded it for you automatically.

You might reasonably wonder where it's downloaded from. While you can use Docker perfectly well by just building and running local images, it's much more useful if you can push and pull images from a *container registry*. The registry allows you to store images and retrieve them using a unique name (like `cloudnatived/demo:hello`).

The default registry for the `docker container run` command is Docker Hub, but you can specify a different one, or set up your own.

For now, let's stick with Docker Hub. While you can download and use any public container image from Docker Hub, to push your own images you'll need an account (called a *Docker ID*). Follow the instructions at *https://hub.docker.com/* to create your Docker ID.

Authenticating to the Registry

Once you've got your Docker ID, the next step is to connect your local Docker daemon with Docker Hub, using your ID and password:

```
docker login
Login with your Docker ID to push and pull images from Docker Hub. If you don't
have a Docker ID, head over to https://hub.docker.com to create one.
Username: YOUR_DOCKER_ID
Password: YOUR_DOCKER_PASSWORD
Login Succeeded
```

Naming and Pushing Your Image

In order to be able to push a local image to the registry, you need to name it using this format: `YOUR_DOCKER_ID/myhello`.

To create this name, you don't need to rebuild the image; instead, run this command:

```
docker image tag myhello YOUR_DOCKER_ID/myhello
```

This is so that when you push the image to the registry, Docker knows which account to store it in.

Go ahead and push the image to Docker Hub, using this command:

```
docker image push YOUR_DOCKER_ID/myhello
The push refers to repository [docker.io/YOUR_DOCKER_ID/myhello]
b2c591f16c33: Pushed
latest: digest:
        sha256:7ac57776e2df70d62d7285124fbff039c9152d1bdfb36c75b5933057cefe4fc7
size: 528
```

Running Your Image

Congratulations! Your container image is now available to run anywhere (at least, anywhere with access to the internet), using the command:

```
docker container run -p 9999:8888 YOUR_DOCKER_ID/myhello
```

Hello, Kubernetes

Now that you've built and pushed your first container image, you can run it using the docker container run command, but that's not very exciting. Let's do something a little more adventurous and run it in Kubernetes.

There are lots of ways to get a Kubernetes cluster, and we'll explore some of them in more detail in Chapter 3. If you already have access to a Kubernetes cluster, that's great, and if you like you can use it for the rest of the examples in this chapter.

If not, don't worry. Docker Desktop includes Kubernetes support (Linux users, see "Minikube" on page 31 instead). To enable it, open the Docker Desktop Preferences, select the Kubernetes tab, and check Enable (see Figure 2-1).

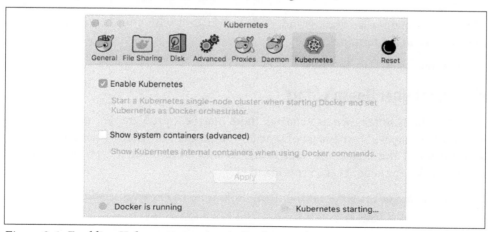

Figure 2-1. Enabling Kubernetes support in Docker Desktop

It will take a few minutes to install and start Kubernetes. Once that's done, you're ready to run the demo app!

Running the Demo App

Let's start by running the demo image you built earlier. Open a terminal and run the kubectl command with the following arguments:

```
kubectl run demo --image=YOUR_DOCKER_ID/myhello --port=9999 --labels app=demo
pod/demo created
```

Don't worry about the details of this command for now: it's basically the Kubernetes equivalent of the docker container run command you used earlier in this chapter to run the demo image. If you haven't built your own image yet, you can use ours: --image=cloudnatived/demo:hello.

Recall that you needed to forward port 9999 on your local machine to the container's port 8888 in order to connect to it with your web browser. You'll need to do the same thing here, using kubectl port-forward:

```
kubectl port-forward pod/demo 9999:8888
Forwarding from 127.0.0.1:9999 -> 8888
Forwarding from [::1]:9999 -> 8888
```

Leave this command running and open a new terminal to carry on.

Connect to *http://localhost:9999/* with your browser to see the Hello, 世界 message.

It may take a few seconds for the container to start and for the app to be available. If it isn't ready after half a minute or so, try this command:

```
kubectl get pods --selector app=demo
NAME          READY    STATUS     RESTARTS    AGE
demo          1/1      Running    0           9m
```

When the container is running and you connect to it with your browser, you'll see this message in the terminal:

```
Handling connection for 9999
```

If the Container Doesn't Start

If the STATUS is not shown as Running, there may be a problem. For example, if the status is ErrImagePull or ImagePullBackoff, it means Kubernetes wasn't able to find and download the image you specified. You may have made a typo in the image name; check your kubectl run command.

If the status is ContainerCreating, then all is well; Kubernetes is still downloading and starting the image. Just wait a few seconds and check again.

Once you are done, you'll want to clean up your demo pod:

```
kubectl delete pod demo
pod "demo" deleted
```

Minikube

If you don't want to use, or can't use, the Kubernetes support in Docker Desktop, there is an alternative: the well-loved Minikube. Like Docker Desktop, Minikube provides a single-node Kubernetes cluster that runs on your own machine (in fact, in a virtual machine, but that doesn't matter).

To install Minikube, follow these Minikube installation instructions (*https://kuber netes.io/docs/tasks/tools/install-minikube/*).

Summary

If, like us, you quickly grow impatient with wordy essays about why Kubernetes is so great, we hope you enjoyed getting to grips with some practical tasks in this chapter. If you're an experienced Docker or Kubernetes user already, perhaps you'll forgive the refresher course. We want to make sure that everybody feels quite comfortable with building and running containers in a basic way, and that you have a Kubernetes environment you can play and experiment with, before getting on to more advanced things.

Here's what you should take away from this chapter:

- All the source code examples (and many more) are available in the demo repository (*https://github.com/cloudnativedevops/demo*) that accompanies this book.

- The Docker tool lets you build containers locally, push them to or pull them from a container registry such as Docker Hub, and run container images locally on your machine.

- A container image is completely specified by a Dockerfile: a text file that contains instructions about how to build the container.

- Docker Desktop lets you run a small (single-node) Kubernetes cluster on your machine, which is nonetheless capable of running any containerized application. Minikube is another option.

- The kubectl tool is the primary way of interacting with a Kubernetes cluster, and can be used either *imperatively* (to run a public container image, for example, and implicitly creating the necessary Kubernetes resources), or *declaratively*, to apply Kubernetes configuration in the form of YAML manifests.

CHAPTER 3

Getting Kubernetes

> Perplexity is the beginning of knowledge.
>
> —Kahlil Gibran

Kubernetes is the operating system of the cloud native world, providing a reliable and scalable platform for running containerized workloads. But how should you run Kubernetes? Should you host it yourself? On cloud instances? On bare-metal servers? Or should you use a managed Kubernetes service? Or a managed platform that's based on Kubernetes, but extends it with workflow tools, dashboards, and web interfaces?

That's a lot of questions for one chapter to answer, but we'll try.

It's worth noting that we won't be particularly concerned here with the technical details of operating Kubernetes itself, such as building, tuning, and troubleshooting clusters. There are many excellent resources to help you with that, of which we particularly recommend Kubernetes cofounder Brendan Burns's book *Managing Kubernetes: Operating Kubernetes Clusters in the Real World* (O'Reilly).

Instead, we'll focus on helping you understand the basic architecture of a cluster, and give you the information you need to decide how to run Kubernetes. We'll outline the pros and cons of managed services, and look at some of the popular vendors.

If you want to run your own Kubernetes cluster, we list some of the best installation tools available to help you set up and manage clusters.

Cluster Architecture

You know that Kubernetes connects multiple servers into a *cluster*, but what is a cluster, and how does it work? The technical details don't matter for the purposes of this book, but you should understand the basic components of Kubernetes and how they fit together, in order to understand what your options are when it comes to building or buying Kubernetes clusters.

The Control Plane

The cluster's brain is called the *control plane*, and it runs all the tasks required for Kubernetes to do its job: scheduling containers, managing Services, serving API requests, and so on (see Figure 3-1).

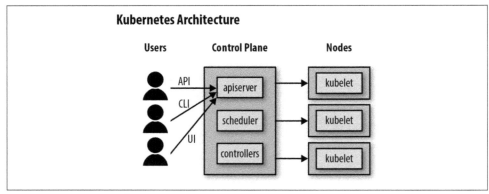

Figure 3-1. How a Kubernetes cluster works

The control plane is actually made up of several components:

kube-apiserver
> This is the frontend server for the control plane, handling API requests.

etcd
> This is the database where Kubernetes stores all its information: what nodes exist, what resources exist on the cluster, and so on.

kube-scheduler
> This decides where to run newly created Pods.

kube-controller-manager
> This is responsible for running resource controllers, such as Deployments.

cloud-controller-manager
> This interacts with the cloud provider (in cloud-based clusters), managing resources such as load balancers and disk volumes.

The members of the cluster which run the control plane components are called *master nodes*.

Node Components

Cluster members that run user workloads are called *worker nodes* (Figure 3-2).

Each worker node in a Kubernetes cluster runs these components:

kubelet
> This is responsible for driving the container runtime to start workloads that are scheduled on the node, and monitoring their status.

kube-proxy
> This does the networking magic that routes requests between Pods on different nodes, and between Pods and the internet.

Container runtime
> This actually starts and stops containers and handles their communications. Usually Docker, but Kubernetes supports other container runtimes, such as rkt and CRI-O.

Other than running different software components, there's no intrinsic difference between master nodes and worker nodes. Master nodes don't usually run user workloads, though, except in very small clusters (like Docker Desktop or Minikube).

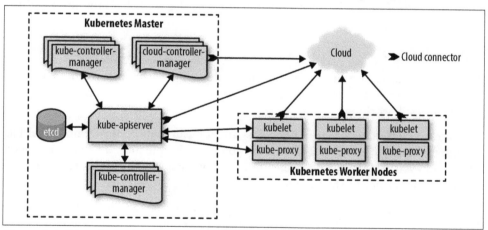

Figure 3-2. How the Kubernetes components fit together

High Availability

A correctly configured Kubernetes control plane has multiple master nodes, making it *highly available*; that is, if any individual master node fails or is shut down, or one of the control plane components on it stops running, the cluster will still work properly. A highly available control plane will also handle the situation where the master nodes are working properly, but some of them cannot communicate with the others, due to a network failure (known as a *network partition*).

The etcd database is replicated across multiple nodes, and can survive the failure of individual nodes, so long as a quorum of over half the original number of etcd replicas is still available.

If all of this is configured correctly, the control plane can survive a reboot or temporary failure of individual master nodes.

Control plane failure

A damaged control plane doesn't necessarily mean that your applications will go down, although it might well cause strange and errant behavior.

For example, if you were to stop all the master nodes in your cluster, the Pods on the worker nodes would keep on running—at least for a while. But you would be unable to deploy any new containers or change any Kubernetes resources, and controllers such as Deployments would stop working.

Therefore, high availability of the control plane is critical to a properly functioning cluster. You need to have enough master nodes available that the cluster can maintain a *quorum* even if one fails; for production clusters, the workable minimum is three (see "The smallest cluster" on page 96).

Worker node failure

By contrast, the failure of any worker node doesn't really matter. Kubernetes will detect the failure and reschedule the node's Pods somewhere else, so long as the control plane is still working.

If a large number of nodes fail at once, this might mean that the cluster no longer has enough resources to run all the workloads you need. Fortunately, this doesn't happen often, and even if it does, Kubernetes will keep as many of your Pods running as it can while you replace the missing nodes.

It's worth bearing in mind, though, that the fewer worker nodes you have, the greater the proportion of the cluster's capacity each one represents. You should assume that a single node failure will happen at any time, especially in the cloud, and two simultaneous failures are not unheard of.

A rare, but entirely possible, kind of failure is losing a whole cloud *availability zone*. Cloud vendors like AWS and Google Cloud provide multiple availability zones in each region, each corresponding roughly to a single data center. For this reason, rather than having all your worker nodes in the same zone, it's a good idea to distribute them across two or even three zones.

Trust, but verify

Although high availability should enable your cluster to survive losing one master, or a few worker nodes, it's always wise to *actually test* this. During a scheduled maintenance window, or outside of peak hours, try rebooting a worker and see what happens. (Hopefully, nothing, or nothing that's visible to users of your applications.)

For a more demanding test, reboot one of the master nodes. (Managed services such as Google Kubernetes Engine, which we'll discuss later in the chapter, don't allow you to do this, for obvious reasons.) Still, a production-grade cluster should survive this with no problems whatsoever.

The Costs of Self-Hosting Kubernetes

The most important decision facing anyone who's considering running production workloads in Kubernetes is *buy or build?* Should you run your own clusters, or pay someone else to run them? Let's look at some of the options.

The most basic choice of all is self-hosted Kubernetes. By *self-hosted* we mean that you, personally, or a team in your organization, install and configure Kubernetes, on machines that you own or control, just as you might do with any other software that you use, such as Redis, PostgreSQL, or Nginx.

This is the option that gives you the maximum flexibility and control. You can decide what versions of Kubernetes to run, what options and features are enabled, when and whether to upgrade clusters, and so on. But there are some significant downsides, as we'll see in the next section.

It's More Work Than You Think

The self-hosted option also requires the maximum resources, in terms of people, skills, engineering time, maintenance, and troubleshooting. Just setting up a working Kubernetes cluster is pretty simple, but that's a long way from a cluster that's ready for production. You need to consider at least the following questions:

- Is the control plane highly available? That is, if a master node goes down or becomes unresponsive, does your cluster still work? Can you still deploy or update apps? Will your running applications still be fault-tolerant without the control plane? (See "High Availability" on page 35.)

- Is your pool of worker nodes highly available? That is, if an outage should take down several worker nodes, or even a whole cloud availability zone, will your workloads stop running? Will your cluster keep working? Will it be able to automatically provision new nodes to heal itself, or will it require manual intervention?

- Is your cluster set up *securely*? Do its internal components communicate using TLS encryption and trusted certificates? Do users and applications have minimal rights and permissions for cluster operations? Are container security defaults set properly? Do nodes have unnecessary access to control plane components? Is access to the underlying etcd database properly controlled and authenticated?

- Are all services in your cluster secure? If they're accessible from the internet, are they properly authenticated and authorized? Is access to the cluster API strictly limited?

- Is your cluster *conformant*? Does it meet the standards for Kubernetes clusters defined by the Cloud Native Computing Foundation? (See "Conformance Checking" on page 102 for details.)

- Are your cluster nodes fully *config-managed*, rather than being set up by imperative shell scripts and then left alone? The operating system and kernel on each node needs to be updated, have security patches applied, and so on.

- Is the data in your cluster properly backed up, including any persistent storage? What is your restore process? How often do you test restores?

- Once you have a working cluster, how do you maintain it over time? How do you provision new nodes? Roll out config changes to existing nodes? Roll out Kubernetes updates? Scale in response to demand? Enforce policies?

Distributed systems engineer and writer Cindy Sridharan has estimated (*https://twit ter.com/copyconstruct/status/1020880388464377856*) that it takes around a million dollars in engineer salary to get Kubernetes up and running in a production configuration from scratch ("And you still might not get there"). That figure should give any technical leader food for thought when considering self-hosted Kubernetes.

It's Not Just About the Initial Setup

Now bear in mind that you need to pay attention to these factors not just when setting up the first cluster for the first time, but for all your clusters for all time. When you make changes or upgrades to your Kubernetes infrastructure, you need to consider the impact on high availability, security, and so on.

You'll need to have monitoring in place to make sure the cluster nodes and all the Kubernetes components are working properly, and an alerting system so that staff can be paged to deal with any problems, day or night.

Kubernetes is still in rapid development, and new features and updates are being released all the time. You'll need to keep your cluster up to date with those, and understand how the changes affect your existing setup. You may need to reprovision your cluster to get the full benefit of the latest Kubernetes functionality.

It's also not enough to read a few books or articles, configure the cluster the right way, and leave it at that. You need to test and verify the configuration on a regular basis—by killing a master node and making sure everything still works, for example.

Automated resilience testing tools such as Netflix's Chaos Monkey can help with this, by randomly killing nodes, Pods, or network connections every so often. Depending on the reliability of your cloud provider, you may find that Chaos Monkey is unnecessary, as regular real-world failures will also test the resilience of your cluster and the services running on it (see "Chaos Testing" on page 107).

Tools Don't Do All the Work for You

There are tools—lots and lots of tools—to help you set up and configure Kubernetes clusters, and many of them advertise themselves as being more or less point-and-click, zero-effort, instant solutions. The sad fact is that in our opinion, the large majority of these tools solve only the easy problems, and ignore the hard ones.

On the other hand, powerful, flexible, enterprise-grade commercial tools tend to be very expensive, or not even available to the public, since there's more money to be made selling a managed service than there is selling a general-purpose cluster management tool.

Kubernetes Is Hard

Despite the widespread notion that it's simple to set up and manage, the truth is that *Kubernetes is hard*. Considering what it does, it's remarkably simple and well-designed, but it has to deal with very complex situations, and that leads to complex software.

Make no mistake, there is a significant investment of time and energy involved in both learning how to manage your own clusters properly, and actually doing it from day to day, month to month. We don't want to discourage you from using Kubernetes, but we want you to have a clear understanding of what's involved in running Kubernetes yourself. This will help you to make an informed decision about the costs and benefits of self-hosting, as opposed to using managed services.

Administration Overhead

If your organization is large, with resources to spare for a dedicated Kubernetes cluster operations team, this may not be such a big problem. But for small to medium enterprises, or even startups with a handful of engineers, the administration overhead of running your own Kubernetes clusters may be prohibitive.

Given a limited budget and number of staff available for IT operations, what proportion of your resources do you want to spend on administering Kubernetes itself? Would those resources be better used to support your business's workloads instead? Can you operate Kubernetes more cost-effectively with your own staff, or by using a managed service?

Start with Managed Services

You might be a little surprised that, in a Kubernetes book, we recommend that you don't run Kubernetes! At least, don't run it yourself. For the reasons we've outlined in the previous sections, we think that using managed services is likely to be far more cost-effective than self-hosting Kubernetes clusters. Unless you want to do something strange and experimental with Kubernetes that isn't supported by any managed provider, there are basically no good reasons to go the self-hosted route.

In our experience, and that of many of the people we interviewed for this book, a managed service is the best way to run Kubernetes, period.

If you're considering whether Kubernetes is even an option for you, using a managed service is a great way to try it out. You can get a fully working, secure, highly available, production-grade cluster in a few minutes, for a few dollars a day. (Most cloud providers even offer a free tier that lets you run a Kubernetes cluster for weeks or months without incurring any charges.) Even if you decide, after a trial period, that you'd prefer to run your own Kubernetes cluster, the managed services will show you how it should be done.

On the other hand, if you've already experimented with setting up Kubernetes yourself, you'll be delighted with how much easier managed services make the process. You probably didn't build your own house; why build your own cluster, when it's cheaper and quicker to have someone else do it, and the results are better?

In the next section, we'll outline some of the most popular managed Kubernetes services, tell you what we think of them, and recommend our favorite. If you're still not convinced, the second half of the chapter will explore Kubernetes installers you can use to build your own clusters (see "Kubernetes Installers" on page 44).

We should say at this point that neither of the authors is affiliated with any cloud provider or commercial Kubernetes vendor. Nobody's paying us to recommend their product or service. The opinions here are our own, based on personal experience, and the views of hundreds of Kubernetes users we spoke to while writing this book.

Naturally, things move quickly in the Kubernetes world, and the managed services marketplace is especially competitive. Expect the features and services described here to change rapidly. The list presented here is not complete, but we've tried to include the services we feel are the best, the most widely used, or otherwise important.

Managed Kubernetes Services

Managed Kubernetes services relieve you of almost all the administration overhead of setting up and running Kubernetes clusters, particularly the control plane. Effectively, a managed service means you pay for someone else (such as Google) to run the cluster for you.

Google Kubernetes Engine (GKE)

As you'd expect from the originators of Kubernetes, Google offers a fully managed Kubernetes service (*https://cloud.google.com/kubernetes-engine*) that is completely integrated with the Google Cloud Platform. Just choose the number of worker nodes, and click a button in the GCP web console to create a cluster, or use the Deployment Manager tool to provision one. Within a few minutes, your cluster will be ready to use.

Google takes care of monitoring and replacing failed nodes, auto-applying security patches, and high availability for the control plane and etcd. You can set your nodes to auto-upgrade to the latest version of Kubernetes, during a maintenance window of your choice.

High availability

GKE gives you a production-grade, highly available Kubernetes cluster with none of the setup and maintenance overhead associated with self-hosted infrastructure. Everything is controllable via the Google Cloud API, using Deployment Manager,[1] Terraform, or other tools, or you can use the GCP web console. Naturally, GKE is fully integrated with all the other services in Google Cloud.

For extended high availability, you can create *multizone* clusters, which spread worker nodes across multiple failure zones (roughly equivalent to individual data centers). Your workloads will keep on running, even if a whole failure zone is affected by an outage.

Regional clusters take this idea even further, by distributing multiple master nodes across failure zones, as well as workers.

---

1 Deployment Manager is Google's command-line tool for managing cloud resources; not to be confused with Kubernetes Deployments.

Cluster Autoscaling

GKE also offers an attractive cluster autoscaling option (see "Autoscaling" on page 102). With autoscaling enabled, if there are pending workloads that are waiting for a node to become available, the system will add new nodes automatically to accommodate the demand.

Conversely, if there is spare capacity, the autoscaler will consolidate Pods onto a smaller number of nodes and remove the unused nodes. Since billing for GKE is based on the number of worker nodes, this helps you control costs.

GKE is best-of-breed

Google has been in the Kubernetes business longer than anybody else, and it shows. GKE is, in our opinion, the best managed Kubernetes service available. If you already have infrastructure in Google Cloud, it makes sense to use GKE to run Kubernetes. If you're already established on another cloud, it needn't stop you using GKE if you want to, but you should look first at managed options within your existing cloud provider.

If you haven't made a cloud provider decision yet, GKE is a persuasive argument in favor of choosing Google Cloud.

Amazon Elastic Container Service for Kubernetes (EKS)

Amazon has also been providing managed container cluster services for a long time, but until very recently the only option was Elastic Container Service (ECS), Amazon's proprietary technology.

While perfectly usable, ECS (*https://aws.amazon.com/eks*) is not as powerful or flexible as Kubernetes, and evidently even Amazon has decided that the future is Kubernetes, with the launch of Elastic Container Service for Kubernetes (EKS). (Yes, *EKS* ought to stand for *Elastic Kubernetes Service*, but it doesn't.)

It's not quite as seamless (*https://blog.hasura.io/gke-vs-aks-vs-eks-411f080640dc*) an experience as Google Kubernetes Engine, so be prepared to do more of the setup work yourself.

If you already have infrastructure in AWS, or run containerized workloads in the older ECS service that you want to move to Kubernetes, then EKS is a sensible choice. As the newest entry into the managed Kubernetes marketplace, though, it has some distance to go to catch up to the Google and Microsoft offerings.

Azure Kubernetes Service (AKS)

Although Microsoft came a little later to the cloud business than Amazon or Google, they're catching up fast. Azure Kubernetes Service (AKS) (*https://azure.micro*

soft.com/en-us/services/kubernetes-service/) offers most of the features of its competitors, such as Google's GKE. You can create clusters from the web interface or using the Azure `az` command-line tool.

As with GKE and EKS, you have no access to the master nodes, which are managed internally, and your billing is based on the number of worker nodes in your cluster, along with any service charges associated with the hosted master nodes.

OpenShift

OpenShift (*https://www.openshift.com/*) is more than just a managed Kubernetes service: it's a full Platform-as-a-Service (PaaS) product, which aims to manage the whole software development life cycle, including continuous integration and build tools, test runner, application deployment, monitoring, and orchestration.

OpenShift can be deployed to bare-metal servers, virtual machines, private clouds, and public clouds, so you can create a single Kubernetes cluster that spans all these environments. This makes it a good choice for very large organizations, or those with very heterogeneous infrastructure.

IBM Cloud Kubernetes Service

Naturally, the venerable IBM is not to be left out in the field of managed Kubernetes services. IBM Cloud Kubernetes Service (*https://www.ibm.com/cloud/container-service*) is pretty simple and straightforward, allowing you to set up a vanilla Kubernetes cluster in IBM Cloud.

You can access and manage your IBM Cloud cluster through the default Kubernetes CLI and the provided command-line tool, or a basic GUI. There are no real killer features that differentiate IBM's offering from the other major cloud providers, but it's a logical option if you're already using IBM Cloud.

Turnkey Kubernetes Solutions

While managed Kubernetes services are a good fit for most business requirements, there may be some circumstances in which using managed services isn't an option. There is a growing class of *turnkey* offerings, which aim to give you a ready-to-use, production-grade Kubernetes cluster by just clicking a button in a web browser.

Turnkey Kubernetes solutions are attractive both to large enterprises (because they can have a commercial relationship with the vendor) and small companies with scarce engineering and operations resources. Here are a few of the options in the turnkey space.

Containership Kubernetes Engine (CKE)

CKE (*https://blog.containership.io/introducing-containership-kubernetes-engine/*) is another web-based interface for provisioning Kubernetes in the public cloud. It lets you get a cluster up and running with sensible defaults, or customize almost every aspect of the cluster for more demanding requirements.

Kubernetes Installers

If managed or turnkey clusters won't work for you, then you'll need to consider some level of Kubernetes self-hosting: that is, setting up and running Kubernetes yourself on your own machines.

It's very unlikely that you'll deploy and run Kubernetes completely from scratch, except for learning and demo purposes. The vast majority of people use one or more of the available Kubernetes installer tools or services to set up and manage their clusters.

kops

kops (*https://kubernetes.io/docs/setup/custom-cloud/kops/*) is a command-line tool for automated provisioning of Kubernetes clusters. It's part of the Kubernetes project, and has been around a long time as an AWS-specific tool, but is now adding beta support for Google Cloud, and support for other providers is planned.

kops supports building high-availability clusters, which makes it suitable for production Kubernetes deployments. It uses declarative configuration, just like Kubernetes resources themselves, and it can not only provision the necessary cloud resources and set up a cluster, but also scale it up and down, resize nodes, perform upgrades, and do other useful admin tasks.

Like everything in the Kubernetes world, kops is under rapid development, but it's a relatively mature and sophisticated tool that is widely used. If you're planning to run self-hosted Kubernetes in AWS, kops is a good choice.

Kubespray

Kubespray (*https://github.com/kubernetes-sigs/kubespray*) (formerly known as Kargo), a project under the Kubernetes umbrella, is a tool for easily deploying production-ready clusters. It offers lots of options, including high availability, and support for multiple platforms.

Kubespray is focused on installing Kubernetes on existing machines, especially on-premise and bare-metal servers. However, it's also suitable for any cloud environment, including private cloud (virtual machines that run on your own servers).

TK8

TK8 (*https://github.com/kubernauts/tk8*) is a command-line tool for provisioning Kubernetes clusters that leverages both Terraform (for creating cloud servers) and Kubespray (for installing Kubernetes on them). Written in Go (of course), it supports installation on AWS, OpenStack, and bare-metal servers, with support for Azure and Google Cloud in the pipeline.

TK8 not only builds a Kubernetes cluster, but will also install optional add-ons for you, including Jmeter Cluster for load testing, Prometheus for monitoring, Jaeger, Linkerd or Zipkin for tracing, Ambassador API Gateway with Envoy for ingress and load balancing, Istio for service mesh support, Jenkins-X for CI/CD, and Helm or Kedge for packaging on Kubernetes.

Kubernetes The Hard Way

Kelsey Hightower's *Kubernetes The Hard Way* (*https://github.com/kelseyhightower/kubernetes-the-hard-way*) tutorial is perhaps best considered not as a Kubernetes setup tool or installation guide, but an opinionated walkthrough of the process of building a Kubernetes cluster which illustrates the complexity of the moving parts involved. Nonetheless, it's very instructive, and it's an exercise worth doing for anyone considering running Kubernetes, even as a managed service, just to get a sense of how it all works under the hood.

kubeadm

kubeadm (*https://kubernetes.io/docs/setup/independent/create-cluster-kubeadm/*) is part of the Kubernetes distribution, and it aims to help you install and maintain a Kubernetes cluster according to best practices. kubeadm does not provision the infrastructure for the cluster itself, so it's suitable for installing Kubernetes on bare-metal servers or cloud instances of any flavor.

Many of the other tools and services we'll mention in this chapter use kubeadm internally to handle cluster admin operations, but there's nothing to stop you using it directly, if you want to.

Tarmak

Tarmak (*https://blog.jetstack.io/blog/introducing-tarmak/*) is a Kubernetes cluster life cycle management tool that is focused on making it easy and reliable to modify and upgrade cluster nodes. While many tools deal with this by simply replacing the node, this can take a long time and often involves moving a lot of data around between nodes during the rebuild process. Instead, Tarmak can repair or upgrade the node in place.

Tarmak uses Terraform under the hood to provision the cluster nodes, and Puppet to manage configuration on the nodes themselves. This makes it quicker and safer to roll out changes to node configuration.

Rancher Kubernetes Engine (RKE)

RKE (*https://github.com/rancher/rke*) aims to be a simple, fast Kubernetes installer. It doesn't provision the nodes for you, and you have to install Docker on the nodes yourself before you can use RKE to install the cluster. RKE supports high availability of the Kubernetes control plane.

Puppet Kubernetes Module

Puppet is a powerful, mature, and sophisticated general configuration management tool that is very widely used, and has a large open source module ecosystem. The officially supported Kubernetes module (*https://forge.puppet.com/puppetlabs/kubernetes*) installs and configures Kubernetes on existing nodes, including high availability support for both the control plane and etcd.

Kubeformation

Kubeformation (*https://github.com/hasura/kubeformation/*) is an online Kubernetes configurator that lets you choose the options for your cluster using a web interface, and will then generate configuration templates for your particular cloud provider's automation API (for example, Deployment Manager for Google Cloud, or Azure Resource Manager for Azure). Support for other cloud providers is in the pipeline.

Using Kubeformation is perhaps not as simple as some other tools, but because it is a wrapper around existing automation tools such as Deployment Manager, it is very flexible. If you already manage your Google Cloud infrastructure using Deployment Manager, for example, Kubeformation will fit into your existing workflow perfectly.

Buy or Build: Our Recommendations

This has necessarily been a quick tour of some of the options available for managing Kubernetes clusters, because the range of offerings is large and varied, and growing all the time. However, we can make a few recommendations based on commonsense principles. One of these is the philosophy of *run less software* (*https://blog.inter com.com/run-less-software*).

Run Less Software

There are three pillars of the Run Less Software philosophy, all of which will help you manipulate time and defeat your enemies.

---

1. Choose standard technology

2. Outsource undifferentiated heavy lifting

3. Create enduring competitive advantage

—Rich Archbold

While using innovative new technologies is fun and exciting, it doesn't always make sense from a business point of view. Using *boring* software that everybody else is using is generally a good bet. It probably works, it's probably well-supported, and you're not going to be the one taking the risks and dealing with the inevitable bugs.

If you're running containerized workloads and cloud native applications, Kubernetes is the boring choice, in the best possible way. Given that, you should opt for the most mature, stable, and widely used Kubernetes tools and services.

Undifferentiated heavy lifting is a term coined at Amazon to denote all the hard work and effort that goes into things like installing and managing software, maintaining infrastructure, and so on. There's nothing special about this work; it's the same for you as it is for every other company out there. It costs you money, instead of making you money.

The *run less software* philosophy says that you should outsource undifferentiated heavy lifting, because it'll be cheaper in the long run, and it frees up resources you can use to work on your core business.

Use Managed Kubernetes if You Can

With the *run less software* principles in mind, we recommend that you outsource your Kubernetes cluster operations to a managed service. Installing, configuring, maintaining, securing, upgrading, and making your Kubernetes cluster reliable is undifferentiated heavy lifting, so it makes sense for almost all businesses not to do it themselves:

> *Cloud native* is not a cloud provider, it's not Kubernetes, it's not containers, it's not a technology. It's the practice of accelerating your business by not running stuff that doesn't differentiate you.
>
> —Justin Garrison

In the managed Kubernetes space, Google Kubernetes Engine (GKE) is the clear winner. While other cloud providers may catch up in a year or two, Google is still way ahead and will remain so for some time to come.

For companies that need to be independent of a single cloud provider, and want 24-hour-a-day technical support from a trusted provider is worth looking at.

But What About Vendor Lock-in?

If you commit to a managed Kubernetes service from a particular vendor, such as Google Cloud, will that lock you in to the vendor and reduce your options in the future? Not necessarily. Kubernetes is a standard platform, so any applications and services you build to run on Google Kubernetes Engine will also work on any other certified Kubernetes provider's system. Just using Kubernetes in the first place is a big step toward escaping vendor lock-in.

Does managed Kubernetes make you more prone to lock-in than running your own Kubernetes cluster? We think it's the other way around. Self-hosting Kubernetes involves a lot of machinery and configuration to maintain, all of which is intimately tied in to a specific cloud provider's API. Provisioning AWS virtual machines to run Kubernetes, for example, requires completely different code than the same operation on Google Cloud. Some Kubernetes setup assistants, like the ones we've mentioned in this chapter, support multiple cloud providers, but many don't.

Part of the point of Kubernetes is to abstract away the technical details of the cloud platform, and present developers with a standard, familiar interface that works the same way whether it happens to be running on Azure or Google Cloud. As long as you design your applications and automation to target Kubernetes itself, rather than the underlying cloud infrastructure, you're as free from vendor lock-in as you can reasonably be.

Use Standard Kubernetes Self-Hosting Tools if You Must

If you have special requirements which mean that managed Kubernetes offerings won't work for you, only then should you consider running Kubernetes yourself.

If that's the case, you should go with the most mature, powerful, and widely used tools available. We recommend kops or Kubespray, depending on your requirements.

If you know that you'll be staying with a single cloud provider long-term, especially if it's AWS, use kops.

On the other hand, if you need your cluster to span multiple clouds or platforms, including bare-metal servers, and you want to keep your options open, you should use Kubespray.

When Your Choices Are Limited

There may be business, rather than technical, reasons, why fully managed Kubernetes services aren't an option for you. If you have an existing business relationship with a hosting company or cloud provider that doesn't offer a managed Kubernetes service, that will necessarily limit your choices.

However, it may be possible for you to use a turnkey solution instead. These options provide a managed service for your Kubernetes master nodes, but connect them to worker nodes running on your own infrastructure. Since most of the administration overhead of Kubernetes is in setting up and maintaining the master nodes, this is a good compromise.

Bare-Metal and On-Prem

It may come as a surprise to you that being cloud native doesn't actually require being *in the cloud*, in the sense of outsourcing your infrastructure to a public cloud provider such as Azure or AWS.

Many organizations run part or all of their infrastructure on bare-metal hardware, whether colocated in data centers or on-premises. Everything we've said in this book about Kubernetes and containers applies just as well to in-house infrastructure as it does to the cloud.

You can run Kubernetes on your own hardware machines; if your budget is limited, you can even run it on a stack of Raspberry Pis (Figure 3-3). Some businesses run a *private cloud*, consisting of virtual machines hosted by on-prem hardware.

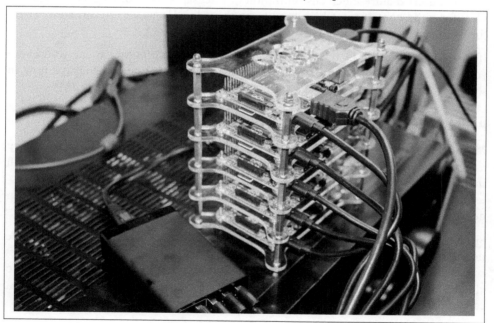

Figure 3-3. Kubernetes on a budget: a Raspberry Pi cluster (photo by David Merrick)

Clusterless Container Services

If you really want to minimize the overhead of running container workloads, there's yet another level above fully managed Kubernetes services. These are so-called *clusterless* services, such as Azure Container Instances or Amazon's Fargate. Although there really is a cluster under the hood, you don't have access to it via tools like kubectl. Instead, you specify a container image to run, and a few parameters like the CPU and memory requirements of your application, and the service does the rest.

Amazon Fargate

According to Amazon, "Fargate is like EC2, but instead of a virtual machine, you get a container." Unlike ECS, there's no need to provision cluster nodes yourself and then connect them to a control plane. You just define a task, which is essentially a set of instructions for how to run your container image, and launch it. Pricing is per-second based on the amount of CPU and memory resources that the task consumes.

It's probably fair to say that Fargate (*https://amzn.to/2SgQS9N*) makes sense for simple, self-contained, long-running compute tasks or batch jobs (such as data crunching) that don't require much customization or integration with other services. It's also ideal for build containers, which tend to be short-lived, and for any situation where the overhead of managing worker nodes isn't justified.

If you're already using ECS with EC2 worker nodes, switching to Fargate will relieve you of the need to provision and manage those nodes. Fargate is available now in some regions for running ECS tasks, and is scheduled to support EKS by 2019.

Azure Container Instances (ACI)

Microsoft's Azure Container Instances (ACI) (*https://azure.microsoft.com/en-gb/serv ices/container-instances/*) service is similar to Fargate, but also offers integration with the Azure Kubernetes Service (AKS). For example, you can configure your AKS cluster to provision temporary extra Pods inside ACI to handle spikes or bursts in demand.

Similarly, you can run batch jobs in ACI in an ad hoc way, without having to keep idle nodes around when there's no work for them to do. Microsoft calls this idea *serverless containers*, but we find that terminology both confusing (*serverless* usually refers to cloud functions, or functions-as-a-service) and inaccurate (there are servers; you just can't access them).

ACI is also integrated with Azure Event Grid, Microsoft's managed event routing service. Using Event Grid, ACI containers can communicate with cloud services, cloud functions, or Kubernetes applications running in AKS.

You can create, run, or pass data to ACI containers using Azure Functions. The advantage of this is that you can run any workload from a cloud function, not just those using the officially supported (*blessed*) languages, such as Python or JavaScript.

If you can containerize your workload, you can run it as a cloud function, with all the associated tooling. For example, Microsoft Flow allows even nonprogrammers to build up workflows graphically, connecting containers, functions, and events.

Summary

Kubernetes is everywhere! Our journey through the extensive landscape of Kubernetes tools, services, and products has been necessarily brief, but we hope you found it useful.

While our coverage of specific products and features is as up to date as we can make it, the world moves pretty fast, and we expect a lot will have changed even by the time you read this.

However, we think the basic point stands: it's not worth managing Kubernetes clusters yourself if a service provider can do it better and cheaper.

In our experience of consulting for companies migrating to Kubernetes, this is often a surprising idea, or at least not one that occurs to a lot of people. We often find that organizations have taken their first steps with self-hosted clusters, using tools like kops, and hadn't really thought about using a managed service such as GKE. It's well worth thinking about.

More things to bear in mind:

- Kubernetes clusters are made up of *master nodes*, which run the *control plane*, and *worker nodes*, which run your workloads.
- Production clusters must be *highly available*, meaning that the failure of a master node won't lose data or affect the operation of the cluster.
- It's a long way from a simple demo cluster to one that's ready for critical production workloads. High availability, security, and node management are just some of the issues involved.
- Managing your own clusters requires a significant investment of time, effort, and expertise. Even then, you can still get it wrong.
- Managed services like Google Kubernetes Engine do all the heavy lifting for you, at much lower cost than self-hosting.
- Turnkey services are a good compromise between self-hosted and fully managed Kubernetes. Turnkey providers manage the master nodes for you, while you run worker nodes on your own machines.

- If you have to host your own cluster, kops is a mature and widely used tool that can provision and manage production-grade clusters on AWS and Google Cloud.

- You should use managed Kubernetes if you can. This is the best option for most businesses in terms of cost, overhead, and quality.

- If managed services aren't an option, consider using turnkey services as a good compromise.

- Don't self-host your cluster without sound business reasons. If you do self-host, don't underestimate the engineering time involved for the initial setup and ongoing maintenance overhead.

CHAPTER 4

Working with Kubernetes Objects

I can't understand why people are frightened of new ideas. I'm frightened of the old ones.

—John Cage

In Chapter 2, you built and deployed an application to Kubernetes. In this chapter, you'll learn about the fundamental Kubernetes objects involved in that process: Pods, Deployments, and Services. You'll also find out how to use the essential Helm tool to manage application in Kubernetes.

After working through the example in "Running the Demo App" on page 30, you should have a container image running in the Kubernetes cluster, but how does that actually work? Under the hood, the `kubectl run` command creates a Kubernetes resource called a *Deployment*. So what's that? And how does a Deployment actually run your container image?

Deployments

Think back to how you ran the demo app with Docker. The `docker container run` command started the container, and it ran until you killed it with `docker stop`.

But suppose that the container exits for some other reason; maybe the program crashed, or there was a system error, or your machine ran out of disk space, or a cosmic ray hit your CPU at the wrong moment (unlikely, but it does happen). Assuming this is a production application, that means you now have unhappy users, until someone can get to a terminal and type `docker container run` to start the container again.

That's an unsatisfactory arrangement. What you really want is a kind of supervisor program, which continually checks that the container is running, and if it ever stops, starts it again immediately. On traditional servers, you can use a tool like systemd, runit, or supervisord to do this; Docker has something similar, and you won't be surprised to know that Kubernetes has a supervisor feature too: the *Deployment*.

Supervising and Scheduling

For each program that Kubernetes has to supervise, it creates a corresponding Deployment object, which records some information about the program: the name of the container image, the number of replicas you want to run, and whatever else it needs to know to start the container.

Working together with the Deployment resource is a kind of Kubernetes component called a *controller*. Controllers watch the resources they're responsible for, making sure they're present and working. If a given Deployment isn't running enough replicas, for whatever reason, the controller will create some new ones. (If there were too many replicas for some reason, the controller would shut down the excess ones. Either way, the controller makes sure that the real state matches the desired state.)

Actually, a Deployment doesn't manage replicas directly: instead, it automatically creates an associated object called a ReplicaSet, which handles that. We'll talk more about ReplicaSets in a moment in "ReplicaSets" on page 56, but since you generally interact only with Deployments, let's get more familiar with them first.

Restarting Containers

At first sight, the way Deployments behave might be a little surprising. If your container finishes its work and exits, the Deployment will restart it. If it crashes, or if you kill it with a signal, or terminate it with kubectl, the Deployment will restart it. (This is how you should think about it conceptually; the reality is a little more complicated, as we'll see.)

Most Kubernetes applications are designed to be long-running and reliable, so this behavior makes sense: containers can exit for all sorts of reasons, and in most cases all a human operator would do is restart them, so that's what Kubernetes does by default.

It's possible to change this policy for an individual container: for example, to never restart it, or to restart it only on failure, not if it exited normally (see "Restart Policies" on page 151). However, the default behavior (restart always) is usually what you want.

A Deployment's job is to watch its associated containers and make sure that the specified number of them is always running. If there are fewer, it will start more. If there are too many, it will terminate some. This is much more powerful and flexible than a traditional supervisor-type program.

Querying Deployments

You can see all the Deployments active in your current namespace (see "Using Name-spaces" on page 77) by running the following command:

```
kubectl get deployments
NAME    DESIRED   CURRENT   UP-TO-DATE   AVAILABLE   AGE
demo    1         1         1            1           21h
```

To get more detailed information on this specific Deployment, run the following command:

```
kubectl describe deployments/demo
Name:               demo
Namespace:          default
CreationTimestamp:  Tue, 08 May 2018 12:20:50 +0100
...
```

As you can see, there's a lot of information here, most of which isn't important for now. Let's look more closely at the `Pod Template` section, though:

```
Pod Template:
  Labels:  app=demo
  Containers:
   demo:
    Image:        cloudnatived/demo:hello
    Port:         8888/TCP
    Host Port:    0/TCP
    Environment:  <none>
    Mounts:       <none>
  Volumes:        <none>
```

You know that a Deployment contains the information Kubernetes needs to run the container, and here it is. But what's a Pod Template? Actually, before we answer that, what's a Pod?

Pods

A Pod is the Kubernetes object that represents a group of one or more containers (*pod* is also the name for a group of whales, which fits in with the vaguely seafaring flavor of Kubernetes metaphors).

Why doesn't a Deployment just manage an individual container directly? The answer is that sometimes a set of containers needs to be scheduled together, running on the same node, and communicating locally, perhaps sharing storage.

For example, a blog application might have one container that syncs content with a Git repository, and an Nginx web server container that serves the blog content to users. Since they share data, the two containers need to be scheduled together in a

Pod. In practice, though, many Pods only have one container, as in this case. (See "What Belongs in a Pod?" on page 138 for more about this.)

So a Pod specification (*spec* for short) has a list of `Containers`, and in our example there is only one container, `demo`:

```
demo:
  Image:         cloudnatived/demo:hello
  Port:          8888/TCP
  Host Port:     0/TCP
  Environment:   <none>
  Mounts:        <none>
```

The `Image` spec will be, in your case, **YOUR_DOCKER_ID**/myhello, and together with the port number, that's all the information the Deployment needs to start the Pod and keep it running.

And that's an important point. The `kubectl run` command didn't actually create the Pod directly. Instead it created a Deployment, and *then* the Deployment started the Pod. The Deployment is a declaration of your desired state: "A Pod should be running with the `myhello` container inside it."

ReplicaSets

We said that Deployments start Pods, but there's a little more to it than that. In fact, Deployments don't manage Pods directly. That's the job of the ReplicaSet object.

A ReplicaSet is responsible for a group of identical Pods, or *replicas*. If there are too few (or too many) Pods, compared to the specification, the ReplicaSet controller will start (or stop) some Pods to rectify the situation.

Deployments, in turn, manage ReplicaSets, and control how the replicas behave when you update them—by rolling out a new version of your application, for example (see "Deployment Strategies" on page 241). When you update the Deployment, a new ReplicaSet is created to manage the new Pods, and when the update is completed, the old ReplicaSet and its Pods are terminated.

In Figure 4-1, each ReplicaSet (V1, V2, V3) represents a different version of the application, with its corresponding Pods.

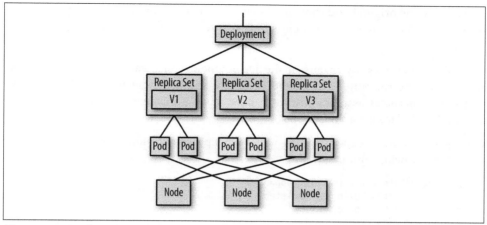

Figure 4-1. Deployments, ReplicaSets, and Pods

Usually, you won't interact with ReplicaSets directly, since Deployments do the work for you—but it's useful to know what they are.

Maintaining Desired State

Kubernetes controllers continually check the desired state specified by each resource against the actual state of the cluster, and make any necessary adjustments to keep them in sync. This process is called the *reconciliation loop*, because it loops forever, trying to reconcile the actual state with the desired state.

For example, when you first create the demo Deployment, there is no demo Pod running. So Kubernetes will start the required Pod immediately. If it were ever to stop, Kubernetes will start it again, so long as the Deployment still exists.

Let's verify that right now by stopping the Pod manually. First, check that the Pod is indeed running:

```
kubectl get pods --selector app=demo
NAME                     READY   STATUS    RESTARTS   AGE
demo-54df94b7b7-qgtc6    1/1     Running   1          22h
```

Now, run the following command to stop the Pod:

```
kubectl delete pods --selector app=demo
pod "demo-54df94b7b7-qgtc6" deleted
```

List the Pods again:

```
kubectl get pods --selector app=demo
NAME                     READY   STATUS        RESTARTS   AGE
demo-54df94b7b7-hrspp    1/1     Running       0          5s
demo-54df94b7b7-qgtc6    0/1     Terminating   1          22h
```

You can see the original Pod shutting down (its status is `Terminating`), but it's already been replaced by a new Pod, which is only five seconds old. That's the reconciliation loop at work.

You told Kubernetes, by means of the Deployment you created, that the `demo` Pod must *always* be running. It takes you at your word, and even if you delete the Pod yourself, Kubernetes assumes you must have made a mistake, and helpfully starts a new Pod to replace it for you.

Once you've finished experimenting with the Deployment, shut it down and clean up using the following command:

```
kubectl delete all --selector app=demo
pod "demo-54df94b7b7-hrspp" deleted
service "demo" deleted
deployment.apps "demo" deleted
```

The Kubernetes Scheduler

We've said things like *the Deployment will create Pods* and *Kubernetes will start the required Pod*, without really explaining how that happens.

The Kubernetes *scheduler* is the component responsible for this part of the process. When a Deployment (via its associated ReplicaSet) decides that a new replica is needed, it creates a Pod resource in the Kubernetes database. Simultaneously, this Pod is added to a queue, which is like the scheduler's inbox.

The scheduler's job is to watch its queue of unscheduled Pods, grab the next Pod from it, and find a node to run it on. It will use a few different criteria, including the Pod's resource requests, to choose a suitable node, assuming there is one available (we'll talk more about this process in Chapter 5).

Once the Pod has been scheduled on a node, the kubelet running on that node picks it up and takes care of actually starting its containers (see "Node Components" on page 35).

When you deleted a Pod in "Maintaining Desired State" on page 57, it was the node's ReplicaSet that spotted this and started a replacement. It *knows* that a `demo` Pod should be running on its node, and if it doesn't find one, it will start one. (What would happen if you shut the node down altogether? Its Pods would become unscheduled and go back into the scheduler's queue, to be reassigned to other nodes.)

Stripe engineer Julia Evans has written a delightfully clear explanation of how scheduling works in Kubernetes (*https://jvns.ca/blog/2017/07/27/how-does-the-kubernetes-scheduler-work/*).

Resource Manifests in YAML Format

Now that you know how to run an application in Kubernetes, is that it? Are you done? Not quite. Using the `kubectl run` command to create a Deployment is useful, but limited. Suppose you want to change something about the Deployment spec: the image name or version, say. You could delete the existing Deployment (using `kubectl delete`) and create a new one with the right fields. But let's see if we can do better.

Because Kubernetes is inherently a *declarative* system, continuously reconciling actual state with desired state, all you need to do is change the desired state—the Deployment spec—and Kubernetes will do the rest. How do you do that?

Resources Are Data

All Kubernetes resources, such as Deployments or Pods, are represented by records in its internal database. The reconciliation loop watches the database for any changes to those records, and takes the appropriate action. In fact, all the `kubectl run` command does is add a new record in the database corresponding to a Deployment, and Kubernetes does the rest.

But you don't need to use `kubectl run` in order to interact with Kubernetes. You can also create and edit the resource *manifest* (the specification for the desired state of the resource) directly. You can keep the manifest file in a version control system, and instead of running imperative commands to make on-the-fly changes, you can change your manifest files and then tell Kubernetes to read the updated data.

Deployment Manifests

The usual format for Kubernetes manifest files is YAML, although it can also understand the JSON format. So what does the YAML manifest for a Deployment look like?

Have a look at our example for the demo application (*hello-k8s/k8s/deployment.yaml*):

```yaml
apiVersion: apps/v1
kind: Deployment
metadata:
  name: demo
  labels:
    app: demo
spec:
  replicas: 1
  selector:
    matchLabels:
      app: demo
  template:
    metadata:
      labels:
        app: demo
```

```
spec:
  containers:
    - name: demo
      image: cloudnatived/demo:hello
      ports:
        - containerPort: 8888
```

At first glance, this looks complicated, but it's mostly boilerplate. The only interesting parts are the same information that you've already seen in various forms: the container image name and port. When you gave this information to kubectl run earlier, it created the equivalent of this YAML manifest behind the scenes and submitted it to Kubernetes.

Using kubectl apply

To use the full power of Kubernetes as a declarative infrastructure as code system, submit YAML manifests to the cluster yourself, using the kubectl apply command.

Try it with our example Deployment manifest, *hello-k8s/k8s/deployment.yaml*.[1]

Run the following commands in your copy of the demo repo:

```
cd hello-k8s
kubectl apply -f k8s/deployment.yaml
deployment.apps "demo" created
```

After a few seconds, a demo Pod should be running:

```
kubectl get pods --selector app=demo
NAME                    READY   STATUS    RESTARTS   AGE
demo-6d99bf474d-z9zv6   1/1     Running   0          2m
```

We're not quite done, though, because in order to connect to the demo Pod with a web browser, we're going to create a Service, which is a Kubernetes resource that lets you connect to your deployed Pods (more on this in a moment).

First, let's explore what a Service is, and why we need one.

Service Resources

Suppose you want to make a network connection to a Pod (such as our example application). How do you do that? You could find out the Pod's IP address and connect directly to that address and the app's port number. But the IP address may change when the Pod is restarted, so you'll have to keep looking it up to make sure it's up to date.

---

1 *k8s*, pronounced *kates*, is a common abbreviation for *Kubernetes*, following the geeky pattern of abbreviating words as a *numeronym*: their first and last letters, plus the number of letters in between (*k-8-s*). See also *i18n* (internationalization), *a11y* (accessibility), and *o11y* (observability).

Worse, there may be multiple replicas of the Pod, each with different addresses. Every other application that needs to contact the Pod would have to maintain a list of those addresses, which doesn't sound like a great idea.

Fortunately, there's a better way: a Service resource gives you a single, unchanging IP address or DNS name that will be automatically routed to any matching Pod. Later on in "Ingress Resources" on page 173 we will talk about the Ingress resource, which allows for more advanced routing and using TLS certificates.

But for now, let's take a closer look at how a Kubernetes Service works.

You can think of a Service as being like a web proxy or a load balancer, forwarding requests to a set of *backend* Pods (Figure 4-2). However, it isn't restricted to web ports: a Service can forward traffic from any port to any other port, as detailed in the ports part of the spec.

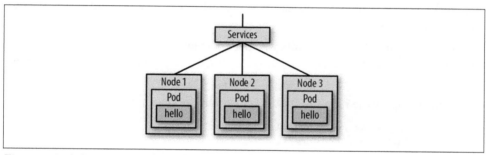

Figure 4-2. A Service provides a persistent endpoint for a group of Pods

Here's the YAML manifest of the Service for our demo app:

```
apiVersion: v1
kind: Service
metadata:
  name: demo
  labels:
    app: demo
spec:
  ports:
  - port: 8888
    protocol: TCP
    targetPort: 8888
  selector:
    app: demo
  type: ClusterIP
```

You can see that it looks somewhat similar to the Deployment resource we showed earlier. However, the kind is Service, instead of Deployment, and the spec just includes a list of ports, plus a selector and a type.

If you zoom in a little, you can see that the Service is forwarding its port 8888 to the Pod's port 8888:

```
...
ports:
- port: 8888
  protocol: TCP
  targetPort: 8888
```

The `selector` is the part that tells the Service how to route requests to particular Pods. Requests will be forwarded to any Pods matching the specified set of labels; in this case, just `app: demo` (see "Labels" on page 155). In our example, there's only one Pod that matches, but if there were multiple Pods, the Service would send each request to a randomly selected one.[2]

In this respect, a Kubernetes Service is a little like a traditional load balancer, and, in fact, both Services and Ingresses can automatically create cloud load balancers (see "Ingress Resources" on page 173).

For now, the main thing to remember is that a Deployment manages a set of Pods for your application, and a Service gives you a single entry point for requests to those Pods.

Go ahead and apply the manifest now, to create the Service:

```
kubectl apply -f k8s/service.yaml
service "demo" created
```

```
kubectl port-forward service/demo 9999:8888
Forwarding from 127.0.0.1:9999 -> 8888
Forwarding from [::1]:9999 -> 8888
```

As before, `kubectl port-forward` will connect the `demo` pod to a port on your local machine, so that you can connect to *http://localhost:9999/* with your web browser.

Once you're satisfied that everything is working correctly, run the following command to clean up before moving on to the next section:

```
kubectl delete -f k8s/
```

 You can use `kubectl delete` with a label selector, as we did earlier on, to delete all resources that match the selector (see "Labels" on page 155). Alternatively, you can use `kubectl delete -f`, as here, with a directory of manifests. All the resources described by the manifest files will be deleted.

---

2 This is the default load balancing algorithm; Kubernetes versions 1.10+ support other algorithms too, such as *least connection*. See *https://kubernetes.io/blog/2018/07/09/ipvs-based-in-cluster-load-balancing-deep-dive/*.

Querying the Cluster with kubectl

The `kubectl` tool is the Swiss Army knife of Kubernetes: it applies configuration, creates, modifies, and destroys resources, and can also query the cluster for information about the resources that exist, as well as their status.

We've already seen how to use `kubectl get` to query Pods and Deployments. You can also use it to see what nodes exist in your cluster:

```
kubectl get nodes
NAME          STATUS   ROLES    AGE     VERSION
my-machine    Ready    <none>   3d20h   v1.18.4-1+6f17be3f1fd54a
```

If you want to see resources of all types, use `kubectl get all`. (In fact, this doesn't show literally *all* resources, just the most common types, but we won't quibble about that for now.)

To see comprehensive information about an individual Pod (or any other resource), use `kubectl describe`:

```
kubectl describe pod/demo-dev-6c96484c48-69vss
Name:          demo-dev-6c96484c48-69vss
Namespace:     default
Node:          docker-for-desktop/10.0.2.15
Start Time:    Wed, 06 Jun 2018 10:48:50 +0100
...
Containers:
  demo:
    Container ID:   docker://646aaf7c4baf6d...
    Image:          cloudnatived/demo:hello
...
Conditions:
  Type           Status
  Initialized    True
  Ready          True
  PodScheduled   True
...
Events:
  Type     Reason      Age    From                Message
  ----     ------      ----   ----                -------
  Normal   Scheduled   1d     default-scheduler   Successfully assigned demo-dev...
  Normal   Pulling     1d     kubelet             pulling image "cloudnatived/demo...
...
```

In the example output, you can see that kubectl gives you some basic information about the container itself, including its image identifier and status, along with an ordered list of events that have happened to the container. (We'll learn a lot more about the power of kubectl in Chapter 7.)

Taking Resources to the Next Level

You now know everything you need to know to deploy applications to Kubernetes clusters using declarative YAML manifests. But there's a lot of repetition in these files: for example, you've repeated the name demo, the label selector app: demo, and the port 8888 several times.

Shouldn't you be able to just specify those values once, and then reference them wherever they occur through the Kubernetes manifests?

For example, it would be great to be able to define variables called something like container.name and container.port, and then use them wherever they're needed in the YAML files. Then, if you needed to change the name of the app or the port number it listens on, you'd only have to change them in one place, and all the manifests would be updated automatically.

Fortunately, there's a tool for that, and in the final section of this chapter we'll show you a little of what it can do.

Helm: A Kubernetes Package Manager

One popular package manager for Kubernetes is called Helm, and it works just the way we've described in the previous section. You can use the helm command-line tool to install and configure applications (your own or anyone else's), and you can create packages called Helm *charts*, which completely specify the resources needed to run the application, its dependencies, and its configurable settings.

Helm is part of the Cloud Native Computing Foundation family of projects (see "Cloud Native" on page 15), which reflects its stability and widespread adoption.

It's important to realize that a Helm chart, unlike the binary software packages used by tools like APT or Yum, doesn't actually include the container image itself. Instead, it simply contains metadata about where the image can be found, just as a Kubernetes Deployment does.

When you install the chart, Kubernetes itself will locate and download the binary container image from the place you specified. In fact, a Helm chart is really just a convenient wrapper around Kubernetes YAML manifests.

Installing Helm

Follow the Helm installation instructions (*https://helm.sh/docs/intro/install/*) for your operating system.

To verify that Helm is installed and working, run:

```
helm version
version.BuildInfo{Version:"v3.2.3",
GitCommit:"8f832046e258e2cb800894579b1b3b50c2d83492",
GitTreeState:"clean", GoVersion:"go1.13.12"}
```

Once this command succeeds, you're ready to start using Helm.

Installing a Helm Chart

What would the Helm chart for our demo application look like? In the *hello-helm3* directory, you'll see a *k8s* subdirectory, which in the previous example (`hello-k8s`) contained just the Kubernetes manifest files to deploy the application. Now it contains a Helm chart, in the *demo* directory:

```
ls k8s/demo
Chart.yaml              prod-values.yaml staging-values.yaml    templates
values.yaml
```

We'll see what all these files are for in "What's Inside a Helm Chart?" on page 222, but for now, let's use Helm to install the demo application. First, clean up the resources from any previous deployments:

```
kubectl delete all --selector app=demo
```

Then run the following command:

```
helm install demo ./k8s/demo
NAME: demo
LAST DEPLOYED: Fri Jul  3 08:06:01 2020
NAMESPACE: default
STATUS: deployed
REVISION: 1
TEST SUITE: None
```

You can see that Helm has created a Deployment resource (which starts a Pod) and a Service, just as in the previous example. The `helm install` command also creates a Kubernetes Secret with a Type of `helm.sh/release` to track the release .

Charts, Repositories, and Releases

These are the three most important Helm terms you need to know:

- A *chart* is a Helm package, containing all the resource definitions necessary to run an application in Kubernetes.

- A *repository* is a place where charts can be collected and shared.
- A *release* is a particular instance of a chart running in a Kubernetes cluster.

One chart can often be installed many times into the same cluster. For example, you might be running multiple copies of the Nginx web server chart, each serving a different site. Each separate instance of the chart is a distinct release.

Listing Helm Releases

To check what releases you have running at any time, run `helm list`:

```
helm list
NAME  NAMESPACE  REVISION  UPDATED         STATUS    CHART       APP VERSION
demo  default    1         2020-07-03 ...  deployed  demo-1.0.1
```

To see the exact status of a particular release, run `helm status` followed by the name of the release. You'll see the same information that you did when you first deployed the release.

Later in the book, we'll show you how to build your own Helm charts for your applications (see "What's Inside a Helm Chart?" on page 222). For now, just know that Helm is a handy way to install applications from public charts.

 You can see the full list of public Helm charts (*https://github.com/helm/charts/tree/master/stable*) on GitHub.

You can also get a list of available charts by running `helm search repo` with no arguments (or `helm search repo redis` to search for a Redis chart, for example).

Summary

This isn't a book about Kubernetes internals (sorry, no refunds). Our aim is to show you what Kubernetes can *do*, and bring you quickly to the point where you can run real workloads in production. However, it's useful to know at least some of the main pieces of machinery you'll be working with, such as Pods and Deployments. In this chapter we've briefly introduced some of the most important ones.

As fascinating as the technology is to geeks like us, though, we're also interested in getting stuff done. Therefore, we haven't exhaustively covered every kind of resource Kubernetes provides, because there are a *lot*, and many of them you almost certainly won't need (at least, not yet).

The key points we think you need to know right now:

- The Pod is the fundamental unit of work in Kubernetes, specifying a single container or group of communicating containers that are scheduled together.

- A Deployment is a high-level Kubernetes resource that declaratively manages Pods, deploying, scheduling, updating, and restarting them when necessary.

- A Service is the Kubernetes equivalent of a load balancer or proxy, routing traffic to its matching Pods via a single, well-known, durable IP address or DNS name.

- The Kubernetes scheduler watches for a Pod that isn't yet running on any node, finds a suitable node for it, and instructs the kubelet on that node to run the Pod.

- Resources like Deployments are represented by records in Kubernetes's internal database. Externally, these resources can be represented by text files (known as *manifests*) in YAML format. The manifest is a declaration of the desired state of the resource.

- kubectl is the main tool for interacting with Kubernetes, allowing you to apply manifests, query resources, make changes, delete resources, and do many other tasks.

- Helm is a Kubernetes package manager. It simplifies configuring and deploying Kubernetes applications, allowing you to use a single set of values (such as the application name or listen port) and a set of templates to generate Kubernetes YAML files, instead of having to maintain the raw YAML files yourself.

CHAPTER 5

Managing Resources

Nothing is enough to the man for whom enough is too little.

—Epicurus

In this chapter we'll look at how to make the most of your cluster: how to manage and optimize resource usage, how to manage the life cycle of containers, and how to partition the cluster using namespaces. We'll also outline some techniques and best practices for keeping down the cost of your cluster, while getting the most for your money.

You'll learn how to use resource requests, limits, and defaults, and how to optimize them with the Vertical Pod Autoscaler; how to use readiness probes, liveness probes, and Pod disruption budgets to manage containers; how to optimize cloud storage; and how and when to use preemptible or reserved instances to control costs.

Understanding Resources

Suppose you have a Kubernetes cluster of a given capacity, with a reasonable number of nodes of the right kind of size. How do you get the most bang for your buck out of it? That is, how do you get the best possible utilization of the available cluster resources for your workload, while still ensuring that you have enough headroom to deal with demand spikes, node failures, and bad deployments?

To answer this, put yourself in the place of the Kubernetes scheduler and try to see things from its point of view. The scheduler's job is to decide where to run a given Pod. Are there any nodes with enough free resources to run the Pod?

This question is impossible to answer unless the scheduler knows how much resource the Pod will need to run. A Pod that needs 1 GiB of memory cannot be scheduled on a node with only 100 MiB of free memory.

Similarly, the scheduler has to be able to take action when a greedy Pod is grabbing too many resources and starving other Pods on the same node. But how much is too much? In order to schedule Pods effectively, the scheduler has to know the minimum and maximum allowable resource requirements for each Pod.

That's where Kubernetes resource requests and limits come in. Kubernetes understands how to manage two kinds of resources: CPU and memory. There are other important types of resources, too, such as network bandwidth, disk I/O operations (IOPS), and disk space, and these may cause contention in the cluster, but Kubernetes doesn't yet have a way to describe Pods' requirements for these.

Resource Units

CPU usage for Pods is expressed, as you might expect, in units of CPUs. One Kubernetes CPU unit is equivalent to one AWS vCPU, one Google Cloud Core, one Azure vCore, or one *hyperthread* on a bare-metal processor that supports hyperthreading. In other words, *1 CPU* in Kubernetes terms means what you think it does.

Because most Pods don't need a whole CPU, requests and limits are usually expressed in *millicpus* (sometimes called *millicores*). Memory is measured in bytes, or more handily, *mebibytes* (MiB).

Resource Requests

A Kubernetes *resource request* specifies the minimum amount of that resource that the Pod needs to run. For example, a resource request of 100m (100 millicpus) and 250Mi (250 MiB of memory) means that the Pod cannot be scheduled on a node with less than those resources available. If there isn't any node with enough capacity available, the Pod will remain in a pending state until there is.

For example, if all your cluster nodes have two CPU cores and 4 GiB of memory, a container that requests 2.5 CPUs will never be scheduled, and neither will one that requests 5 GiB of memory.

Let's see what resource requests would look like, applied to our demo application:

```
spec:
  containers:
  - name: demo
    image: cloudnatived/demo:hello
    ports:
    - containerPort: 8888
    resources:
      requests:
        memory: "10Mi"
        cpu: "100m"
```

Resource Limits

A *resource limit* specifies the maximum amount of resource that a Pod is allowed to use. A Pod that tries to use more than its allocated CPU limit will be *throttled*, reducing its performance.

A Pod that tries to use more than the allowed memory limit, though, will be terminated. If the terminated Pod can be rescheduled, it will be. In practice, this may mean that the Pod is simply restarted on the same node.

Some applications, such as network servers, can consume more and more resources over time in response to increasing demand. Specifying resource limits is a good way to prevent such hungry Pods from using more than their fair share of the cluster's capacity.

Here's an example of setting resource limits on the demo application:

```
spec:
  containers:
  - name: demo
    image: cloudnatived/demo:hello
    ports:
    - containerPort: 8888
    resources:
      limits:
        memory: "20Mi"
        cpu: "250m"
```

Knowing what limits to set for a particular application is a matter of observation and judgment (see "Optimizing Pods" on page 83).

Kubernetes allows resources to be *overcommitted*; that is, the sum of all the resource limits of containers on a node can exceed the total resources of that node. This is a kind of gamble: the scheduler is betting that, most of the time, most containers will not need to hit their resource limits.

If this gamble fails, and total resource usage starts approaching the maximum capacity of the node, Kubernetes will start being more aggressive in terminating containers. Under conditions of resource pressure, containers that have exceeded their requests, but not their limits, may still be terminated.[1]

All other things being equal, if Kubernetes needs to terminate Pods, it will start with the ones that have most exceeded their requests. Pods that are within their requests will not be terminated except in very rare circumstances where Kubernetes would otherwise be unable to run its system components, such as the kubelet.

---

[1] It's possible to customize this behavior for individual containers using Quality of Service (*https://kubernetes.io/docs/tasks/configure-pod-container/quality-service-pod/*) (QoS) classes.

Best Practice

Always specify resource requests and limits for your containers. This helps Kubernetes schedule and manage your Pods properly.

Keep Your Containers Small

We mentioned in "Minimal Container Images" on page 26 that keeping your container images as small as possible is a good idea, for lots of reasons:

- Small containers build faster.
- The images take up less storage.
- Image pulls are faster.
- The attack surface is reduced.

If you're using Go, you're already way ahead, because Go can compile your application into a single statically linked binary. If there's only one file in your container, it's about as small as it can be!

Managing the Container Life Cycle

We've seen that Kubernetes can best manage your Pods when it knows what their CPU and memory requirements are. But it also has to know when a container is working: that is, when it's functioning properly and ready to handle requests.

It's quite common for containerized applications to get into a stuck state, where the process is still running, but it's not serving any requests. Kubernetes needs a way to detect this situation, so that it can restart the container to fix the problem.

Liveness Probes

Kubernetes lets you specify a *liveness* probe as part of the container spec: a health check that determines whether or not the container is alive (that is, working).

For an HTTP server container, the liveness probe specification usually looks something like this:

```
livenessProbe:
  httpGet:
    path: /healthz
    port: 8888
  initialDelaySeconds: 3
  periodSeconds: 3
```

The `httpGet` probe makes an HTTP request to a URI and port you specify; in this case, `/healthz` on port 8888.

If your application doesn't have a specific endpoint for a health check, you could use /, or any valid URL for your application. It's common practice, though, to create a /healthz endpoint just for this purpose. (Why the z? Just to make sure it doesn't collide with an existing path like `health`, which could be a page about health information, for example).

If the application responds with an HTTP 2xx or 3xx status code, Kubernetes considers it alive. If it responds with anything else, or doesn't respond at all, the container is considered dead, and will be restarted.

Probe Delay and Frequency

How soon should Kubernetes start checking your liveness probe? No application can start instantly. If Kubernetes tried the liveness probe immediately after starting the container, it would probably fail, causing the container to be restarted—and this loop would repeat forever!

The `initialDelaySeconds` field lets you tell Kubernetes how long to wait before trying the first liveness probe, avoiding this *loop of death* situation.

Similarly, it wouldn't be a good idea for Kubernetes to hammer your application with requests for the `healthz` endpoint thousands of times a second. The `periodSeconds` field specifies how often the liveness probe should be checked; in this example, every three seconds.

Other Types of Probes

`httpGet` isn't the only kind of probe available; for network servers that don't speak HTTP, you can use `tcpSocket`:

```
livenessProbe:
  tcpSocket:
    port: 8888
```

If a TCP connection to the specified port succeeds, the container is alive.

You can also run an arbitrary command on the container, using an *exec* probe:

```
livenessProbe:
  exec:
    command:
    - cat
    - /tmp/healthy
```

The exec probe runs the specified command inside the container, and the probe succeeds if the command succeeds (that is, exits with a zero status). exec is usually more useful as a readiness probe, and we'll see how they're used in the next section.

gRPC Probes

Although many applications and services communicate via HTTP, it's increasingly popular to use the gRPC (*https://grpc.io/*) protocol instead, especially for microservices. gRPC is an efficient, portable, binary network protocol developed by Google and hosted by the Cloud Native Computing Foundation.

httpGet probes will not work with gRPC servers, and although you could use a tcpSocket probe instead, that only tells you that you can make a connection to the socket, not that the server itself is working.

gRPC has a standard health checking protocol, which most gRPC services support, and to interrogate this health check with a Kubernetes liveness probe you can use the grpc-health-probe tool (*https://kubernetes.io/blog/2018/10/01/health-checking-grpc-servers-on-kubernetes/*). If you add the tool to your container, you can check it using an exec probe.

Readiness Probes

Related to the liveness probe, but with different semantics, is the *readiness probe*. Sometimes an application needs to signal to Kubernetes that it's temporarily unable to handle requests; perhaps because it's performing some lengthy initialization process, or waiting for some subprocess to complete. The readiness probe serves this function.

If your application doesn't start listening for HTTP until it's ready to serve, your readiness probe can be the same as your liveness probe:

```
readinessProbe:
  httpGet:
    path: /healthz
    port: 8888
  initialDelaySeconds: 3
  periodSeconds: 3
```

A container that fails its readiness probe will be removed from any Services that match the Pod. This is like taking a failing node out of a load balancer pool: no traffic will be sent to the Pod until its readiness probe starts succeeding again.

Normally, when a Pod starts, Kubernetes will start sending it traffic as soon as the container is in a running state. However, if the container has a readiness probe, Kubernetes will wait until the probe succeeds before sending it any requests, so that users won't see errors from unready containers. This is critically important for zero-downtime upgrades (see "Deployment Strategies" on page 241 for more about these).

A container that is not ready will still be shown as `Running`, but the `READY` column will show one or more unready containers in the Pod:

```
kubectl get pods
NAME              READY   STATUS    RESTARTS   AGE
readiness-test    0/1     Running   0          56s
```

 Readiness probes should only return HTTP 200 OK status. Although Kubernetes itself considers both 2xx and 3xx status codes as *ready*, cloud load balancers may not. If you're using an Ingress resource coupled with a cloud load balancer (see "Ingress Resources" on page 173), and your readiness probe returns a 301 redirect, for example, the load balancer may flag all your Pods as unhealthy. Make sure your readiness probes only return a 200 status code.

File-Based Readiness Probes

Alternatively, you could have the application create a file on the container's filesystem called something like */tmp/healthy*, and use an `exec` readiness probe to check for the presence of that file.

This kind of readiness probe can be useful, because if you want to take the container temporarily out of service to debug a problem, you can attach to the container and delete the */tmp/healthy* file. The next readiness probe will fail, and Kubernetes will remove the container from any matching Services. (A better way to do this, though, is to adjust the container's labels so that it no longer matches the service: see "Service Resources" on page 60.)

You can now inspect and troubleshoot the container at your leisure. Once you're done, you can either terminate the container and deploy a fixed version, or put the probe file back in place, so that the container will start receiving traffic again.

 Best Practice

Use readiness probes and liveness probes to let Kubernetes know when your application is ready to handle requests, or when it has a problem and needs to be restarted.

minReadySeconds

By default, a container or Pod is considered ready the moment its readiness probe succeeds. In some cases, you may want to run the container for a short while to make sure it is stable. During a deployment, Kubernetes waits until each new Pod is ready before starting the next (see "Rolling Updates" on page 241). If a faulty container crashes straight away, this will halt the rollout, but if it takes a few seconds to crash, all its replicas might be rolled out before you discover the problem.

To avoid this, you can set the minReadySeconds field on the container. A container or Pod will not be considered ready until its readiness probe has been up for minReady Seconds (default 0).

Pod Disruption Budgets

Sometimes Kubernetes needs to stop your Pods even though they're alive and ready (a process called *eviction*). Perhaps the node they're running on is being drained prior to an upgrade, for example, and the Pods need to be moved to another node.

However, this needn't result in downtime for your application, provided enough replicas can be kept running. You can use the PodDisruptionBudget resource to specify, for a given application, how many Pods you can afford to lose at any given time.

For example, you might specify that no more than 10% of your application's Pods can be disrupted at once. Or perhaps you want to specify that Kubernetes can evict any number of Pods, provided that at least three replicas are always running.

minAvailable

Here's an example of a PodDisruptionBudget that specifies a minimum number of Pods to be kept running, using the minAvailable field:

```
apiVersion: policy/v1beta1
kind: PodDisruptionBudget
metadata:
  name: demo-pdb
spec:
  minAvailable: 3
  selector:
    matchLabels:
      app: demo
```

In this example, minAvailable: 3 specifies that at least three Pods matching the label app: demo should always be running. Kubernetes can evict as many demo Pods as it wants, so long as there are always at least three left.

maxUnavailable

Conversely, you can use maxUnavailable to limit the total number or percentage of Pods that Kubernetes is allowed to evict:

```
apiVersion: policy/v1beta1
kind: PodDisruptionBudget
metadata:
  name: demo-pdb
spec:
  maxUnavailable: 10%
  selector:
```

```
    matchLabels:
       app: demo
```

Here, no more than 10% of demo Pods are allowed to be evicted at any one time. This only applies to so-called *voluntary evictions*, though; that is to say, evictions initiated by Kubernetes. If a node suffers a hardware failure or gets deleted, for example, the Pods on it will be involuntarily evicted, even if that would violate the disruption budget.

Since Kubernetes will tend to spread Pods evenly across nodes, all other things being equal, this is worth bearing in mind when considering how many nodes your cluster needs. If you have three nodes, the failure of one could result in the loss of a third of all your Pods, and that may not leave enough to maintain an acceptable level of service (see "High Availability" on page 35).

Best Practice

Set PodDisruptionBudgets for your business-critical applications to make sure there are always enough replicas to maintain the service, even when Pods are evicted.

Using Namespaces

Another very useful way of managing resource usage across your cluster is to use *namespaces*. A Kubernetes namespace is a way of partitioning your cluster into separate subdivisions, for whatever purpose you like.

For example, you might have a prod namespace for production applications, and a test namespace for trying things out. As the term *namespace* suggests, names in one namespace are not visible from a different namespace.

This means that you could have a service called demo in the prod namespace, and a different service called demo in the test namespace, and there won't be any conflict.

To see the namespaces that exist on your cluster, run the following command:

```
kubectl get namespaces
NAME            STATUS     AGE
default         Active     1y
kube-public     Active     1y
kube-system     Active     1y
```

You can think of namespaces as being a bit like folders on your computer's hard disk. While you *could* keep all your files in the same folder, it would be inconvenient. Looking for a particular file would be time-consuming, and it wouldn't be easy to see which files belong with which others. A namespace groups related resources together, and makes it easier to work with them. Unlike folders, however, namespaces can't be nested.

Working with Namespaces

So far when working with Kubernetes we've always used the *default namespace*. If you don't specify a namespace when running a `kubectl` command, such as `kubectl run`, your command will operate on the default namespace. If you're wondering what the `kube-system` namespace is, that's where the Kubernetes internal system components run, so that they're segregated from your own applications.

If, instead, you specify a namespace with the `--namespace` flag (or `-n` for short), your command will use that namespace. For example, to get a list of Pods in the `prod` namespace, run:

```
kubectl get pods --namespace prod
```

What Namespaces Should I Use?

It's entirely up to you how to divide your cluster into namespaces. One idea that makes intuitive sense is to have one namespace per application, or per team. For example, you might create a `demo` namespace to run the demo application in. You can create a namespace using a Kubernetes Namespace resource like the following:

```
apiVersion: v1
kind: Namespace
metadata:
  name: demo
```

To apply this resource manifest, use the `kubectl apply -f` command (see "Resource Manifests in YAML Format" on page 59 for more about this.) You'll find the YAML manifests for all the examples in this section in the demo application repo, in the *hello-namespace* directory:

```
cd demo/hello-namespace
ls k8s
deployment.yaml    limitrange.yaml    namespace.yaml    resourcequota.yaml
service.yaml
```

You could go further and create namespaces for each environment your app runs in, such as `demo-prod`, `demo-staging`, `demo-test`, and so on. You could use a namespace as a kind of temporary *virtual cluster*, and delete the namespace when you're finished with it. But be careful! Deleting a namespace deletes all the resources within it. You really don't want to run that command against the wrong namespace. (See "Introducing Role-Based Access Control (RBAC)" on page 202 for how to grant or deny user permissions on individual namespaces.)

In the current version of Kubernetes, there is no way to *protect* a resource such as a namespace from being deleted (though a proposal (*https://github.com/kubernetes/kubernetes/issues/10179*) for such a feature is under discussion). So don't delete namespaces unless they really are temporary, and you're sure they don't contain any production resources.

Best Practice

Create separate namespaces for each of your applications or each logical component of your infrastructure. Don't use the default namespace: it's too easy to make mistakes.

If you need to block all network traffic in or out of a particular namespace, you can use Kubernetes Network Policies (*https://kubernetes.io/docs/concepts/services-networking/network-policies/*) to enforce this.

Service Addresses

Although namespaces are isolated from one another, they can still communicate with Services in other namespaces. You may recall from "Service Resources" on page 60 that every Kubernetes Service has an associated DNS name that you can use to talk to it. Connecting to the hostname demo will connect you to the Service whose name is demo. How does that work across different namespaces?

Service DNS names always follow this pattern:

```
SERVICE.NAMESPACE.svc.cluster.local
```

The .svc.cluster.local part is optional, and so is the namespace. But if you want to talk to the demo Service in the prod namespace, for example, you can use:

```
demo.prod
```

Even if you have a dozen different Services called demo, each in its own namespace, you can add the namespace to the DNS name for the Service to specify exactly which one you mean.

Resource Quotas

As well as restricting the CPU and memory usage of individual containers, which you learned about in "Resource Requests" on page 70, you can (and should) restrict the resource usage of a given namespace. The way to do this is to create a ResourceQuota in the namespace. Here's an example ResourceQuota:

```
apiVersion: v1
kind: ResourceQuota
metadata:
  name: demo-resourcequota
spec:
  hard:
    pods: "100"
```

Applying this manifest to a particular namespace (for example, demo) sets a hard limit of 100 Pods running at once in that namespace. (Note that the metadata.name of the ResourceQuota can be anything you like. The namespaces it affects depends on which namespaces you apply the manifest to.)

```
cd demo/hello-namespace
kubectl create namespace demo
namespace "demo" created
kubectl apply --namespace demo -f k8s/resourcequota.yaml
resourcequota "demo-resourcequota" created
```

Now Kubernetes will block any API operations in the demo namespace that would exceed the quota. The example ResourceQuota limits the namespace to 100 Pods, so if there are 100 Pods already running and you try to start a new one, you will see an error message like this:

```
Error from server (Forbidden): pods "demo" is forbidden: exceeded quota:
demo-resourcequota, requested: pods=1, used: pods=100, limited: pods=100
```

Using ResourceQuotas is a good way to stop applications in one namespace from grabbing too many resources and starving those in other parts of the cluster.

Although you can also limit the total CPU and memory usage of Pods in a namespace, we don't recommend this. If you set these totals quite low, they'll likely cause you unexpected and hard-to-spot problems when your workloads are getting close to the limit. If you set them very high, there's not much point in setting them at all.

However, a Pod limit is useful to prevent a misconfiguration or typing error from generating a potentially unlimited number of Pods. It's easy to forget to clean up some object from a regular task, and find one day that you've got thousands of them clogging up your cluster.

Best Practice

Use ResourceQuotas in each namespace to enforce a limit on the number of Pods that can run in the namespace.

To check if a ResourceQuota is active in a particular namespace, use the kubectl get resourcequotas command:

```
kubectl get resourcequotas -n demo
NAME                  AGE
demo-resourcequota    15d
```

Default Resource Requests and Limits

It's not always easy to know what your container's resource requirements are going to be in advance. You can set default requests and limits for all containers in a namespace using a LimitRange resource:

```
apiVersion: v1
kind: LimitRange
metadata:
  name: demo-limitrange
spec:
  limits:
  - default:
      cpu: "500m"
      memory: "256Mi"
    defaultRequest:
      cpu: "200m"
      memory: "128Mi"
    type: Container
```

As with ResourceQuotas, the `metadata.name` of the LimitRange can be whatever you want. It doesn't correspond to a Kubernetes namespace, for example. A LimitRange or ResourceQuota takes effect in a particular namespace only when you apply the manifest to that namespace.

Any container in the namespace that doesn't specify a resource limit or request will inherit the default value from the LimitRange. For example, a container with no `cpu` request specified will inherit the value of `200m` from the LimitRange. Similarly, a container with no `memory` limit specified will inherit the value of `256Mi` from the Limit-Range.

In theory, then, you could set the defaults in a LimitRange and not bother to specify requests or limits for individual containers. However, this isn't good practice: it should be possible to look at a container spec and see what its requests and limits are, without having to know whether or not a LimitRange is in effect. Use the LimitRange only as a backstop to prevent problems with containers whose owners forgot to specify requests and limits.

Best Practice

Use LimitRanges in each namespace to set default resource requests and limits for containers, but don't rely on them; treat them as a backstop. Always specify explicit requests and limits in the container spec itself.

Optimizing Cluster Costs

In "Cluster Sizing and Scaling" on page 95, we outlined some considerations for choosing the initial size of your cluster, and scaling it over time as your workloads evolve. But assuming that your cluster is correctly sized and has sufficient capacity, how should you run it in the most cost-effective way?

Optimizing Deployments

Do you really need quite so many replicas? It may seem an obvious point, but every Pod in your cluster uses up some resources that are thus unavailable to some other Pod.

It can be tempting to run a large number of replicas for everything, so that quality of service will never be reduced if individual Pods fail, or during rolling upgrades. Also, the more replicas, the more traffic your apps can handle.

But you should use replicas wisely. Your cluster can only run a finite number of Pods. Give them to applications that really need maximum availability and performance.

If it really doesn't matter that a given Deployment is down for a few seconds during an upgrade, it doesn't need a lot of replicas. A surprisingly large number of applications and services can get by perfectly well with one or two replicas.

Review the number of replicas configured for each Deployment, and ask:

- What are the business requirements for performance and availability for this service?
- Can we meet those requirements with fewer replicas?

If an app is struggling to handle demand, or users get too many errors when you upgrade the Deployment, it needs more replicas. But in many cases you can reduce the size of a Deployment considerably before you get to the point where the degradation starts to be noticeable.

Best Practice

Use the minimum number of Pods for a given Deployment that will satisfy your performance and availability requirements. Gradually reduce the number of replicas to just above the point where your service level objectives are met.

Optimizing Pods

Earlier in this chapter, in "Resource Requests" on page 70, we emphasized the importance of setting the correct resource requests and limits for your containers. If the resource requests are too small, you'll soon know about it: Pods will start failing. If they are too large, however, the first time you find about it may be when you get your monthly cloud bill.

You should regularly review the resource requests and limits for your various workloads, and compare them against what was actually used.

Most managed Kubernetes services offer some kind of dashboard showing the CPU and memory usage of your containers over time—we'll see more about this in "Monitoring Cluster Status" on page 213.

You can also build your own dashboards and statistics using Prometheus and Grafana, and we'll cover this in detail in Chapter 15.

Setting the optimal resource requests and limits is something of an art, and the answer will be different for every kind of workload. Some containers may be idle most of the time, occasionally spiking their resource usage to handle a request; others may be constantly busy, and gradually use more and more memory until they hit their limits.

In general, you should set the resource limits for a container to a little above the maximum it uses in normal operation. For example, if a given container's memory usage over a few days never exceeds 500 MiB of memory, you might set its memory limit to 600 MiB.

> Should containers have limits at all? One school of thought says that containers should have *no* limits in production, or that the limits should be set so high that the containers will never exceed them. With very large and resource-hungry containers that are expensive to restart, this may make some sense, but we think it's better to set limits anyway. Without them, a container that has a memory leak, or that uses too much CPU, can gobble up all the resources available on a node, starving other containers.
>
> To avoid this *resource Pac-Man* scenario, set a container's limits to a little more than 100% of normal usage. This will ensure it's not killed as long as it's working properly, but still minimize the blast radius if something goes wrong.

Request settings are less critical than limits, but they still should not be set too high (as the Pod will never be scheduled), or too low (as Pods that exceed their requests are first in line for eviction).

Vertical Pod Autoscaler

There is a Kubernetes add-on called the Vertical Pod Autoscaler (*https://github.com/kubernetes/autoscaler/tree/master/vertical-pod-autoscaler*), which can help you work out the ideal values for resource requests. It will watch a specified Deployment and automatically adjust the resource requests for its Pods based on what they actually use. It has a dry-run mode that will just make suggestions, without actually modifying the running Pods, and this can be helpful.

Optimizing Nodes

Kubernetes can work with a wide range of node sizes, but some will perform better than others. To get the best cluster capacity for your money, you need to observe how your nodes perform in practice, under real demand conditions, with your specific workloads. This will help you determine the most cost-effective instance types.

It's worth remembering that every node has to have an operating system on it, which consumes disk, memory, and CPU resources. So do the Kubernetes system components and the container runtime. The smaller the node, the bigger a proportion of its total resources this overhead represents.

Larger nodes, therefore, can be more cost-effective, because a greater proportion of their resources are available for your workloads. The trade-off is that losing an individual node has a bigger effect on your cluster's available capacity.

Small nodes also have a higher percentage of *stranded resources*: chunks of memory space and CPU time that are unused, but too small for any existing Pod to claim them.

A good rule of thumb (*https://medium.com/@dyachuk/why-do-kubernetes-clusters-in-aws-cost-more-than-they-should-fa510c1964c6*) is that nodes should be big enough to run at least five of your typical Pods, keeping the proportion of stranded resources to around 10% or less. If the node can run 10 or more Pods, stranded resources will be below 5%.

The default limit in Kubernetes is 110 Pods per node. Although you can increase this limit by adjusting the `--max-pods` setting of the `kubelet`, this may not be possible with some managed services, and it's a good idea to stick to the Kubernetes defaults unless there is a strong reason to change them.

The Pods-per-node limit means that you may not be able to take advantage of your cloud provider's largest instance sizes. Instead, consider running a larger number of smaller nodes (*https://medium.com/@brendanrius/scaling-kubernetes-for-25m-users-a7937e3536a0*) to get better utilization. For example, instead of 6 nodes with 8 vCPUs, run 12 nodes with 4 vCPUs.

Look at the percentage resource utilization of each node, using your cloud provider's dashboard or `kubectl top nodes`. The bigger the percentage of CPU in use, the better the utilization. If the larger nodes in your cluster have better utilization, you may be well advised to remove some of the smaller nodes and replace them with larger ones.

On the other hand, if larger nodes have low utilization, your cluster may be over capacity and you can therefore either remove some nodes, or make them smaller, reducing the total bill.

Best Practice

Larger nodes tend to be more cost-effective, because less of their resources are consumed by system overhead. Size your nodes by looking at real-world utilization figures for your cluster, aiming for between 10 and 100 Pods per node.

Optimizing Storage

One cloud cost that is often overlooked is that of disk storage. Cloud providers offer varying amounts of disk space with each of their instance sizes, and the price of large-scale storage varies too.

While it's possible to achieve quite high CPU and memory utilization using Kubernetes resource requests and limits, the same is not true of storage, and many cluster nodes are significantly over-provisioned with disk space.

Not only do many nodes have more storage space than they need, the class of storage can also be a factor. Most cloud providers offer different classes of storage depending on the number of I/O operations per second (IOPS), or bandwidth, allocated.

For example, databases that use persistent disk volumes often need a very high IOPS rating, for fast, high-throughput storage access. This is expensive. You can save on cloud costs by provisioning low-IOPS storage for workloads that don't need so much bandwidth. On the other hand, if your application is performing poorly because it's spending a lot of time waiting for storage I/O, you may want to provision more IOPS to handle this.

Your cloud or Kubernetes provider console can usually show you how many IOPS are actually being used on your nodes, and you can use these figures to help you decide where to cut costs.

Ideally, you would be able to set resource requests for containers that need high bandwidth or large amounts of storage. However, Kubernetes does not currently support this, though support for IOPS requests may be added in the future.

Best Practice

Don't use instance types with more storage than you need. Provision the smallest, lowest-IOPS disk volumes you can, based on the throughput and space that you actually use.

Cleaning Up Unused Resources

As your Kubernetes clusters grow, you will find many unused, or *lost* resources hanging around in dark corners. Over time, if these lost resources are not cleaned up, they will start to represent a significant fraction of your overall costs.

At the highest level, you may find cloud instances that are not part of any cluster; it's easy to forget to terminate a machine when it's no longer in use.

Other types of cloud resources, such as load balancers, public IPs, and disk volumes, also cost you money even though they're not in use. You should regularly review your usage of each type of resource, to find and remove unused instances.

Similarly, there may be Deployments and Pods in your Kubernetes cluster that are not actually referenced by any Service, and so cannot receive traffic.

Even container images that are not running take up disk space on your nodes. Fortunately, Kubernetes will automatically clean up unused images when the node starts running short of disk space.[2]

Using owner metadata

One helpful way to minimize unused resources is to have an organization-wide policy that each resource must be tagged with information about its owner. You can use Kubernetes annotations to do this (see "Labels and Annotations" on page 158).

For example, you could annotate each Deployment like this:

```
apiVersion: apps/v1
kind: Deployment
metadata:
  name: my-brilliant-app
  annotations:
    example.com/owner: "Customer Apps Team"
...
```

The owner metadata should specify the person or team to be contacted about this resource. This is useful anyway, but it's especially handy for identifying abandoned or unused resources. (Note that it's a good idea to prefix custom annotations with the

---

2 You can customize this behavior by adjusting the kubelet garbage collection (*https://kubernetes.io/docs/concepts/cluster-administration/kubelet-garbage-collection/*) settings.

domain name of your company, such as `example.com`, to prevent collisions with other annotations that might have the same name.)

You can regularly query the cluster for all resources that do not have an owner annotation and make a list of them for potential termination. An especially strict policy might terminate all unowned resources immediately. Don't be too strict, though, especially at first: developer goodwill is as important a resource as cluster capacity, if not more so.

Best Practice

Set owner annotations on all your resources, giving information about who to contact if there's a problem with this resource, or if it seems abandoned and liable for termination.

Finding underutilized resources

Some resources may be receiving very low levels of traffic, or none at all. Perhaps they became disconnected from a Service front end due to a change in labels, or maybe they were temporary or experimental.

Every Pod should expose the number of requests it receives as a metric (see Chapter 16 for more about this). Use these metrics to find Pods that are getting low or zero traffic, and make a list of resources that can potentially be terminated.

You can also check the CPU and memory utilization figures for each Pod in your web console and find the least-utilized Pods in your cluster. Pods which don't do anything probably aren't a good use of resources.

If the Pods have owner metadata, contact their owners to find out whether these Pods are actually needed (for example, they might be for an application still in development).

You could use another custom Kubernetes annotation (perhaps `example.com/lowtraffic`) to identify Pods that receive no requests, but are still needed for one reason or another.

Best Practice

Regularly review your cluster to find underutilized or abandoned resources and eliminate them. Owner annotations can help.

Cleaning up completed Jobs

Kubernetes Jobs (see "Jobs" on page 168) are Pods that run once to completion and are not restarted. However, the Job objects still exist in the Kubernetes database, and once there are a significant number of completed Jobs, this can affect API performance. A handy tool for cleaning up completed Jobs is kube-job-cleaner (*https:// github.com/hjacobs/kube-job-cleaner*).

Checking Spare Capacity

There should always be enough spare capacity in the cluster to handle the failure of a single worker node. To check this, try draining your biggest node (see "Scaling down" on page 101). Once all Pods have been evicted from the node, check that all your applications are still in a working state with the configured number of replicas. If this is not the case, you need to add more capacity to the cluster.

If there isn't room to reschedule its workloads when a node fails, your services could be degraded at best, and unavailable at worst.

Using Reserved Instances

Some cloud providers offer different instance classes depending on the machine's life cycle. *Reserved* instances offer a trade-off between price and flexibility.

For example, AWS reserved instances are about half the price of *on-demand* instances (the default type). You can reserve instances for various periods: a year, three years, and so on. AWS reserved instances have a fixed size, so if it turns out in three months time that you need a larger instance, your reservation will be mostly wasted.

The Google Cloud equivalent of reserved instances is *Committed Use Discounts*, which allow you to prepay for a certain number of vCPUs and an amount of memory. This is more flexible than AWS reservations, as you can use more resources than you have reserved; you just pay the normal on-demand price for anything not covered by your reservation.

Reserved instances and committed use discounts can be a good choice when you know your requirements for the foreseeable future. However, there's no refund for reservations that you don't end up using, and you have to pay up front for the whole reservation period. So you should only choose to reserve instances for a period over which your requirements aren't likely to change significantly.

If you can plan a year or two ahead, however, using reserved instances could deliver a considerable saving.

Best Practice

Use reserved instances when your needs aren't likely to change for a year or two—but choose your reservations wisely, because they can't be altered or refunded once they're made.

Using Preemptible (Spot) Instances

Spot instances, as AWS calls them, or *preemptible VMs* in Google's terminology, provide no availability guarantees, and are often limited in life span. Thus, they represent a trade-off between price and availability.

A spot instance is cheap, but may be paused or resumed at any time, and may be terminated altogether. Fortunately, Kubernetes is designed to provide high-availability services despite the loss of individual cluster nodes.

Variable price or variable preemption

Spot instances can therefore be a cost-effective choice for your cluster. With AWS spot instances, the per-hour pricing varies according to demand. When demand is high for a given instance type in a particular region and availability zone, the price will rise.

Google Cloud's preemptible VMs, on the other hand, are billed at a fixed rate, but the rate of preemption varies. Google says that on average, about 5–15% of your nodes will be preempted in a given week (*https://cloud.google.com/compute/docs/instances/preemptible*). However, preemptible VMs can be up to 80% cheaper than on-demand, depending on the instance type.

Preemptible nodes can halve your costs

Using preemptible nodes for your Kubernetes cluster, then, can be a very effective way to reduce costs. While you may need to run a few more nodes to make sure that your workloads can survive preemption, anecdotal evidence suggests that an overall 50% reduction in the cost per node is achievable.

You may also find that using preemptible nodes is a good way to build a little chaos engineering into your cluster (see "Chaos Testing" on page 107)—provided that your application is ready for chaos testing in the first place.

Bear in mind, though, that you should always have enough nonpreemptible nodes to handle your cluster's minimum workload. Never bet more than you can afford to lose. If you have a lot of preemptible nodes, it might be a good idea to use cluster autoscaling to make sure any preempted nodes are replaced as soon as possible (see "Autoscaling" on page 102).

In theory, *all* your preemptible nodes could disappear at the same time. Despite the cost savings, therefore, it's a good idea to limit your preemptible nodes to no more than, say, two-thirds of your cluster.

Best Practice

Keep costs down by using preemptible or spot instances for some of your nodes, but no more than you can afford to lose. Always keep some nonpreemptible nodes in the mix, too.

Using node affinities to control scheduling

You can use Kubernetes *node affinities* to make sure Pods that can't tolerate failure are not scheduled on preemptible nodes (*https://medium.com/google-cloud/using-preemptible-vms-to-cut-kubernetes-engine-bills-in-half-de2481b8e814*) (see "Node Affinities" on page 159).

For example, Google Kubernetes Engine preemptible nodes carry the label `cloud.goo gle.com/gke-preemptible`. To tell Kubernetes to never schedule a Pod on one of these nodes, add the following to the Pod or Deployment spec:

```
affinity:
  nodeAffinity:
    requiredDuringSchedulingIgnoredDuringExecution:
      nodeSelectorTerms:
      - matchExpressions:
        - key: cloud.google.com/gke-preemptible
          operator: DoesNotExist
```

The `requiredDuringScheduling...` affinity is mandatory: a Pod with this affinity will *never* be scheduled on a node that does not match the selector expression (known as a *hard affinity*).

Alternatively, you might want to tell Kubernetes that some of your less critical Pods, which can tolerate occasional failures, should preferentially be scheduled on preemptible nodes. In this case, you can use a *soft affinity* with the opposite sense:

```
affinity:
  nodeAffinity:
    preferredDuringSchedulingIgnoredDuringExecution:
    - preference:
        matchExpressions:
        - key: cloud.google.com/gke-preemptible
          operator: Exists
      weight: 100
```

This effectively means "Please schedule this Pod on a preemptible node if you can; if not, it doesn't matter."

Best Practice

If you're running preemptible nodes, use Kubernetes node affinities to make sure critical workloads are not preempted.

Keeping Your Workloads Balanced

We've talked about the work that the Kubernetes scheduler does, ensuring that workloads are distributed fairly, across as many nodes as possible, and trying to place replica Pods on different nodes for high availability.

In general, the scheduler does a great job, but there are some edge cases you need to watch out for.

For example, suppose you have two nodes, and two services, A and B, each with two replicas. In a balanced cluster, there will be one replica of service A on each node, and one of service B on each node (Figure 5-1). If one node should fail, both A and B will still be available.

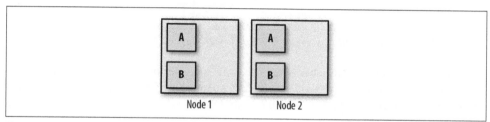

Figure 5-1. Services A and B are balanced across the available nodes

So far, so good. But suppose Node 2 does fail. The scheduler will notice that both A and B need an extra replica, and there's only one node for it to create them on, so it does. Now Node 1 is running two replicas of service A, and two of service B.

Now suppose we spin up a new node to replace the failed Node 2. Even once it's available, there will be no Pods on it. The scheduler never moves running Pods from one node to another.

We now have an unbalanced cluster (*https://itnext.io/keep-you-kubernetes-cluster-balanced-the-secret-to-high-availability-17edf60d9cb7*), where all the Pods are on Node 1, and none are on Node 2 (Figure 5-2).

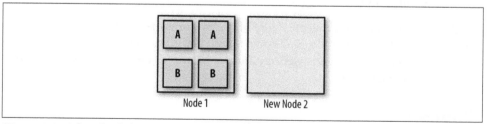

Figure 5-2. After the failure of Node 2, all replicas have moved to Node 1

But it gets worse. Suppose you deploy a rolling update to service A (let's call the new version service A*). The scheduler needs to start two new replicas for service A*, wait for them to come up, and then terminate the old ones. Where will it start the new replicas? On the new Node 2, because it's idle, while Node 1 is already running four Pods. So two new service A* replicas are started on Node 2, and the old ones removed from Node 1 (Figure 5-3).

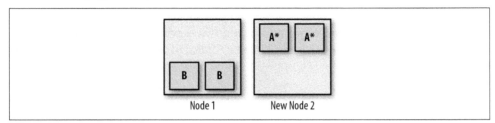

Figure 5-3. After the rollout of service A*, the cluster is still unbalanced

Now you're in a bad situation, because both replicas of service B are on the same node (Node 1), while both replicas of service A* are also on the same node (Node 2). Although you have two nodes, you have no high availability. The failure of either Node 1 or Node 2 will result in a service outage.

The key to this problem is that the scheduler never moves Pods from one node to another unless they are restarted for some reason. Also, the scheduler's goal of placing workloads evenly across nodes is sometimes in conflict with maintaining high availability for individual services.

One way around this is to use a tool called Descheduler (*https://github.com/ kubernetes-incubator/descheduler*). You can run this tool every so often, as a Kubernetes Job, and it will do its best to rebalance the cluster by finding Pods that need to be moved, and killing them.

Descheduler has various strategies and policies that you can configure. For example, one policy looks for underutilized nodes, and kills Pods on other nodes to force them to be rescheduled on the idle nodes.

Another policy looks for duplicate Pods, where two or more replicas of the same Pod are running on the same node, and evicts them. This fixes the problem that arose in our example, where workloads were nominally balanced, but in fact neither service was highly available.

Summary

Kubernetes is pretty good at running workloads for you in a reliable, efficient way with no real need for manual intervention. Providing you give the scheduler accurate estimates of your containers' resource needs, you can largely leave Kubernetes to get on with it.

The time you would have spent fixing operations issues can thus be put to better use, like developing applications. Thanks, Kubernetes!

Understanding how Kubernetes manages resources is key to building and running your cluster correctly. The most important points to take away:

- Kubernetes allocates CPU and memory resources to containers on the basis of *requests* and *limits*.

- A container's requests are the minimum amounts of resources it needs to run. Its limits specify the maximum amount it's allowed to use.

- Minimal container images are faster to build, push, deploy, and start. The smaller the container, the fewer the potential security vulnerabilities.

- Liveness probes tell Kubernetes whether the container is working properly. If a container's liveness probe fails, it will be killed and restarted.

- Readiness probes tell Kubernetes that the container is ready and able to serve requests. If the readiness probe fails, the container will be removed from any Services that reference it, disconnecting it from user traffic.

- PodDisruptionBudgets let you limit the number of Pods that can be stopped at once during *evictions*, preserving high availability for your application.

- Namespaces are a way of logically partitioning your cluster. You might create a namespace for each application, or group of related applications.

- To refer to a Service in another namespace, you can use a DNS address like this: `SERVICE.NAMESPACE`.

- ResourceQuotas let you set overall resource limits for a given namespace.

- LimitRanges specify default resource requests and limits for containers in a namespace.

- Set resource limits so that your applications almost, but don't quite exceed them in normal usage.

- Don't allocate more cloud storage than you need, and don't provision high-bandwidth storage unless it's critical for your application's performance.

- Set owner annotations on all your resources, and scan the cluster regularly for unowned resources.

- Find and clean up resources that aren't being used (but check with their owners).

- Reserved instances can save you money if you can plan your usage long-term.
- Preemptible instances can save you money right now, but be ready for them to vanish at short notice. Use node affinities to keep failure-sensitive Pods away from preemptible nodes.

CHAPTER 6

Operating Clusters

If Tetris has taught me anything, it's that errors pile up and accomplishments disappear.

—Andrew Clay Shafer

Once you have a Kubernetes cluster, how do you know it's in good shape and running properly? How do you scale to cope with demand, but keep cloud costs to a minimum? In this chapter we'll look at the issues involved in operating Kubernetes clusters for production workloads, and some of the tools that can help you.

As we've seen in Chapter 3, there are many important things to consider about your Kubernetes cluster: availability, authentication, upgrades, and so on. If you're using a good managed Kubernetes service, as we recommend, most of these issues should be taken care of for you.

However, what you actually do with the cluster is up to you. In this chapter you'll learn how to size and scale the cluster, check it for conformance, find security problems, and test the resilience of your infrastructure with chaos monkeys.

Cluster Sizing and Scaling

How big does your cluster need to be? With self-hosted Kubernetes clusters, and almost all managed services, the ongoing cost of your cluster depends directly on the number and size of its nodes. If the capacity of the cluster is too small, your workloads won't run properly, or will fail under heavy traffic. If the capacity is too large, you're wasting money.

Sizing and scaling your cluster appropriately is very important, so let's look at some of the decisions involved.

Capacity Planning

One way to make an initial estimate of the capacity you need is to think about how many traditional servers you would need to run the same applications. For example, if your current architecture runs on 10 cloud instances, you probably won't need more than 10 nodes in your Kubernetes cluster to run the same workload, plus another for redundancy. In fact, you probably won't need that many: because it can balance work evenly across machines, Kubernetes can achieve higher utilization than with traditional servers. But it may take some time and practical experience to tune your cluster for optimal capacity.

The smallest cluster

When you're first setting up a cluster, you will probably be using it to play around and experiment, and figure out how to run your application. So you probably don't need to burn money on a large cluster until you have some idea what capacity you're going to need.

The smallest possible Kubernetes cluster is a single node. This will allow you to try out Kubernetes and run small workloads for development, as we saw in Chapter 2. However, a single-node cluster has no resilience against the failure of the node hardware, or of the Kubernetes API server or the *kubelet* (the agent daemon that is responsible for running workloads on each node).

If you're using a managed Kubernetes service like GKE (see "Google Kubernetes Engine (GKE)" on page 41), then you don't need to worry about provisioning master nodes: this is done for you. If, on the other hand, you're building your own cluster, you'll need to decide how many master nodes to use.

The minimum number of master nodes for a resilient Kubernetes cluster is three. One wouldn't be resilient, and two could disagree about which was the leader, so three master nodes are needed.

While you can do useful work on a Kubernetes cluster this small, it's not recommended. A better idea is to add some worker nodes, so that your own workloads aren't competing for resources with the Kubernetes control plane.

Provided your cluster control plane is highly available, you *can* get by with a single worker node, but two is the sensible minimum to protect against node failure, and to allow Kubernetes to run at least two replicas of every Pod. The more nodes the better, especially as the Kubernetes scheduler cannot always ensure that workloads are fully balanced across available nodes (see "Keeping Your Workloads Balanced" on page 91).

Best Practice

Kubernetes clusters need at least three master nodes in order to be highly available, and you may need more to handle the work of larger clusters. Two worker nodes is the minimum required to make your workloads fault-tolerant to the failure of a single node, and three worker nodes is even better.

The biggest cluster

Is there a limit to how large Kubernetes clusters can be? The short answer is yes, but you almost certainly won't have to worry about it; Kubernetes version 1.12 officially supports clusters of up to 5,000 nodes.

Because clustering requires communication between nodes, the number of possible communication paths, and the cumulative load on the underlying database, grows exponentially with the size of the cluster. While Kubernetes *may* still function with more than 5,000 nodes, it's not *guaranteed* to work, or at least to be responsive enough to deal with production workloads.

The Kubernetes documentation advises that supported cluster configurations (*https://kubernetes.io/docs/setup/cluster-large*) must have no more than 5,000 nodes, no more than 150,000 total Pods, no more than 300,000 total containers, and no more than 100 Pods per node. It's worth bearing in mind that the larger the cluster, the bigger the load on the master nodes; if you're responsible for your own master nodes, they'll need to be pretty powerful machines to cope with a cluster of thousands of nodes.

Best Practice

For maximum reliability, keep your Kubernetes clusters smaller than 5,000 nodes and 150,000 Pods (this isn't an issue for most users). If you need more resources, run multiple clusters.

Federated clusters

If you have extremely demanding workloads or need to operate at huge scale, these limits may become a practical problem for you. In this case, you can run multiple Kubernetes clusters, and if necessary *federate* them, so that workloads can be replicated across clusters.

Federation provides the ability to keep two or more clusters synchronized, running identical workloads. This can be useful if you need Kubernetes clusters in different cloud providers, for resilience, or in different geographical locations, to reduce latency for your users. A group of federated clusters can keep running even if an individual cluster fails.

You can read more about cluster federation in the Kubernetes documentation (*https://kubernetes.io/docs/concepts/cluster-administration/federation/*).

For most Kubernetes users, federation isn't something they need to be concerned with, and, indeed, in practice most users at very large scale are able to handle their workloads with multiple unfederated clusters of a few hundred to a few thousand nodes each.

Best Practice

If you need to replicate workloads across multiple clusters, perhaps for geographical redundancy or latency reasons, use federation. Most users don't need to federate their clusters, though.

Do I need multiple clusters?

Unless you're operating at very large scale, as we mentioned in the previous section, you probably don't need more than one or two clusters: maybe one for production, and one for staging and testing.

For convenience and ease of resource management, you can divide your cluster into logical partitions using *namespaces*, which we covered in more detail in "Using Namespaces" on page 77. With a few exceptions, it's not usually worth the administration overhead of managing multiple clusters.

There are some specific situations, such as security and regulatory compliance, where you might want to ensure that services in one cluster are absolutely isolated from those in another (for example, when dealing with protected health information, or when data can't be transmitted from one geographical location to another for legal reasons). In those cases, you need to create separate clusters. For most Kubernetes users, this won't be an issue.

Best Practice

Use a single production and a single staging cluster, unless you really need complete isolation of one set of workloads or teams from another. If you just want to partition your cluster for ease of management, use namespaces instead.

Nodes and Instances

The more capacity a given node has, the more work it can do, where capacity is expressed in terms of the number of CPU cores (virtual or otherwise), available memory, and to a lesser extent disk space. But is it better to run 10 very large nodes, for example, rather than 100 much smaller ones?

Picking the right node size

There's no universally correct node size for Kubernetes clusters. The answer depends on your cloud or hardware provider, and on your specific workloads.

The cost per capacity of different instance sizes can have an effect on the way you decide to size your nodes. For example, some cloud providers may offer a slight discount on larger instance sizes, so that if your workloads are very compute-intensive, it may be cheaper to run them on a few very large nodes instead of many smaller ones.

The number of nodes required in the cluster also affects the choice of node size. To get the advantages that Kubernetes offers, such as Pod replication and high availability, you need to spread work across several nodes. But if nodes have too much spare capacity, that's a waste of money.

If you need, say, at least 10 nodes for high availability, but each node only needs to run a couple of Pods, the node instances can be very small. On the other hand, if you only need two nodes, you can make them quite large and potentially save money with more favorable instance pricing.

Best Practice

Use the most cost-effective node type that your provider offers. Often, larger nodes work out cheaper, but if you only have a handful of nodes, you might want to add some smaller ones, to help with redundancy.

Cloud instance types

Because the Kubernetes components themselves, such as the kubelet, use a given amount of resources, and you will need some spare capacity to do useful work, the smallest instance sizes offered by your cloud provider will probably not be suitable for Kubernetes.

A master node for small clusters (up to around five nodes) should have at least one virtual CPU (vCPU) and 3–4 GiB of memory, with larger clusters requiring more memory and CPUs for each master node. This is equivalent to an `n1-standard-1` instance on Google Cloud, an `m3.medium` on AWS, and a Standard DS1 v2 on Azure.

A single-CPU, 4 GiB instance is also a sensible minimum for a worker node, although, as we've seen, it may sometimes be more cost-effective for you to provision larger nodes. The default node size in Google Kubernetes Engine, for example, is `n1-standard-1`, which has approximately these specs.

For larger clusters, with perhaps a few tens of nodes, it may make sense for you to provision a mix of two or three different instance sizes. This means that Pods with compute-intensive workloads requiring a lot of memory can be scheduled by Kubernetes on large nodes, leaving smaller nodes free to handle smaller Pods (see "Node Affinities" on page 159). This gives the Kubernetes scheduler the maximum freedom of choice when deciding where to run a given Pod.

Heterogeneous nodes

Not all nodes are created equal. You may need some nodes with special properties, such as a graphics processing unit (GPU). GPUs are high-performance parallel processors that are widely used for compute-intensive problems that have nothing to do with graphics, such as machine learning or data analysis.

You can use the *resource limits* functionality in Kubernetes (see "Resource Limits" on page 71) to specify that a given Pod needs at least one GPU, for example. This will ensure that those Pods will run only on GPU-enabled nodes, and get priority over Pods that can run on any node.

Most Kubernetes nodes probably run Linux of one kind or another, which is suitable for almost all applications. Recall that containers are *not* virtual machines, so the process inside a container runs directly on the kernel of the operating system on the underlying node. A Windows binary will not run on a Linux Kubernetes node, for example, so if you need to run Windows containers, you will have to provision Windows nodes for them.

Best Practice

Most containers are built for Linux, so you'll probably want to run mostly Linux-based nodes. You may need to add one or two special types of nodes for specific requirements, such as GPUs or Windows.

Bare-metal servers

One of the most useful properties of Kubernetes is its ability to connect all sorts of machines of different sizes, architectures, and capabilities, to provide a single, unified, logical machine on which workloads can run. While Kubernetes is usually associated with cloud servers, many organizations have large numbers of physical, bare-metal machines in data centers that can potentially be harnessed into Kubernetes clusters.

We saw in Chapter 1 that cloud technology transforms *capex* infrastructure (purchasing machines as a capital expense) to *opex* infrastructure (leasing compute capacity as an operating expense), and this makes financial sense, but if your business already owns a large number of bare-metal servers, you don't need to write them off just yet: instead, consider joining them into a Kubernetes cluster (see "Bare-Metal and On-Prem" on page 49).

Best Practice

If you have hardware servers with spare capacity, or you're not ready to migrate completely to the cloud yet, use Kubernetes to run container workloads on your existing machines.

Scaling the Cluster

Having chosen a sensible starting size for your cluster, and picked the right mix of instance sizes for your worker nodes, is that the end of the story? Almost certainly not: over time, you may need to grow or shrink the cluster to match changes in demand, or in business requirements.

Instance groups

It's easy to add nodes to a Kubernetes cluster. If you're running a self-hosted cluster, a cluster management tool such as kops (see "kops" on page 44) can do it for you. kops has the concept of an *instance group*, which is a set of nodes of a given instance type (for example, m3.medium). Managed services, such as Google Kubernetes Engine, have the same facility, called *node pools*.

You can scale instance groups or node pools either by changing the minimum and maximum size for the group, or by changing the specified instance type, or both.

Scaling down

In principle, there's no problem with scaling down a Kubernetes cluster either. You can tell Kubernetes to *drain* the nodes you want to remove, which will gradually shut down or move any running Pods on those nodes elsewhere.

Most cluster management tools will do the node draining for you automatically, or you can use the kubectl drain command to do it yourself. Providing there is enough spare capacity in the rest of the cluster to reschedule the doomed Pods, once the nodes have been successfully drained, you can terminate them.

To avoid reducing the number of Pod replicas too much for a given service, you can use PodDisruptionBudgets to specify a minimum number of available Pods, or the maximum number of Pods that can be *unavailable* at any time (see "Pod Disruption Budgets" on page 76).

If draining a node would cause Kubernetes to exceed these limits, the drain operation will block until you change the limits or free up some more resources in the cluster.

Draining allows Pods to shut down gracefully, cleaning up after themselves and saving any necessary state. For most applications, this is preferable to simply shutting down the node, which will terminate the Pods immediately.

Best Practice

Don't just shut down nodes when you don't need them anymore. Drain them first to ensure their workloads are migrated to other nodes, and to make sure you have enough spare capacity remaining in the cluster.

Autoscaling

Most cloud providers support *autoscaling*: automatically increasing or reducing the number of instances in a group according to some metric or schedule. For example, AWS autoscaling groups (ASGs) can maintain a minimum and maximum number of instances, so that if one instance fails, another will be started to take its place, or if too many instances are running, some will be shut down.

Alternatively, if your demand fluctuates according to the time of day, you can schedule the group to grow and shrink at specified times. You can also configure the scaling group to grow or shrink dynamically on demand: if the average CPU utilization exceeds 90% over a 15-minute period, for example, instances can be added automatically until the CPU usage falls below the threshold. When demand falls again, the group can be scaled down to save money.

Kubernetes has a Cluster Autoscaler add-on that cluster management tools like kops can take advantage of to enable cloud autoscaling, and managed clusters such as Azure Kubernetes Service also offer autoscaling.

However, it can take some time and experimentation to get your autoscaling settings right, and for many users it may not be necessary at all. Most Kubernetes clusters start small and grow gradually and monotonically by adding a node here and there as resource usage grows.

For large-scale users, though, or applications where demand is highly variable, cluster autoscaling is a very useful feature.

Best Practice

Don't enable cluster autoscaling just because it's there. You probably won't need it unless your workloads or demand are extremely variable. Scale your cluster manually instead, at least until you've been running it for a while and have a sense of how your scale requirements are changing over time.

Conformance Checking

When is Kubernetes not Kubernetes? The flexibility of Kubernetes means there are lots of different ways to set up Kubernetes clusters, and this presents a potential problem. If Kubernetes is to be a universal platform, you should be able to take a workload and run it on any Kubernetes cluster and have it work the way you expect. That means the same API calls and Kubernetes objects have to be available, they have to have the same behavior, they have to work as advertised, and so on.

Fortunately, Kubernetes itself includes a test suite which verifies that a given Kubernetes cluster is *conformant*; that is, it satisfies a core set of requirements for a given Kubernetes version. These conformance tests are very useful for Kubernetes administrators.

If your cluster doesn't pass them, then there is a problem with your setup that needs to be addressed. If it does pass, knowing that it's conformant gives you confidence that applications designed for Kubernetes will work with your cluster, and that things you build on your cluster will work elsewhere too.

CNCF Certification

The Cloud Native Computing Foundation (CNCF) is the official owner of the Kubernetes project and trademark (see "Cloud Native" on page 15), and provides various kinds of certifications for Kubernetes-related products, engineers, and vendors.

Certified Kubernetes

If you use a managed, or partially managed, Kubernetes service, check whether it carries the Certified Kubernetes mark and logo (see Figure 6-1). This indicates that the vendor and service meet the Certified Kubernetes standard (*https://github.com/cncf/ k8s-conformance*), as specified by the Cloud Native Computing Foundation (CNCF).

Figure 6-1. The Certified Kubernetes mark means that the product or service is approved by the CNCF

If the product has *Kubernetes* in the name, it must be certified by the CNCF. This means customers know exactly what they're getting, and can be satisfied that it will be interoperable with other conformant Kubernetes services. Vendors can self-certify their products by running the Sonobuoy conformance checking tool (see "Conformance Testing with Sonobuoy" on page 104).

Certified Kubernetes products also have to track the latest version of Kubernetes, providing updates at least annually. It's not just managed services that can carry the Certified Kubernetes mark; distributions and installer tools can, too.

Certified Kubernetes Administrator (CKA)

To become a Certified Kubernetes Administrator, you need to demonstrate that you have the key skills to manage Kubernetes clusters in production, including installation and configuration, networking, maintenance, knowledge of the API, security, and troubleshooting. Anyone can take the CKA exam, which is administered online, and includes a series of challenging practical tests.

The CKA has a reputation as a tough, comprehensive exam that really tests your skills and knowledge. You can be confident that any engineer who is CKA-certified really knows Kubernetes. If you run your business on Kubernetes, consider putting some of your staff through the CKA program, especially those directly responsible for managing clusters.

Kubernetes Certified Service Provider (KCSP)

Vendors themselves can apply for the Kubernetes Certified Service Provider (KCSP) program. To be eligible, the vendor has to be a CNCF member, provide enterprise support (for example by supplying field engineers to a customer site), contribute actively to the Kubernetes community, and employ three or more CKA-certified engineers.

Best Practice

Look for the Certified Kubernetes mark to make sure that a product meets CNCF standards. Look for vendors to be KCSP-certified, and if you're hiring Kubernetes administrators, look for a CKA qualification.

Conformance Testing with Sonobuoy

If you're managing your own cluster, or even if you're using a managed service but want to double-check that it's configured properly and up to date, you can run the Kubernetes conformance tests to prove it. The standard tool for running these tests is Sonobuoy (*https://github.com/vmware-tanzu/sonobuoy*).

Best Practice

Run Sonobuoy once your cluster is set up for the first time, to verify that it's standards-compliant and that everything works. Run it again every so often to make sure there are no conformance problems.

Validation and Auditing

Cluster conformance is a baseline: any production cluster should certainly be conformant, but there are many common problems with Kubernetes configurations and workloads that conformance testing won't pick up. For example:

- Using excessively large container images can waste a lot of time and cluster resources.
- Deployments that specify only a single Pod replica are not highly available.
- Running processes in containers as root is a potential security risk (see "Container Security" on page 143).

In this section, we'll look at some tools and techniques that can help you find problems with your cluster, and tell you what's causing them.

K8Guard

The K8Guard tool (*https://target.github.io/infrastructure/k8guard-the-guardian-angel-for-kuberentes*), developed at Target, can check for common problems with your Kubernetes cluster and either take corrective action, or just send you a notification about them. You can configure it with your own specific policies for your cluster (for example, you might specify that K8Guard should warn you if any container image is larger than 1 GiB, or if an ingress rule allows access from anywhere).

K8Guard also exports metrics, which can be collected by a monitoring system like Prometheus (more about this in Chapter 16), on things like how many Deployments have policy violations, and also the performance of the Kubernetes API responses. This can help you detect and fix problems early.

It's a good idea to leave K8Guard running on your cluster so that it can warn you about any violations as soon as they happen.

Copper

Copper (*https://copper.sh/*) is a tool for checking your Kubernetes manifests before they're deployed, and flagging common problems or enforcing custom policies. It includes a Domain-Specific Language (DSL) for expressing validation rules and policies.

For example, here is a rule expressed in the Copper language that blocks any container using the `latest` tag (see "The latest Tag" on page 140 for why this is a bad idea):

```
rule NoLatest ensure {
    fetch("$.spec.template.spec.containers..image")
        .as(:image)
        .pick(:tag)
        .contains("latest") == false
}
```

When you run the `copper check` command on a Kubernetes manifest that includes a `latest` container image spec, you'll see a failure message:

```
copper check --rules no_latest.cop --files deployment.yml
Validating part 0
    NoLatest - FAIL
```

It's a good idea to add some Copper rules like this and run the tool as part of your version control system (for example, to validate the Kubernetes manifests before committing, or as part of the automated checks on a pull request).

A related tool, which validates your manifests against the Kubernetes API spec, is kubeval (see "kubeval" on page 236 for more about this).

kube-bench

kube-bench (*https://github.com/aquasecurity/kube-bench*) is a tool for auditing your Kubernetes cluster against a set of benchmarks produced by the Center for Internet Security (CIS). In effect, it verifies that your cluster is set up according to security best practices. Although you probably won't need to, you can configure the tests that kube-bench runs, and even add your own, specified as YAML documents.

Kubernetes Audit Logging

Suppose you find a problem on your cluster, such as a Pod you don't recognize, and you want to know where it came from. How do you find out who did what on the cluster when? The Kubernetes audit log (*https://kubernetes.io/docs/tasks/debug-application-cluster/audit/*) will tell you.

With audit logging enabled, all requests to the cluster API will be recorded, with a timestamp, saying who made the request (which service account), the details of the request, such as which resources it queried, and what the response was.

The audit events can be sent to your central logging system, where you can filter and alert on them as you would for other log data (see Chapter 15). A good managed service such as Google Kubernetes Engine will include audit logging by default, but otherwise you may need to configure the cluster yourself to enable it.

Chaos Testing

We pointed out in "Trust, but verify" on page 37 that the only real way to verify high availability is to kill one or more of your cluster nodes and see what happens. The same applies to the high availability of your Kubernetes Pods and applications. You could pick a Pod at random, for example, terminate it, and check that Kubernetes restarts it, and that your error rate is unaffected.

Doing this manually is time-consuming, and without realizing it you may be unconsciously sparing resources that you know are application-critical. To make it a fair test, the process must be automated.

This kind of automated, random interference with production services is sometimes known as *Chaos Monkey* testing, after the tool of the same name developed by Netflix to test its infrastructure:

> Imagine a monkey entering a data center, these farms of servers that host all the critical functions of our online activities. The monkey randomly rips cables, destroys devices...
>
> The challenge for IT managers is to design the information system they are responsible for so that it can work despite these monkeys, which no one ever knows when they arrive and what they will destroy.
>
> —Antonio Garcia Martinez, *Chaos Monkeys*

Apart from Chaos Monkey itself, which terminates random cloud servers, the Netflix *Simian Army* also includes other *chaos engineering* tools such as Latency Monkey, which introduces communication delays to simulate network issues, Security Monkey, which looks for known vulnerabilities, and Chaos Gorilla, which drops a whole AWS availability zone.

Only Production Is Production

You can apply the Chaos Monkey idea to Kubernetes applications, too. While you can run chaos engineering tools on a staging cluster to avoid disrupting production, that can only tell you so much. To learn about your production environment, you need to test production:

> Many systems are too big, complex, and cost-prohibitive to clone. Imagine trying to spin up a copy of Facebook for testing (with its multiple, globally distributed data centers).
>
> The unpredictability of user traffic makes it impossible to mock; even if you could perfectly reproduce yesterday's traffic, you still can't predict tomorrow's. Only production is production.
>
> —Charity Majors (*https://opensource.com/article/17/8/testing-production*)

It's also important to note that your chaos experiments, to be most useful, need to be automated and continuous. It's no good doing it once and deciding that your system is reliable for evermore:

> The whole point of automating your chaos experiments is so that you can run them again and again to build trust and confidence in your system. Not just surfacing new weaknesses, but also ensuring that you've overcome a weakness in the first place.
>
> —Russ Miles (ChaosIQ) (*https://medium.com/chaosiq/exploring-multi-level-weaknesses-using-automated-chaos-experiments-aa30f0605ce*)

There are several tools you can use for automatically chaos engineering your cluster. Here are a few options.

chaoskube

chaoskube (*https://github.com/linki/chaoskube*) randomly kills Pods in your cluster. By default it operates in dry-run mode, which shows you what it would have done, but doesn't actually terminate anything.

You can configure chaoskube to include or exclude Pods based on labels (see "Labels" on page 155), annotations, and namespaces, and to avoid certain time periods or dates (for example, don't kill anything on Christmas Eve). By default, though, it will potentially kill any Pod in any namespace, including Kubernetes system Pods, and even chaoskube itself.

Once you're happy with your chaoskube filter configuration, you can disable dry-run mode and let it do its work.

chaoskube is simple to install and set up, and it's an ideal tool for getting started with chaos engineering.

kube-monkey

kube-monkey (*https://github.com/asobti/kube-monkey*) runs at a preset time (by default, 8 a.m. on weekdays), and builds a schedule of Deployments that will be targeted during the rest of the day (by default, 10 a.m. to 4 p.m.). Unlike some other tools, kube-monkey works on an opt-in basis: only those Pods that specifically enable kube-monkey using annotations will be targeted.

This means that you can add kube-monkey testing to specific apps or services during their development, and set different levels of frequency and aggression depending on the service. For example, the following annotation on a Pod will set a mean time between failures (MTBF) of two days:

```
kube-monkey/mtbf: 2
```

The `kill-mode` annotation lets you specify how many of a Deployment's Pods will be killed, or a maximum percentage. The following annotations will kill up to 50% of the Pods in the targeted Deployment:

```
kube-monkey/kill-mode: "random-max-percent"
kube-monkey/kill-value: 50
```

PowerfulSeal

PowerfulSeal (*https://github.com/bloomberg/powerfulseal*) is an open source Kubernetes chaos engineering tool that works in two modes: interactive and autonomous. Interactive mode lets you explore your cluster and manually break things to see what happens. It can terminate nodes, namespaces, Deployments, and individual Pods.

Autonomous mode uses a set of policies specified by you: which resources to operate on, which to avoid, when to run (you can configure it to only operate during working hours Monday–Friday, for example), and how aggressive to be (kill a given percentage of all matching Deployments, for example). PowerfulSeal's policy files are very flexible and let you set up almost any imaginable chaos engineering scenario.

Best Practice

If your applications require high availability, run a chaos testing tool such as chaoskube regularly to make sure that unexpected node or Pod failures don't cause problems. Make sure you clear this first with the people responsible for operating the cluster and the applications under test.

Summary

It can be really difficult to know how to size and configure your first Kubernetes clusters. There are a lot of choices you can make, and you don't really know what you'll need until you've actually gained some production experience.

We can't make those decisions for you, but we hope we've at least given you some helpful things to think about when making them:

- Before provisioning your production Kubernetes cluster, think about how many nodes you'll need, and of what size.

- You need at least three master nodes (none, if you're using a managed service) and at least two (ideally three) worker nodes. This can make Kubernetes clusters seem a little expensive at first when you're only running a few small workloads, but don't forget the advantages of built-in resilience and scaling.

- Kubernetes clusters can scale to many thousands of nodes and hundreds of thousands of containers.

- If you need to scale beyond that, use multiple clusters (sometimes you need to do this for security or compliance reasons too). You can join clusters together using federation if you need to replicate workloads across clusters.

- A typical instance size for a Kubernetes node is 1 CPU, 4 GiB RAM. It's good to have a mix of a few different node sizes, though.

- Kubernetes isn't just for the cloud; it runs on bare-metal servers too. If you've got metal sitting around, why not use it?

- You can scale your cluster up and down manually without too much trouble, and you probably won't have to do it very often. Autoscaling is nice to have, but not that important.

- There's a well-defined standard for Kubernetes vendors and products: the CNCF *Certified Kubernetes* mark. If you don't see this, ask why not.

- Chaos testing is a process of knocking out Pods at random and seeing if your application still works. It's useful, but the cloud has a way of doing its own chaos testing anyway, without you asking for it.

CHAPTER 7

Kubernetes Power Tools

My mechanic told me, "I couldn't repair your brakes, so I made your horn louder."
—Steven Wright

People always ask us, "What about all these Kubernetes tools? Do I need them? If so, which ones? And what do they all do?"

In this chapter, we'll explore a small part of the landscape of tools and utilities that help you work with Kubernetes. We'll show you some advanced techniques with kubectl, and a few useful utilities such as jq, kubectx, kubens, kube-ps1, kube-shell, Click, kubed-sh, Stern, and BusyBox.

Mastering kubectl

We've already met kubectl, starting in Chapter 2, and as it's the primary tool for interacting with Kubernetes, you may already be comfortable with the basics. Let's look at some more advanced features of kubectl now, including some tips and tricks that may be new to you.

Shell Aliases

One of the first things that most Kubernetes users do to make their life easier is to create a shell alias for the kubectl command. For example, we have the following alias set up in our *.bash_profile* files:

```
alias k=kubectl
```

Now instead of having to type out kubectl in full for every command, we can just use k:

```
k get pods
```

If there are some kubectl commands that you use a lot, you might like to create aliases for them too. Here are some possible examples:

```
alias kg=kubectl get
alias kgdep=kubectl get deployment
alias ksys=kubectl --namespace=kube-system
alias kd=kubectl describe
```

Google engineer Ahmet Alp Balkan has worked out a logical system of aliases (*https://ahmet.im/blog/kubectl-aliases*) like these, and created a script to generate them all for you (currently around 800 aliases):

You don't have to use those, though; we suggest you start with k, and add aliases that are memorable to you, for the commands you use most frequently.

Using Short Flags

Like most command-line tools, kubectl supports abbreviated forms of many of its flags and switches. This can save you a lot of typing.

For example, you can abbreviate the --namespace flag to just -n (see "Using Namespaces" on page 77):

```
kubectl get pods -n kube-system
```

It's very common to have kubectl operate on resources matching a set of labels, with the --selector flag (see "Labels" on page 155). Fortunately, this can be shortened to -l (labels):

```
kubectl get pods -l "environment=staging"
```

Abbreviating Resource Types

A common use for kubectl is to list resources of various types, such as Pods, Deployments, Services, and namespaces. The usual way to do this is to use kubectl get followed by, for example, deployments.

To speed this up, kubectl supports short forms of these resource types:

```
kubectl get po
kubectl get deploy
kubectl get svc
kubectl get ns
```

Other useful abbreviations include no for nodes, cm for configmaps, sa for serviceaccounts, ds for daemonsets, and pv for persistentvolumes.

Auto-Completing kubectl Commands

If you're using the bash or zsh shells, you can have them auto-complete kubectl commands. Run this command to see instructions on how to enable auto-completion for your shell:

```
kubectl completion -h
```

Follow the instructions, and you should be able to press Tab to complete partial kubectl commands. Try it now:

```
kubectl cl<TAB>
```

The command should complete to kubectl cluster-info.

If you type just kubectl and hit Tab twice, you'll see all the commands available:

```
kubectl <TAB><TAB>
alpha           attach          cluster-info    cordon          describe    ...
```

You can use the same technique to list all the flags that you can use with the current command:

```
kubectl get pods --<TAB><TAB>
--all-namespaces    --cluster=    --label-columns=    ...
```

Usefully, kubectl will also auto-complete the names of Pods, Deployments, namespaces, and so on:

```
kubectl -n kube-system describe pod <TAB><TAB>
event-exporter-v0.1.9-85bb4fd64d-2zjng
kube-dns-autoscaler-79b4b844b9-2wglc
fluentd-gcp-scaler-7c5db745fc-h7ntr
...
```

Getting Help

The best command-line tools include thorough documentation, and kubectl is no exception. You can get a complete overview of the available commands with kubectl -h:

```
kubectl -h
```

You can go further and get detailed documentation on each command, with all the available options, and a set of examples, by typing kubectl COMMAND -h:

```
kubectl get -h
```

Getting Help on Kubernetes Resources

As well as documenting itself, kubectl can also give you help on Kubernetes objects, such as Deployments or Pods. The kubectl explain command will show documentation on the specified type of resource:

```
kubectl explain pods
```

You can get further information on a specific field of a resource, with kubectl explain RESOURCE.FIELD. In fact, you can drill down as far as you like with explain:

```
kubectl explain deploy.spec.template.spec.containers.livenessProbe.exec
```

Alternatively, try kubectl explain --recursive, which shows fields within fields within fields... just be careful you don't get dizzy!

Showing More Detailed Output

You already know that kubectl get will list resources of various types, such as Pods:

```
kubectl get pods
NAME                        READY     STATUS     RESTARTS   AGE
demo-54f4458547-pqdxn       1/1       Running    6          5d
```

You can see extra information, such as the node each Pod is running on, by using the -o wide flag:

```
kubectl get pods -o wide
NAME                     ... IP            NODE
demo-54f4458547-pqdxn    ... 10.76.1.88    gke-k8s-cluster-1-n1-standard...
```

(We've omitted the information that you see without -o wide, just for reasons of space.)

Depending on the resource type, -o wide will show you different information. For example, with nodes:

```
kubectl get nodes -o wide
NAME              ... EXTERNAL-IP       OS-IMAGE       KERNEL-VERSION
gke-k8s-...8l6n   ... 35.233.136.194    Container...    4.14.22+
gke-k8s-...dwtv   ... 35.227.162.224    Container...    4.14.22+
gke-k8s-...67ch   ... 35.233.212.49     Container...    4.14.22+
```

Working with JSON Data and jq

The default output format for kubectl get is plain text, but it can also print information in JSON format:

```
kubectl get pods -n kube-system -o json
{
    "apiVersion": "v1",
    "items": [
```

```
    {
        "apiVersion": "v1",
        "kind": "Pod",
        "metadata": {
            "creationTimestamp": "2018-05-21T18:24:54Z",
            ...
```

Not surprisingly, this produces a lot of output (about 5,000 lines on our cluster). Fortunately, because the output is in the widely used JSON format, you can use other tools to filter it, such as the invaluable jq.

If you don't have jq (*https://stedolan.github.io/jq/manual*) already, install it (*https://stedolan.github.io/jq/download*) in the usual way for your system (brew install jq for macOS, apt install jq for Debian/Ubuntu, and so on).

Once you've got jq installed, you can use it to query and filter kubectl output:

```
kubectl get pods -n kube-system -o json | jq '.items[].metadata.name'
"event-exporter-v0.1.9-85bb4fd64d-2zjng"
"fluentd-gcp-scaler-7c5db745fc-h7ntr"
"fluentd-gcp-v3.0.0-5m627"
"fluentd-gcp-v3.0.0-h5fjg"
...
```

jq is a very powerful tool for querying and transforming JSON data.

For example, to list your busiest nodes, by the number of Pods running on each:

```
kubectl get pods -o json --all-namespaces | jq '.items |
    group_by(.spec.nodeName) | map({"nodeName": .[0].spec.nodeName,
    "count": length}) | sort_by(.count) | reverse'
```

There's a handy online playground (*https://jqplay.org/*) for jq where you can paste in JSON data and try out different jq queries to get the exact result you want.

If you don't have access to jq, kubectl also supports JSONPath queries (*https://kubernetes.io/docs/reference/kubectl/jsonpath/$$*). JSONPath is a JSON query language that isn't quite as powerful as jq, but useful for quick one-liners:

```
kubectl get pods -o=jsonpath={.items[0].metadata.name}
demo-66ddf956b9-pnknx
```

Watching Objects

When you're waiting for a bunch of Pods to start up, it can be annoying to have to keep typing kubectl get pods... every few seconds to see if anything's happened.

kubectl provides the --watch flag (-w for short) to save you having to do this. For example:

```
kubectl get pods --watch
NAME                        READY       STATUS          RESTARTS    AGE
```

```
demo-95444875c-z9xv4    0/1     ContainerCreating   0       1s
... [time passes] ...
demo-95444875c-z9xv4    0/1     Completed           0       2s
demo-95444875c-z9xv4    1/1     Running             0       2s
```

Every time the status of one of the matching Pods changes, you'll see an update in your terminal. (See "Watching Kubernetes Resources with kubespy" on page 121 for a neat way to watch any kind of resource.)

Describing Objects

For really detailed information about Kubernetes objects, you can use the kubectl describe command:

```
kubectl describe pods demo-d94cffc44-gvgzm
```

The Events section can be particularly useful for troubleshooting containers that aren't working properly, as it records each stage of the container's life cycle, along with any errors that occurred.

Working with Resources

So far, you've used kubectl mostly for querying or listing things, as well as applying declarative YAML manifests with kubectl apply. However, kubectl also has a complete set of *imperative* commands: operations that create or modify resources directly.

Imperative kubectl Commands

We showed one example of this in "Running the Demo App" on page 30, using the kubectl run command, which implicitly creates a Deployment to run the specified container.

You can also explicitly create most resources using kubectl create:

```
kubectl create namespace my-new-namespace
namespace "my-new-namespace" created
```

Similarly, kubectl delete will delete a resource:

```
kubectl delete namespace my-new-namespace
namespace "my-new-namespace" deleted
```

The kubectl edit command gives you the power to view and modify any resource:

```
kubectl edit deployments my-deployment
```

This will open your default editor with a YAML manifest file representing the specified resource.

This is a good way to get a detailed look at the configuration of any resource, but you can also make any changes you like in the editor. When you save the file and quit the editor, kubectl will update the resource, exactly as though you had run kubectl apply on the manifest file for the resource.

If you introduced any errors, such as invalid YAML, kubectl will tell you and reopen the file for you to fix the problem.

When Not to Use Imperative Commands

Throughout this book we've emphasized the importance of using *declarative* infrastructure as code. So it shouldn't come as a surprise that we don't recommend you use imperative kubectl commands.

Although they can be very useful for quickly testing things or trying out ideas, the major problem with imperative commands is that you have no single *source of truth*. There's no way to know who ran what imperative commands on the cluster at what time, and what the effect was. As soon as you run any imperative command, the state of the cluster becomes out of sync with the manifest files stored in version control.

The next time someone applies the YAML manifests, whatever changes you made imperatively will be overwritten and lost. This can lead to surprising results, and potentially adverse effects on critical services:

> Alice is on-call, when suddenly there is a large increase in load on the service she is managing. Alice uses the kubectl scale command to increase the number of replicas from 5 to 10. Several days later, Bob edits the YAML manifests in version control to use a new container image, but he doesn't notice that the number of replicas in the file is currently 5, not the 10 that are active in production. Bob proceeds with the rollout, which cuts the number of replicas by half, causing an immediate overload or outage.
>
> —Kelsey Hightower et al., *Kubernetes Up & Running*

Alice forgot to update the files in version control after she made her imperative change, but that's easy to do, especially under the stress of an incident (see "On-call Should Not Be Hell" on page 298). Real life doesn't always follow best practices.

Similarly, before reapplying the manifest files, Bob should have checked the diff using kubectl diff (see "Diffing Resources" on page 119) to see what would change. But if you're not expecting something to be different, it's easy to overlook it. And maybe Bob hasn't read this book.

The best way to avoid this kind of problem is to always make changes by editing and applying the resource files under version control.

Best Practice

Don't use kubectl imperative commands such as `create` or `edit` on production clusters. Instead, always manage resources with version-controlled YAML manifests, applied with `kubectl apply` (or Helm charts).

Generating Resource Manifests

Even though we don't recommend using `kubectl` in imperative mode to make changes to your cluster, imperative commands can be a great time-saver when creating Kubernetes YAML files from scratch.

Rather than typing a lot of boilerplate into an empty file, you can use `kubectl` to give you a head start, by generating the YAML manifest for you:

```
kubectl create deployment  demo --image=cloudnatived/demo:hello
--dry-run=client -o yaml
apiVersion: apps/v1
kind: Deployment
...
```

The `--dry-run=client` flag tells `kubectl` not to actually create the resource, but merely to print out what it would have created. The `-o yaml` flag gives you the resource manifest in YAML format. You can save this output to a file, edit it if you need to, and finally apply it to create the resource in the cluster:

```
kubectl create deployment  demo --image=cloudnatived/demo:hello
--dry-run=client -o yaml
    >deployment.yaml
```

Now make some edits, using your favorite editor, save, and apply the result:

```
kubectl apply -f deployment.yaml
deployment.apps/demo created
```

Exporting Resources

As well as helping you create new resource manifests, `kubectl` can also produce manifest files for resources that already exist in the cluster. For example, maybe you created a Deployment using imperative commands (`kubectl create`), edited and adjusted it to get the settings just right, and now you want to write a declarative YAML manifest for it that you can add to version control.

To do this, use the `-o` flag with `kubectl get`:

```
kubectl create deployment newdemo --image=cloudnatived/demo:hello
deployment.apps/newdemo created
kubectl get deployments newdemo -o yaml >deployment.yaml
```

This output will contain some extra information, like the status section that you can remove before saving with your other manifests, update, and apply with kubectl apply -f.

If you've been using imperative kubectl commands to manage your cluster up to now, and you'd like to switch to the declarative style that we recommend in this book, this is a great way to do it. Export all the resources in your cluster to manifest files using kubectl with the -o flag, as shown in the example, and you'll be all set.

Diffing Resources

Before you apply Kubernetes manifests using kubectl apply, it's very useful to be able to see exactly what would change on the cluster. The kubectl diff command will do this for you.

```
kubectl diff -f deployment.yaml
-   replicas: 10
+   replicas: 5
```

You can use this diff output to check whether the changes you made will actually have the effect you expected. Also, it will warn you if the state of the live resource is out of sync with the YAML manifest, perhaps because someone edited it imperatively since you last applied it.

Best Practice

Use kubectl diff to check what would change before applying any updates to your production cluster.

Working with Containers

Most of what goes on in a Kubernetes cluster happens inside containers, so when things go wrong, it can be hard to see what's happening. Here are a few useful ways to work with running containers using kubectl.

Viewing a Container's Logs

When you're trying to get a container working and it's not behaving as it should, one of the most useful sources of information is the container's logs. In Kubernetes, *logs* are considered to be whatever a container writes to the *standard output* and *standard error* streams; if you were running the program in a terminal, these are what you would see printed in the terminal.

In production applications, especially distributed ones, you'll need to be able to aggregate logs from multiple services, store them in a persistent database, and query and graph them. This is a big topic, and one we'll treat in much more detail in Chapter 15.

Inspecting the log messages from specific containers is still a very useful troubleshooting technique, though, and you can do this directly with kubectl logs, followed by the name of a Pod:

```
kubectl logs -n kube-system --tail=20 kube-dns-autoscaler-69c5cbdcdd-94h7f
autoscaler.go:49] Scaling Namespace: kube-system, Target: deployment/kube-dns
autoscaler_server.go:133] ConfigMap not found: configmaps "kube-dns-autoscaler"
k8sclient.go:117] Created ConfigMap kube-dns-autoscaler in namespace kube-system
plugin.go:50] Set control mode to linear
linear_controller.go:59] ConfigMap version change (old:  new: 526) - rebuilding
```

Most long-running containers will generate a *lot* of log output, so you'll usually want to restrict it to just the most recent lines, using the --tail flag, as in this example. (The container logs will be shown with timestamps, but we've trimmed those here to fit the messages on the page.)

To watch a container as it's running, and stream its log output to your terminal, use the --follow flag (-f for short):

```
kubectl logs --namespace kube-system --tail=10 --follow etcd-docker-for-desktop
etcdserver: starting server... [version: 3.1.12, cluster version: 3.1]
embed: ClientTLS: cert = /var/lib/localkube/certs/etcd/server.crt, key = ...
...
```

As long as you leave the kubectl logs command running, you'll continue to see output from the etcd-docker-for-desktop container.

It can be particularly useful to view the Kubernetes API server's logs; for example, if you have RBAC permission errors (see "Introducing Role-Based Access Control (RBAC)" on page 202), they'll show up here. If you have access to your master nodes, you can find the kube-apiserver Pod in the kube-system namespace and use kubectl logs to see its output.

If you're using a managed service like GKE, where the master nodes are not visible to you, check your provider's documentation to see how to find the control plane logs (for example, on GKE they'll be visible in the Stackdriver Logs Viewer).

When there are multiple containers in a Pod, you can specify which one you want to see the logs for using the --container flag (-c for short):

```
kubectl logs -n kube-system metrics-server
    -c metrics-server-nanny
...
```

For more sophisticated log watching, you may want to use a dedicated tool like Stern instead (see "Stern" on page 130).

Attaching to a Container

When looking at the logs of a container isn't enough, you might need to attach your local terminal to the container instead. This lets you see the container's output directly. To do this, use kubectl attach:

```
kubectl attach demo-54f4458547-fcx2n
Defaulting container name to demo.
Use kubectl describe pod/demo-54f4458547-fcx2n to see all of the containers
in this pod.
If you don't see a command prompt, try pressing enter.
```

Watching Kubernetes Resources with kubespy

When you deploy changes to your Kubernetes manifests, there's often an anxious period of waiting to see what happens next.

Often when you deploy an application, lots of things need to happen behind the scenes, as Kubernetes creates your resources, spins up Pods, and so on.

Because this happens *automagically*, as engineers like to say, it can be difficult to tell what's going on. kubectl get and kubectl describe can give you snapshots of individual resources, but what we'd really like is a way to see the state of Kubernetes resources changing in real time.

Enter kubespy (*https://github.com/pulumi/kubespy*), a neat tool from the Pulumi project.[1] kubespy can watch an individual resource in the cluster and show you what's happening to it over time.

For example, if you point kubespy at a Service resource, it will show you when the Service is created, when it's allocated an IP address, when its endpoints are connected, and so on.

Forwarding a Container Port

We've used kubectl port-forward before, in "Running the Demo App" on page 30, to forward a Kubernetes Service to a port on your local machine. But you can also use it to forward a container port, if you want to connect directly to a specific Pod. Just specify the Pod name and the local and remote ports:

---

1 Pulumi (*https://www.pulumi.com/*) is a cloud native, infrastructure as code framework.

```
kubectl port-forward demo-54f4458547-vm88z 9999:8888
Forwarding from 127.0.0.1:9999 -> 8888
Forwarding from [::1]:9999 -> 8888
```

Now port 9999 on your local machine will be forwarded to port 8888 on the container, and you can connect to it with a web browser, for example.

Executing Commands on Containers

The isolated nature of containers is great when you want to run reliable, secure workloads. But it can be a little inconvenient when something's not working right, and you can't see why.

When you're running a program on your local machine and it misbehaves, you have the power of the command line at your disposal to troubleshoot it: you can look at the running processes with ps, list and display files with ls and cat, and even edit them with vi.

Very often, with a malfunctioning container, it would be useful to have a shell running in the container so that we can do this kind of interactive debugging.

Using the kubectl exec command, you can run a specified command in any container, including a shell:

```
kubectl run alpine --image alpine --command -- sleep 999
deployment.apps "alpine" created

kubectl get pods
NAME                     READY     STATUS     RESTARTS    AGE
alpine-7fd44fc4bf-7gl4n  1/1       Running    0           4s

kubectl exec -it alpine-7fd44fc4bf-7gl4n /bin/sh
/ # ps
PID   USER     TIME    COMMAND
    1 root      0:00 sleep 999
    7 root      0:00 /bin/sh
   11 root      0:00 ps
```

If the Pod has more than one container in it, kubectl exec will run the command in the first container by default. Alternatively, you can specify the container with the -c flag:

```
kubectl exec -it -c container2 POD_NAME /bin/sh
```

(If the container doesn't have a shell, see "Adding BusyBox to Your Containers" on page 124.)

Running Containers for Troubleshooting

As well as running commands on an existing container, sometimes it's handy to be able to run commands like `wget` or `nslookup` in the cluster, to see the results that your application would get. You've already learned how to run containers in the cluster with `kubectl run`, but here are a few useful examples of running one-off container commands for debugging purposes.

First, let's run an instance of the demo application to test against:

```
kubectl run demo --image cloudnatived/demo:hello --expose --port 8888
service/demo created
pod/demo created
```

The `demo` service should have been allocated an IP address and a DNS name of `demo` that is accessible from inside the cluster. Let's check that, using the `nslookup` command running inside a container:

```
kubectl run nslookup --image=busybox:1.28 --rm -it --restart=Never \
--command -- nslookup demo
Server:    10.79.240.10
Address 1: 10.79.240.10 kube-dns.kube-system.svc.cluster.local

Name:      demo
Address 1: 10.79.242.119 demo.default.svc.cluster.local
```

Good news: the DNS name works, so we should be able to make an HTTP request to it using `wget` and see the result:

```
kubectl run wget --image=busybox:1.28 --rm -it --restart=Never \
--command -- wget -qO- http://demo:8888
Hello, 世界
pod "wget" deleted
```

You can see that this pattern of `kubectl run` commands uses a common set of flags:

```
kubectl run NAME --image=IMAGE --rm -it --restart=Never --command -- ...
```

What do these do?

`--rm`

This tells Kubernetes to delete the resources created in this command for attached containers so that it doesn't clutter up your nodes' local storage.

`-it`

This runs the container interactively (`i`), via a terminal (`t`), so that you see the output from the container in your own terminal, and can send keystrokes to it if you need to.

`--restart=Never`
> This tells Kubernetes to skip its usual helpful behavior of restarting a container whenever it exits. Since we only want to run the container one time, we can disable the default restart policy.

`--command --`
> This specifies a command to run, instead of the container's default entrypoint. Everything following the `--` will be passed to the container as a command line, complete with arguments.

Using BusyBox Commands

Although you can run any container available to you, the `busybox` image is particularly useful, because it contains a wealth of the most commonly used Unix commands, such as `cat`, `echo`, `find`, `grep`, and `kill`. You can see a complete list of BusyBox commands (*https://busybox.net/downloads/BusyBox.html*) at their website.

BusyBox also includes a lightweight bash-like shell, called `ash`, which is compatible with standard */bin/sh* shell scripts. So to get an interactive shell in your cluster, you can run:

```
kubectl run busybox --image=busybox:1.28 --rm -it --restart=Never /bin/sh
```

Because the pattern for running commands from the BusyBox image is always the same, you could even make a shell alias for it (see "Shell Aliases" on page 111):

```
alias bb=kubectl run busybox --image=busybox:1.28 --rm -it --restart=Never
    --command --
bb nslookup demo
...
bb wget -qO- http://demo:8888
...
bb sh
If you don't see a command prompt, try pressing enter.
/ #
```

Adding BusyBox to Your Containers

If your container already has a shell in it (for example, if it's built from a Linux base image, such as `alpine`), then you can get shell access on the container by running:

```
kubectl exec -it POD /bin/sh
```

But what if there's no */bin/sh* in the container? For example, if you're using a minimal, scratch image as described in "Understanding Dockerfiles" on page 25.

The simplest way to make your containers easily debuggable, while keeping the images very small, is to copy the `busybox` executable into them at build time. It's only

1 MiB, which is a small price to pay for having a usable shell and a set of Unix utilities.

You learned in the earlier discussion of multistage builds that you can copy a file from a previously built container into a new container using the Dockerfile COPY --from command. A lesser-known feature of this command is that you can also copy a file from any public image, not just one that you built locally.

The following Dockerfile shows how to do this with the demo image:

```
FROM golang:1.14-alpine AS build

WORKDIR /src/
COPY main.go go.* /src/
RUN CGO_ENABLED=0 go build -o /bin/demo

FROM scratch
COPY --from=build /bin/demo /bin/demo
COPY --from=busybox:1.28 /bin/busybox /bin/busybox
ENTRYPOINT ["/bin/demo"]
```

Here, the --from=busybox:1.28 references the public BusyBox library image.[2] You could copy a file from any image you like (such as alpine, for example).

Now you still have a very small container, but you can also get a shell on it, by running:

```
kubectl exec -it POD_NAME /bin/busybox sh
```

Instead of executing /bin/sh directly, you execute /bin/busybox followed by the name of the command you want; in this case, sh.

Installing Programs on a Container

If you need some programs that aren't included in BusyBox, or aren't available in a public container image, you can run a Linux image such as alpine or ubuntu instead, and install whatever you need on it:

```
kubectl run alpine --image alpine --rm -it --restart=Never /bin/sh
If you don't see a command prompt, try pressing enter.
/ # apk --update add emacs
```

Live Debugging with kubesquash

We've talked somewhat loosely about *debugging* containers in this chapter, in the sense of *figuring out what's wrong with them*. But what if you want to attach a real

---

2 Versions of the BusyBox image later than 1.28 have a problem doing DNS lookups (*https://github.com/kubernetes/kubernetes/issues/66924*) in Kubernetes.

debugger, like gdb (the GNU Project debugger) or dlv (the Go debugger) to one of your running processes in a container?

A debugger, such as dlv, is a very powerful tool that can attach to a process, show you which source code lines are being executed, inspect and change the values of local variables, set breakpoints, and step through code line by line. If something mysterious is going on that you can't figure out, it's likely that eventually you'll have to resort to a debugger.

When you're running a program on your local machine, you have direct access to its processes, so this is no problem. If it's in a container, then like most things, it's a little bit more complicated than that.

The kubesquash tool is designed to help you attach a debugger to a container. To install it, follow the instructions (*https://github.com/solo-io/kubesquash*) on GitHub.

Once kubesquash is installed, all you need to do to use it is to give it the name of a running container:

```
/usr/local/bin/kubesquash-osx demo-6d7dff895c-x8pfd
? Going to attach dlv to pod demo-6d7dff895c-x8pfd. continue? Yes
If you don't see a command prompt, try pressing enter.
(dlv)
```

Behind the scenes, kubesquash creates a Pod in the squash namespace that runs the debugger binary, and takes care of attaching it to the running process in the Pod you specified.

For technical reasons (*https://github.com/solo-io/kubesquash/blob/master/cmd/kubes quash/main.go#L13*), kubesquash relies on the ls command being available in the target container. If you're using a scratch container, you can bake in the BusyBox executable to make this work, like we did in "Adding BusyBox to Your Containers" on page 124:

```
COPY --from=busybox:1.28 /bin/busybox /bin/ls
```

Instead of copying the executable to /bin/busybox, we copy it to /bin/ls. This makes kubesquash work perfectly.

We won't go into the details of using dlv here, but if you're writing Kubernetes applications in Go, it's an invaluable tool, and kubesquash is a very easy way to use it with containers.

You can read more about dlv in the official documentation (*https://github.com/derek parker/delve/tree/master/Documentation*).

Contexts and Namespaces

So far in this book we've been working with a single Kubernetes cluster, and all the kubectl commands you've run have naturally applied to that cluster.

So what happens when you have more than one cluster? For example, maybe you have a Kubernetes cluster on your machine, for local testing, and a production cluster in the cloud, and perhaps another remote cluster for staging and development. How does kubectl know which one you mean?

To solve this problem, kubectl has the concept of *contexts*. A context is a combination of a cluster, a user, and a namespace (see "Using Namespaces" on page 77).

When you run kubectl commands, they're always executed in the *current context*. Let's look at an example:

```
kubectl config get-contexts
CURRENT   NAME                 CLUSTER           AUTHINFO        NAMESPACE
          gke                  gke_test_us-w     gke_test_us     myapp
*         docker-for-desktop   docker-for-d      docker-for-d
```

These are the contexts kubectl currently knows about. Each context has a name, and refers to a particular cluster, a username that authenticates to the cluster, and a namespace within the cluster. The docker-for-desktop context, as you might expect, refers to my local Kubernetes cluster.

The current context is shown with a * in the first column (in the example, it's docker-for-desktop). If I run a kubectl command now, it will operate on the Docker Desktop cluster, in the default namespace (because the NAMESPACE column is blank, indicating that the context refers to the default namespace):

```
kubectl cluster-info
Kubernetes master is running at https://192.168.99.100:8443
KubeDNS is running at https://192.168.99.100:8443/api/v1/...

To further debug and diagnose cluster problems, use 'kubectl cluster-info dump'.
```

You can switch to another context using the kubectl config use-context command:

```
kubectl config use-context gke
Switched to context "gke".
```

You could think of contexts as being like bookmarks: they let you switch easily to a particular cluster and a particular namespace. To create a new context, use kubectl config set-context:

```
kubectl config set-context myapp --cluster=gke --namespace=myapp
Context "myapp" created.
```

Now whenever you switch to the myapp context, your current context will be the myapp namespace on the Docker Desktop cluster.

If you forget what your current context is, kubectl config current-context will tell you:

```
kubectl config current-context
myapp
```

kubectx and kubens

If, like us, you type for a living, you probably don't like typing any more keystrokes than you have to. For faster switching of kubectl contexts, you can use the kubectx and kubens tools. Follow the instructions (*https://github.com/ahmetb/kubectx*) on Git-Hub to install both kubectx and kubens.

Now you can use the kubectx command to switch contexts:

```
kubectx docker-for-desktop
Switched to context "docker-for-desktop".
```

One nice feature of kubectx is that kubectx - will switch to your previous context, so you can quickly toggle between two contexts:

```
kubectx -
Switched to context "gke".
kubectx -
Switched to context "docker-for-desktop".
```

Just kubectx on its own will list all the contexts you have stored, with the current context highlighted.

Switching namespaces is something you'll probably do more often than switching contexts, so the kubens tool is ideal for this:

```
kubens
default
kube-public
kube-system

kubens kube-system
Context "docker-for-desktop" modified.
Active namespace is "kube-system".

kubens -
Context "docker-for-desktop" modified.
Active namespace is "default".
```

The kubectx and kubens tools do one thing well, and they're very useful additions to your Kubernetes toolbox.

kube-ps1

If you use the bash or zsh shells, there's a little utility (*https://github.com/jonmosco/kube-ps1*) that will add the current Kubernetes context to your prompt.

With kube-ps1 installed, you can't forget which context you're in:

```
source "/usr/local/opt/kube-ps1/share/kube-ps1.sh"
PS1="[$(kube_ps1)]$ "
[(❈ |docker-for-desktop:default)]
kubectx cloudnativedevops
Switched to context "cloudnativedevops".
(❈ |cloudnativedevops:cloudnativedevopsblog)
```

Kubernetes Shells and Tools

While using kubectl in an ordinary shell is perfectly sufficient for most things you'll want to do with a Kubernetes cluster, there are other options.

kube-shell

If kubectl auto-completion isn't fancy enough for you, there's always kube-shell, a wrapper for kubectl that provides a pop-up menu of possible completions for each command (see Figure 7-1).

```
kube-shell> kubectl get pods cluster
                         pod
                         poddisruptionbudget
                         podsecuritypolicy
                         podtemplate
                         componentstatus
                         endpoints
                         networkpolicy
 [F4] Cluster: minikube [F5] Namespace: kube-system User: minikube [F9] In-line help: ON [F10] Exit
```

Figure 7-1. kube-shell is an interactive Kubernetes client

Click

A more sophisticated Kubernetes terminal experience is provided by Click (*https://databricks.com/blog/2018/03/27/introducing-click-the-command-line-interactive-controller-for-kubernetes.html*).

Click is like an interactive version of kubectl, which *remembers* the current object you're working with. For example, when you want to find and describe a Pod in kubectl, you usually have to list all the matching Pods first, then copy and paste the unique name of the Pod you're interested in into a new command.

Instead, with Click, you can select any resource from a list by typing its number (for example, 1 for the first item). That's now the current resource, and the next Click command will operate on that resource by default. To make finding the object you want easier, Click supports searching by regular expressions.

Click is a powerful tool that provides a very pleasant environment for working with Kubernetes. While it's described as *beta and experimental*, it's already perfectly usable for everyday cluster administration tasks, and it's well worth trying out.

kubed-sh

While kube-shell and Click provide essentially local shells that know a little about Kubernetes, kubed-sh (pronounced *kube-dash*) is a more intriguing idea: a shell that runs, in some sense, *on* the cluster itself.

kubed-sh will pull and run the necessary containers to execute JavaScript, Ruby, or Python programs on your current cluster. You can create, for example, a Ruby script on your local machine, and use kubed-sh to execute the script as a Kubernetes Deployment.

Stern

While kubectl logs is a useful command (see "Viewing a Container's Logs" on page 119), it's not as convenient as it could be. For example, before you can use it, you first have to find out the unique name of the Pod and container whose logs you want to see, and specify these on the command line, which generally means at least one copy and paste.

Also, if you're using -f to follow logs from a particular container, whenever the container is restarted, your log stream will stop. You'll have to find out the new name of the container and run kubectl logs again to follow it. And you can only follow logs from one Pod at a time.

A more sophisticated log-streaming tool would allow you to specify a group of Pods with a regular expression matching their names, or a set of labels, and it would be able to keep on streaming logs even if individual containers are restarted.

Fortunately, that's exactly what the Stern (*https://github.com/wercker/stern*) tool does. Stern tails the logs from all Pods matching a regular expression (for example demo.*). If there are multiple containers within the Pod, Stern will show you log messages from each, prefixed by its name.

The `--since` flag lets you limit the output to recent messages (within the last 10 minutes, in the example).

Instead of matching specific Pod names with a regular expression, you can use any Kubernetes label selector expression, just as with `kubectl`. Combined with the `--all-namespaces` flag, this is ideal for watching logs from multiple containers.

Building Your Own Kubernetes Tools

Combined with query tools like `jq` and the standard set of Unix utilities (`cut`, `grep`, `xargs`, and friends), `kubectl` can be used for some fairly sophisticated scripting of Kubernetes resources. As we've seen in this chapter, there are also many third-party tools available that you can use as part of automated scripts.

This approach has its limits, however. It's fine to cook up ingenious one-liners and ad hoc shell scripts for interactive debugging and exploration, but they can be hard to understand and maintain.

For real systems programs, automating your production workflows, we strongly recommend you use a real systems programming language. Go is the logical choice, since it was good enough for the Kubernetes authors, and naturally Kubernetes includes a full-featured client library (*https://github.com/kubernetes/client-go*) for use in Go programs.

Because the `client-go` library gives you complete access to the Kubernetes API, you can do anything with it that `kubectl` can do, and more. The following snippet shows how to list all the Pods in your cluster, for example:

```
...
podList, err := clientset.CoreV1().Pods("").List(metav1.ListOptions{})
if err != nil {
        log.Fatal(err)
}
fmt.Println("There are", len(podList.Items), "pods in the cluster:")
for _, i := range podList.Items {
        fmt.Println(i.ObjectMeta.Name)
}
...
```

You can also create or delete Pods, Deployments, or any other resources. You can even implement your own custom resource types.

If you need a feature that's missing from Kubernetes, you can implement it yourself, using the client library.

Other programming languages, such as Ruby, Python, and PHP, also have Kubernetes client libraries (*https://kubernetes.io/docs/reference/using-api/client-libraries/*) you can use in the same way.

Summary

There is a bewildering profusion of Kubernetes tools available, and more are released every week. You could be forgiven for feeling a little weary when reading about yet another tool you apparently can't do without.

The fact is, you don't need most of these tools. Kubernetes itself, via `kubectl`, can do most everything you want it to. The rest is just for fun and convenience.

Nobody knows everything, but everybody knows something. In writing this chapter, we've incorporated tips and tricks from lots of experienced Kubernetes engineers, from books, blog posts, and documentation, and one or two little discoveries of our own. Everybody we've shown it to, no matter how expert, learned at least one useful thing. That makes us happy.

It's worth taking a little time to get familiar with `kubectl` and explore its possibilities; it's the most important Kubernetes tool you have, and you'll be using it a lot.

Here are a few of the most important things to know:

- `kubectl` includes complete and exhaustive documentation on itself, available with `kubectl -h`, and on every Kubernetes resource, field, or feature, using `kubectl explain`.

- When you want to do complicated filtering and transformations on `kubectl` output, for example in scripts, select JSON format with `-o json`. Once you have JSON data, you can use power tools like `jq` to query it.

- The `--dry-run=client` option to `kubectl`, combined with `-o YAML` to get YAML output, lets you use imperative commands to generate Kubernetes manifests. This is a big time-saver when creating manifest files for new applications, for example.

- You can turn existing resources into YAML manifests, too, using the `-o` flag to `kubectl get`.

- `kubectl diff` will tell you what *would* change if you applied a manifest, without actually changing it.

- You can see the output and error messages from any container with `kubectl logs`, stream them continuously with the `--follow` flag, or do more sophisticated multi-Pod log tailing with Stern.

- To troubleshoot problem containers, you can attach to them with `kubectl attach` or get a shell on the container with `kubectl exec -it ... /bin/sh`.

- You can run any public container image with `kubectl run` to help solve problems, including the multitalented BusyBox tool, which contains all your favorite Unix commands.

- Kubernetes contexts are like bookmarks, marking your place in a particular cluster and namespace. You can switch conveniently between contexts and namespaces using the kubectx and kubens tools.

- Click is a powerful Kubernetes shell that gives you all the functionality of kubectl, but with added state: it remembers the currently selected object from one command to the next, so you don't have to specify it every time.

- Kubernetes is designed to be automated and controlled by code. When you need to go beyond what kubectl provides, the Kubernetes client-go library gives you complete control over every aspect of your cluster using Go code.

CHAPTER 8

Running Containers

If you have a tough question that you can't answer, start by tackling a simpler question that you can't answer.

—Max Tegmark

In previous chapters, we've focused mostly on the operational aspects of Kubernetes: where to get your clusters, how to maintain them, and how to manage your cluster resources. Let's turn now to the most fundamental Kubernetes object: the *container*. We'll look at how containers work on a technical level, how they relate to Pods, and how to deploy container images to Kubernetes.

In this chapter, we'll also cover the important topic of container security, and how to use the security features in Kubernetes to deploy your applications in a secure way, according to best practices. Finally, we'll look at how to mount disk volumes on Pods, allowing containers to share and persist data.

Containers and Pods

We've already introduced Pods in Chapter 2, and talked about how Deployments use ReplicaSets to maintain a set of replica Pods, but we haven't really looked at Pods themselves in much detail. Pods are the unit of scheduling in Kubernetes. A Pod object represents a container or group of containers, and everything that runs in Kubernetes does so by means of a Pod:

A Pod represents a collection of application containers and volumes running in the same execution environment. Pods, not containers, are the smallest deployable artifact in a Kubernetes cluster. This means all of the containers in a Pod always land on the same machine.

—Kelsey Hightower et al., *Kubernetes Up & Running*

So far in this book the terms *Pod* and *container* have been used more or less interchangeably: the demo application Pod only has one container in it. In more complex applications, though, it's quite likely that a Pod will include two or more containers. So let's look at how that works, and see when and why you might want to group containers together in Pods.

What Is a Container?

Before asking why you might want to have multiple containers in a Pod, let's take a moment to revisit what a container actually is.

You know from "The Coming of Containers" on page 7 that a container is a standardized package that contains a piece of software together with its dependencies, configuration, data, and so on: everything it needs to run. How does that actually work, though?

In Linux and most other operating systems, everything that runs on a machine does so by means of a *process*. A process represents the binary code and memory state of a running application, such as Chrome, iTunes, or Visual Studio Code. All processes exist in the same global namespace: they can all see and interact with each other, they all share the same pool of resources, such as CPU, memory, and filesystem. (A Linux namespace is a bit like a Kubernetes namespace, though not the same thing technically.)

From the operating system's point of view, a container represents an isolated process (or group of processes) that exists in its own namespace. Processes inside the container can't see processes outside it, and vice versa. A container can't access resources belonging to another container, or processes outside of a container. The container boundary is like a ring fence that stops processes running wild and using up each other's resources.

As far as the process inside the container is concerned, it's running on its own machine, with complete access to all its resources, and there are no other processes running. You can see this if you run a few commands inside a container:

```
kubectl run busybox --image busybox:1.28 --rm -it --restart=Never /bin/sh
If you don't see a command prompt, try pressing enter.
/ # ps ax
PID   USER     TIME  COMMAND
    1 root      0:00 /bin/sh
    8 root      0:00 ps ax

/ # hostname
busybox
```

Normally, the `ps ax` command will list all processes running on the machine, and there are usually a lot of them (a few hundred on a typical Linux server). But there are only two processes shown here: /bin/sh, and ps ax. The only processes visible inside the container, therefore, are the ones actually running in the container.

Similarly, the hostname command, which would normally show the name of the host machine, returns busybox: in fact, this is the name of the container. So it looks to the busybox container as if it's running on a machine called busybox, and it has the whole machine to itself. This is true for each of the containers running on the same machine.

It's a fun exercise to create a container yourself, without the benefit of a container runtime like Docker. Liz Rice's excellent talk on "What is a container, really?" (*https://youtu.be/HPuvDm8IC-4*) shows how to do this from scratch in a Go program.

What Belongs in a Container?

There's no technical reason you can't run as many processes as you want to inside a container: you could run a complete Linux distribution, with multiple running applications, network services, and so on, all inside the same container. This is why you sometimes hear containers referred to as *lightweight virtual machines*. But this isn't the best way to use containers, because then you don't get the benefits of resource isolation.

If processes don't need to know about each other, then they don't need to run in the same container. A good rule of thumb with a container is that it should *do one thing*. For example, our demo application container listens on a network port, and sends the string Hello, 世界 to anyone who connects to it. That's a simple, self-contained service: it doesn't rely on any other programs or services, and in turn, nothing relies on it. It's a perfect candidate for having its own container.

A container also has an *entrypoint*: a command that is run when the container starts. That usually results in the creation of a single process to run the command, though some applications often start a few subprocesses to act as helpers or workers. To start multiple separate processes in a container, you'd need to write a wrapper script to act as the entrypoint, which would in turn start the processes you want.

Each container should run just one main process. If you're running a large group of unrelated processes in a container, you're not taking full advantage of the power of containers, and you should think about splitting your application up into multiple, communicating containers.

What Belongs in a Pod?

Now that you know what a container is, you can see why it's useful to group them together in Pods. A Pod represents a group of containers that need to communicate and share data with each other; they need to be scheduled together, they need to be started and stopped together, and they need to run on the same physical machine.

A good example of this is an application that stores data in a local cache, such as Memcached (*https://memcached.org/about*). You'll need to run two processes: your application, and the memcached server process that handles storing and retrieving data. Although you could run both processes inside a single container, that's unnecessary: they only need to communicate via a network socket. Better to split them into two separate containers, each of which only needs to worry about building and running its own process.

In fact, you can use a public Memcached container image, available from Docker Hub, which is already set up to work as part of a Pod with another container.

So you create a Pod with two containers: Memcached, and your application. The application can talk to Memcached by making a network connection, and because the two containers are in the same Pod, that connection will always be local: the two containers will always run on the same node.

Similarly, imagine a blog application, which consists of a web server container, such as Nginx, and a Git synchronizer container, which clones a Git repo containing the blog data: HTML files, images, and so on. The blog container writes data to disk, and because containers in a Pod can share a disk volume, the data can also be available to the Nginx container to serve over HTTP:

> In general, the right question to ask yourself when designing Pods is, "Will these containers work correctly if they land on different machines?" If the answer is "no", a Pod is the correct grouping for the containers. If the answer is "yes", multiple Pods is the probably the correct solution.
>
> —Kelsey Hightower et al., *Kubernetes Up & Running*

The containers in a Pod should all be working together to do one job. If you only need one container to do that job, fine: use one container. If you need two or three, that's OK. If you have more than that, you might want to think about whether the containers could actually be split into separate Pods.

Container Manifests

We've outlined what containers are, what should go in a container, and when containers should be grouped together in Pods. So how do we actually run a container in Kubernetes?

When you created your first Deployment, in "Deployment Manifests" on page 59, it contained a `template.spec` section specifying the container to run (only one container, in that example):

```
spec:
  containers:
  - name: demo
    image: cloudnatived/demo:hello
    ports:
    - containerPort: 8888
```

Here's an example of what the `template.spec` section for a Deployment with two containers would look like:

```
spec:
  containers:
  - name: container1
    image: example/container1
  - name: container2
    image: example/container2
```

The only required fields in each container's spec are the `name` and `image`: a container has to have a name, so that other resources can refer to it, and you have to tell Kubernetes what image to run in the container.

Image Identifiers

You've already used some different container image identifiers so far in this book; for example, `cloudnatived/demo:hello`, `alpine`, and `busybox:1.28`.

There are actually four different parts to an image identifier: the *registry hostname*, the *repository namespace*, the *image repository*, and the *tag*. All but the image name are optional. An image identifier using all of those parts looks like this:

`docker.io/cloudnatived/demo:hello`

- The registry hostname in this example is `docker.io`; in fact, that's the default for Docker images, so we don't need to specify it. If your image is stored in another registry, though, you'll need to give its hostname. For example, Google Container Registry images are prefixed by `gcr.io`.

- The repository namespace is `cloudnatived`: that's us (hello!). If you don't specify the repository namespace, then the default namespace (called `library`) is used. This is a set of official images (*https://docs.docker.com/docker-hub/official_repos*), which are approved and maintained by Docker, Inc. Popular official images include OS base images (`alpine`, `ubuntu`, `debian`, `centos`), language environments (`golang`, `python`, `ruby`, `php`, `java`), and widely used software (`mongo`, `mysql`, `nginx`, `redis`).

- The image repository is `demo`, which identifies a particular container image within the registry and namespace. (See also "Container Digests" on page 140.)
- The tag is `hello`. Tags identify different versions of the same image.

It's up to you what tags to put on a container: some common choices include:

- A semantic version tag, like `v1.3.0`. This usually refers to the version of the application.
- A Git SHA tag, like `5ba6bfd....` This identifies the specific commit in the source repo that was used to build the container (see "Git SHA Tags" on page 256).
- The environment it represents, such as `staging` or `production`.

You can add as many tags as you want to a given image.

The latest Tag

If you don't specify a tag when pulling an image, the default tag is `latest`. For example, when you run an `alpine` image, with no tag specified, you'll get `alpine:latest`.

The `latest` tag is a default tag that's added to an image when you build or push it without specifying a tag. It doesn't necessarily identify the most recent image; just the most recent image that wasn't explicitly tagged. This makes `latest` rather unhelpful (*https://vsupalov.com/docker-latest-tag*) as an identifier.

That's why it's important to always use a specific tag when deploying production containers to Kubernetes. When you're just running a quick one-off container, for troubleshooting or experimentation, like the `alpine` container, it's fine to omit the tag and get the latest image. For real applications, though, you want to make sure that if you deploy the Pod tomorrow, you'll get the exact same container image as when you deployed it today:

> You should avoid using the `latest` tag when deploying containers in production, because this makes it hard to track which version of the image is running and hard to roll back.
>
> —The Kubernetes documentation (*https://kubernetes.io/docs/concepts/configuration/overview/#using-labels*)

Container Digests

As we've seen, the `latest` tag doesn't always mean what you think it will, and even a semantic version or Git SHA tag doesn't uniquely and permanently identify a particular container image. If the maintainer decides to push a different image with the same tag, the next time you deploy, you'll get that updated image. In technical terms, a tag is *nondeterministic*.

Sometimes it's desirable to have deterministic deployments: in other words, to guarantee that a deployment will always reference the exact container image you specified. You can do this using the container's *digest*: a cryptographic hash of the image's contents that immutably identifies that image.

Images can have many tags, but only one digest. This means that if your container manifest specifies the image digest, you can guarantee deterministic deployments. An image identifier with a digest looks like this:

```
cloudnatived/
demo@sha256:aeae1e551a6cbd60bcfd56c3b4ffec732c45b8012b7cb758c6c4a34...
```

Base Image Tags

When you reference a base image in a Dockerfile, if you don't specify a tag, you'll get `latest`, just as you do when deploying a container. Because of the tricky semantics of `latest`, as we've seen, it's a good idea to use a specific base image tag instead, like `alpine:3.8`.

When you make a change to your application and rebuild its container, you don't want to also get unexpected changes as a result of a newer public base image. That may cause problems that are hard to find and debug.

To make your builds as reproducible as possible, use a specific tag or digest.

 We've said that you should avoid using the `latest` tag, but it's fair to note that there's some room for disagreement about this. Even the present authors have different preferences. Always using `latest` base images means that if some change to the base image breaks your build, you'll find out right away. On the other hand, using specific image tags means that you only have to upgrade your base image when *you* want to, not when the upstream maintainers decide to. It's up to you.

Ports

You've already seen the `ports` field used with our demo application: it specifies the network port numbers the application will listen on. This is just informational, and has no significance to Kubernetes, but it's good practice to include it.

Resource Requests and Limits

We've already covered resource requests and limits for containers in detail, in Chapter 5, so a brief recap here will suffice.

Each container can supply one or more of the following as part of its spec:

- `resources.requests.cpu`
- `resources.requests.memory`
- `resources.limits.cpu`
- `resources.limits.memory`

Although requests and limits are specified on individual containers, we usually talk in terms of the Pod's resource requests and limits. A Pod's resource request is the sum of the resource requests for all containers in that Pod, and so on.

Image Pull Policy

As you know, before a container can be run on a node, the image has to be *pulled*, or downloaded, from the appropriate container registry. The `imagePullPolicy` field on a container governs how often Kubernetes will do this. It can take one of three values: `Always`, `IfNotPresent`, or `Never`:

- `Always` will pull the image every time the container is started. Assuming that you specify a tag, which you should (see "The latest Tag" on page 140), then this is unnecessary, and wastes time and bandwidth.
- `IfNotPresent`, the default, is correct for most situations. If the image is not already present on the node, it will be downloaded. After that, unless you change the image spec, the saved image will be used every time the container starts, and Kubernetes will not attempt to redownload it.
- `Never` will never update the image at all. With this policy, Kubernetes will never fetch the image from a registry: if it's already present on the node, it will be used, but if it's not, the container will fail to start. You're unlikely to want this.

If you run into strange problems (for example, a Pod not updating when you've pushed a new container image), check your image pull policy.

Environment Variables

Environment variables are a common, if limited, way to pass information to containers at runtime. Common, because all Linux executables have access to environment variables, and even programs that were written long before containers existed can use their environment for configuration. Limited, because environment variables can only be string values: no arrays, no keys and values, no structured data in general. The total size of a process's environment is also limited to 32 KiB, so you can't pass large data files in the environment.

To set an environment variable, list it in the container's env field:

```
containers:
- name: demo
  image: cloudnatived/demo:hello
  env:
  - name: GREETING
    value: "Hello from the environment"
```

If the container image itself specifies environment variables (set in the Dockerfile, for example), then the Kubernetes env settings will override them. This can be useful for altering the default configuration of a container.

> A more flexible way of passing configuration data to containers is to use a Kubernetes ConfigMap or Secret object: see Chapter 10 for more about these.

Container Security

You might have noticed in "What Is a Container?" on page 136 that when we looked at the process list in the container with the `ps ax` command, the processes were all running as the `root` user. In Linux and other Unix-derived operating systems, `root` is the superuser, which has privileges to read any data, modify any file, and perform any operation on the system.

While on a full Linux system some processes need to run as root (for example `init`, which manages all other processes), that's not usually the case with a container.

Indeed, running processes as the `root` user when you don't need to is a bad idea. It contravenes the *principle of least privilege* (*https://en.wikipedia.org/wiki/Princi ple_of_least_privilege*). This says that a program should only be able to access the information and resources that it actually needs to do its job.

Programs have bugs; this is a fact of life apparent to anyone who's written one. Some bugs allow malicious users to hijack the program to do things it's not supposed to, like read secret data, or execute arbitrary code. To mitigate this, it's important to run containers with the minimum possible privileges.

This starts with not allowing them to run as `root`, but instead assigning them an *ordinary* user: one that has no special privileges, such as reading other users' files:

> Just like you wouldn't (or shouldn't) run anything as root on your server, you shouldn't run anything as root in a container on your server. Running binaries that were created elsewhere requires a significant amount of trust, and the same is true for binaries in containers.

—Marc Campbell (*https://medium.com/@mccode/processes-in-containers-should-not-run-as-root-2feae3f0df3b*)

It's also possible for attackers to exploit bugs in the container runtime to "escape" from the container, and get the same powers and privileges on the host machine that they did in the container.

Running Containers as a Non-Root User

Here's an example of a container spec that tells Kubernetes to run the container as a specific user:

```
containers:
- name: demo
  image: cloudnatived/demo:hello
  securityContext:
    runAsUser: 1000
```

The value for `runAsUser` is a *UID* (a numerical user identifier). On many Linux systems, UID 1000 is assigned to the first non-root user created on the system, so it's generally safe to choose values of 1000 or above for container UIDs. It doesn't matter whether or not a Unix user with that UID *exists* in the container, or even if there is an operating system in the container; this works just as well with scratch containers.

Docker also allows you to specify a user in the Dockerfile to run the container's process, but you needn't bother to do this. It's easier and more flexible to set the `runAsUser` field in the Kubernetes spec.

If a `runAsUser` UID is specified, it will override any user configured in the container image. If there is no `runAsUser`, but the container specifies a user, Kubernetes will run it as that user. If no user is specified either in the manifest or the image, the container will run as `root` (which, as we've seen, is a bad idea).

For maximum security, you should choose a different UID for each container. That way, if a container should be compromised somehow, or accidentally overwrite data, it only has permission to access its own data, and not that of other containers.

On the other hand, if you want two or more containers to be able to access the same data (via a mounted volume, for example), you should assign them the same UID.

Blocking Root Containers

To help prevent this situation, Kubernetes allows you to block containers from running if they would run as the root user.

The `runAsNonRoot: true` setting will do this:

```
containers:
- name: demo
```

```
image: cloudnatived/demo:hello
securityContext:
  runAsNonRoot: true
```

When Kubernetes runs this container, it will check to see if the container wants to run as root. If so, it will refuse to start it. This will protect you against forgetting to set a non-root user in your containers, or running third-party containers that are configured to run as root.

If this happens, you'll see the Pod status shown as `CreateContainerConfigError`, and when you `kubectl describe` the Pod, you'll see this error:

```
Error: container has runAsNonRoot and image will run as root
```

Best Practice

Run containers as non-root users, and block root containers from running, using the `runAsNonRoot: true` setting.

Setting a Read-Only Filesystem

Another useful security context setting is `readOnlyRootFilesystem`, which will prevent the container from writing to its own filesystem. It's possible to imagine a container taking advantage of a bug in Docker or Kubernetes, for example, where writing to its filesystem could affect files on the host node. If its filesystem is read-only, that can't happen; the container will get an I/O error:

```
containers:
- name: demo
  image: cloudnatived/demo:hello
  securityContext:
    readOnlyRootFilesystem: true
```

Many containers don't need to write anything to their own filesystem, so this setting won't interfere with them. It's good practice (*https://kubernetes.io/blog/2016/08/security-best-practices-kubernetes-deployment/*) to always set `readOnlyRootFilesystem` unless the container really does need to write to files.

Disabling Privilege Escalation

Normally, Linux binaries run with the same privileges as the user that executes them. There is an exception, though: binaries that use the `setuid` mechanism can temporarily gain the privileges of the user that *owns* the binary (usually `root`).

This is a potential problem in containers, since even if the container is running as a regular user (UID 1000, for example), if it contains a `setuid` binary, that binary can gain root privileges by default.

To prevent this, set the `allowPrivilegeEscalation` field of the container's security policy to `false`:

```
containers:
- name: demo
  image: cloudnatived/demo:hello
  securityContext:
    allowPrivilegeEscalation: false
```

To control this setting across the whole cluster, rather than for an individual container, see "Pod Security Policies" on page 148.

Modern Linux programs don't need `setuid`; they can use a more flexible and fine-grained privilege mechanism called *capabilities* to achieve the same thing.

Capabilities

Traditionally, Unix programs had two levels of privileges: *normal* and *superuser*. Normal programs have no more privileges than the user who runs them, while superuser programs can do anything, bypassing all kernel security checks.

The Linux capabilities mechanism improves on this by defining various specific things that a program can do: load kernel modules, perform direct network I/O operations, access system devices, and so on. Any program that needs a specific privilege can be granted it, but no others.

For example, a web server that listens on port 80 would normally need to run as `root` to do this; port numbers below 1024 are considered privileged *system* ports. Instead, the program can be granted the `NET_BIND_SERVICE` capability, which allows it to bind to any port, but gives it no other special privileges.

The default set of capabilities for Docker containers is fairly generous. This is a pragmatic decision based on a trade-off of security against usability: giving containers *no* capabilities by default would require operators to set capabilities on many containers in order for them to run.

On the other hand, the principle of least privilege says that a container should have no capabilities it doesn't need. Kubernetes security contexts allow you to drop any capabilities from the default set, and add ones as they're needed, like this example shows:

```
containers:
- name: demo
  image: cloudnatived/demo:hello
  securityContext:
    capabilities:
      drop: ["CHOWN", "NET_RAW", "SETPCAP"]
      add: ["NET_ADMIN"]
```

The container will have the CHOWN, NET_RAW, and SETPCAP capabilities removed, and the NET_ADMIN capability added.

The Docker documentation (*https://docs.docker.com/engine/reference/run/#runtime-privilege-and-linux-capabilities*) lists all the capabilities that are set on containers by default, and that can be added as necessary.

For maximum security, you should drop all capabilities for every container, and only add specific capabilities if they're needed:

```
containers:
- name: demo
  image: cloudnatived/demo:hello
  securityContext:
    capabilities:
      drop: ["all"]
      add: ["NET_BIND_SERVICE"]
```

The capability mechanism puts a hard limit on what processes inside the container can do, even if they're running as root. Once a capability has been dropped at the container level, it can't be regained, even by a malicious process with maximum privileges.

Pod Security Contexts

We've covered security context settings at the level of individual containers, but you can also set some of them at the Pod level:

```
apiVersion: v1
kind: Pod
...
spec:
  securityContext:
    runAsUser: 1000
    runAsNonRoot: false
    allowPrivilegeEscalation: false
```

These settings will apply to all containers in the Pod, unless the container overrides a given setting in its own security context.

Best Practice

Set security contexts on all your Pods and containers. Disable privilege escalation and drop all capabilities. Add only the specific capabilities that a given container needs.

Pod Security Policies

Rather than have to specify all the security settings for each individual container or Pod, you can specify them at the cluster level using a PodSecurityPolicy resource. A PodSecurityPolicy looks like this:

```
apiVersion: policy/v1beta1
kind: PodSecurityPolicy
metadata:
  name: example
spec:
  privileged: false
  # The rest fills in some required fields.
  seLinux:
    rule: RunAsAny
  supplementalGroups:
    rule: RunAsAny
  runAsUser:
    rule: RunAsAny
  fsGroup:
    rule: RunAsAny
  volumes:
  - *
```

This simple policy blocks any privileged containers (those with the `privileged` flag set in their `securityContext`, which would give them almost all the capabilities of a process running natively on the node).

It's a little more complicated to use PodSecurityPolicies, as you have to create the policies, grant the relevant service accounts access to the policies via RBAC (see "Introducing Role-Based Access Control (RBAC)" on page 202), and enable the PodSecurityPolicy admission controller in your cluster. For larger infrastructures, though, or where you don't have direct control over the security configuration of individual Pods, PodSecurityPolicies are a good idea.

You can read about how to create and enable PodSecurityPolicies in the Kubernetes documentation (*https://kubernetes.io/docs/concepts/policy/pod-security-policy/*).

Pod Service Accounts

Pods run with the permissions of the default service account for the namespace, unless you specify otherwise (see "Applications and Deployment" on page 205). If you need to grant extra permissions for some reason (such as viewing Pods in other namespaces), create a dedicated service account for the app, bind it to the required roles, and configure the Pod to use the new service account.

To do that, set the `serviceAccountName` field in the Pod spec to the name of the service account:

```
apiVersion: v1
kind: Pod
...
spec:
  serviceAccountName: deploy-tool
```

Volumes

As you may recall, each container has its own filesystem, which is accessible only to that container, and is *ephemeral*: any data that is not part of the container image will be lost when the container is restarted.

Often, this is fine; the demo application, for example, is a stateless server which therefore needs no persistent storage. Nor does it need to share files with any other container.

More complex applications, though, may need both the ability to share data with other containers in the same Pod, and to have it persist across restarts. A Kubernetes Volume object can provide both of these.

There are many different types of Volume that you can attach to a Pod. Whatever the underlying storage medium, a Volume mounted on a Pod is accessible to all the containers in the Pod. Containers that need to communicate by sharing files can do so using a Volume of one kind or another. We'll look at some of the more important types in the following sections.

emptyDir Volumes

The simplest Volume type is `emptyDir`. This is a piece of ephemeral storage that starts out empty—hence the name—and stores its data on the node (either in memory, or on the node's disk). It persists only as long as the Pod is running on that node.

An `emptyDir` is useful when you want to provision some extra storage for a container, but it's not critical to have the data persist forever or move with the container if it should be scheduled on another node. Some examples include caching downloaded files or generated content, or using a scratch workspace for data processing jobs.

Similarly, if you just want to share files between containers in a Pod, but don't need to keep the data around for a long time, an `emptyDir` Volume is ideal.

Here's an example of a Pod that creates an `emptyDir` Volume and mounts it on a container:

```
apiVersion: v1
kind: Pod
...
spec:
  volumes:
```

```
  - name: cache-volume
    emptyDir: {}
containers:
- name: demo
  image: cloudnatived/demo:hello
  volumeMounts:
  - mountPath: /cache
    name: cache-volume
```

First, in the `volumes` section of the Pod spec, we create an `emptyDir` Volume named `cache-volume`:

```
volumes:
- name: cache-volume
  emptyDir: {}
```

Now the `cache-volume` Volume is available for any container in the Pod to mount and use. To do that, we list it in the `volumeMounts` section of the `demo` container:

```
name: demo
image: cloudnatived/demo:hello
volumeMounts:
- mountPath: /cache
  name: cache-volume
```

The container doesn't have to do anything special to use the new storage: anything it writes to the path /cache will be written to the Volume, and will be visible to other containers that mount the same Volume. All containers mounting the Volume can read and write to it.

> Be careful writing to shared Volumes. Kubernetes doesn't enforce any locking on disk writes. If two containers try to write to the same file at once, data corruption can result. To avoid this, either implement your own write-lock mechanism, or use a Volume type that supports locking, such as `nfs` or `glusterfs`.

Persistent Volumes

While an ephemeral `emptyDir` Volume is ideal for cache and temporary file-sharing, some applications need to store persistent data; for example, any kind of database. In general, we don't recommend that you run databases in Kubernetes. You're almost always better served by using a cloud service instead: for example, most cloud providers have managed solutions for relational databases such as MySQL and PostgreSQL, as well as key-value (*NoSQL*) stores.

As we saw in "Kubernetes Doesn't Do It All" on page 13, Kubernetes is best at managing stateless applications, which means no persistent data. Storing persistent data significantly complicates the Kubernetes configuration for your app, uses extra cloud resources, and it also needs to be backed up.

However, if you need to use persistent volumes with Kubernetes, the PersistentVolume resource is what you're looking for. We won't go into great detail about them here, because the details tend to be specific to your cloud provider; you can read more about PersistentVolumes in the Kubernetes documentation (*https://kubernetes.io/docs/concepts/storage/persistent-volumes/*).

The most flexible way to use PersistentVolumes in Kubernetes is to create a PersistentVolumeClaim object. This represents a request for a particular type and size of PersistentVolume; for example, a 10 GiB Volume of high-speed, read-write storage.

The Pod can then add this PersistentVolumeClaim as a Volume, where it will be available for containers to mount and use:

```
volumes:
- name: data-volume
  persistentVolumeClaim:
    claimName: data-pvc
```

You can create a pool of PersistentVolumes in your cluster to be claimed by Pods in this way. Alternatively, you can set up *dynamic provisioning* (*https://kubernetes.io/docs/concepts/storage/dynamic-provisioning/*): when a PersistentVolumeClaim like this is mounted, a suitable chunk of storage will be automatically provisioned and connected to the Pod.

Restart Policies

We saw in "Running Containers for Troubleshooting" on page 123 that Kubernetes always restarts a Pod when it exits, unless you tell it otherwise. The default restart policy is thus `Always`, but you can change this to `OnFailure` (restart only if the container exited with a nonzero status), or `Never`:

```
apiVersion: v1
kind: Pod
...
spec:
  restartPolicy: OnFailure
```

If you want to run a Pod to completion and then have it exit, rather than being restarted, you can use a Job resource to do this (see "Jobs" on page 168).

Image Pull Secrets

As you know, Kubernetes will download your specified image from the container registry if it isn't already present on the node. However, what if you're using a private registry? How can you give Kubernetes the credentials to authenticate to the registry?

The `imagePullSecrets` field on a Pod allows you to configure this. First, you need to store the registry credentials in a Secret object (see "Kubernetes Secrets" on page 189 for more about this). Now you can tell Kubernetes to use this Secret when pulling any containers in the Pod. For example, if your Secret is named `registry-creds`:

```
apiVersion: v1
kind: Pod
...
spec:
  imagePullSecrets:
  - name: registry-creds
```

The exact format of the registry credentials data is described in the Kubernetes documentation (*https://kubernetes.io/docs/tasks/configure-pod-container/pull-image-private-registry/*).

You can also attach `imagePullSecrets` to a service account (see "Pod Service Accounts" on page 148). Any Pods created using this service account will automatically have the attached registry credentials available.

Summary

In order to understand Kubernetes, you first need to understand containers. In this chapter, we've outlined the basic idea of what a container is, how they work together in Pods, and what options are available for you to control how containers run in Kubernetes.

The bare essentials:

- A Linux container, at the kernel level, is an isolated set of processes, with ring-fenced resources. From inside a container, it looks as though the container has a Linux machine to itself.

- Containers are not virtual machines. Each container should run one primary process.

- A Pod usually contains one container that runs a primary application, plus optional *helper* containers that support it.

- Container image specifications can include a registry hostname, a repository namespace, an image repository, and a tag; for example `docker.io/cloudna tived/demo:hello`. Only the image name is required.

- For reproducible deployments, always specify a tag for the container image. Otherwise, you'll get whatever happens to be `latest`.

- Programs in containers should not run as the `root` user. Instead, assign them an ordinary user.

- You can set the `runAsNonRoot: true` field on a container to block any container that wants to run as `root`.

- Other useful security settings on containers include `readOnlyRootFilesystem: true` and `allowPrivilegeEscalation: false`.
- Linux capabilities provide a fine-grained privilege control mechanism, but the default capabilities for containers are too generous. Start by dropping all capabilities for containers, then grant specific capabilities if a container needs them.
- Containers in the same Pod can share data by reading and writing a mounted Volume. The simplest Volume is of type `emptyDir`, which starts out empty and preserves its contents only as long as the Pod is running.
- A PersistentVolume, on the other hand, preserves its contents as long as needed. Pods can dynamically provision new PersistentVolumes using PersistentVolume-Claims.

CHAPTER 9

Managing Pods

There are no big problems, there are just a lot of little problems.

—Henry Ford

In the previous chapter we covered containers in some detail, and explained how containers are composed to form Pods. There are a few other interesting aspects of Pods, which we'll turn to in this chapter, including labels, guiding Pod scheduling using node affinities, barring Pods from running on certain nodes with taints and tolerations, keeping Pods together or apart using Pod affinities, and orchestrating applications using Pod controllers such as DaemonSets and StatefulSets.

We'll also cover some advanced networking options including Ingress resources, Istio, and Envoy.

Labels

You know that Pods (and other Kubernetes resources) can have labels attached to them, and that these play an important role in connecting related resources (for example, sending requests from a Service to the appropriate backends). Let's take a closer look at labels and selectors in this section.

What Are Labels?

Labels are key/value pairs that are attached to objects, such as pods. Labels are intended to be used to specify identifying attributes of objects that are meaningful and relevant to users, but do not directly imply semantics to the core system.

—The Kubernetes documentation (*https://kubernetes.io/docs/concepts/overview/ working-with-objects/labels/*)

In other words, labels exist to tag resources with information that's meaningful to us, but they don't mean anything to Kubernetes. For example, it's common to label Pods with the application they belong to:

```
apiVersion: v1
kind: Pod
metadata:
  labels:
    app: demo
```

Now, by itself, this label has no effect. It's still useful as documentation: someone can look at this Pod and see what application it's running. But the real power of a label comes when we use it with a *selector*.

Selectors

A selector is an expression that matches a label (or set of labels). It's a way of specifying a group of resources by their labels. For example, a Service resource has a selector that identifies the Pods it will send requests to. Remember our demo Service from "Service Resources" on page 60?

```
apiVersion: v1
kind: Service
...
spec:
  ...
  selector:
    app: demo
```

This is a very simple selector that matches any resource that has the app label with a value of demo. If a resource doesn't have the app label at all, it won't match this selector. If it has the app label, but its value is not demo, it won't match the selector either. Only suitable resources (in this case, Pods) with the label app: demo will match, and all such resources will be selected by this Service.

Labels aren't just used for connecting Services and Pods; you can use them directly when querying the cluster with kubectl get, using the --selector flag:

```
kubectl get pods --all-namespaces --selector app=demo
NAMESPACE   NAME                      READY   STATUS    RESTARTS   AGE
demo        demo-5cb7d6bfdd-9dckm     1/1     Running   0          20s
```

You may recall from "Using Short Flags" on page 112 that --selector can be abbreviated to just -l (for *labels*).

If you want to see what labels are defined on your Pods, use the --show-labels flag to kubectl get:

```
kubectl get pods --show-labels
NAME                    ... LABELS
demo-5cb7d6bfdd-9dckm   ... app=demo,environment=development
```

More Advanced Selectors

Most of the time, a simple selector like app: demo (known as an *equality selector*) will be all you need. You can combine different labels to make more specific selectors:

```
kubectl get pods -l app=demo,environment=production
```

This will return only Pods that have *both* app: demo and environment: production labels. The YAML equivalent of this (in a Service, for example) would be:

```
selector:
  app: demo
  environment: production
```

Equality selectors like this are the only kind available with a Service, but for interactive queries with kubectl, or more sophisticated resources such as Deployments, there are other options.

One is selecting for label *inequality*:

```
kubectl get pods -l app!=demo
```

This will return all Pods that have an app label with a different value to demo, or that don't have an app label at all.

You can also ask for label values that are in a *set*:

```
kubectl get pods -l environment in (staging, production)
```

The YAML equivalent would be:

```
selector:
  matchExpressions:
  - {key: environment, operator: In, values: [staging, production]}
```

You can also ask for label values not in a given set:

```
kubectl get pods -l environment notin (production)
```

The YAML equivalent of this would be:

```
selector:
  matchExpressions:
  - {key: environment, operator: NotIn, values: [production]}
```

You can see another example of using matchExpressions in "Using node affinities to control scheduling" on page 90.

Other Uses for Labels

We've seen how to link Pods to Services using an `app` label (actually, you can use any label, but `app` is common). But what other uses are there for labels?

In our Helm chart for the demo application (see "What's Inside a Helm Chart?" on page 222) we set a `environment` label, which can be, for example, `staging` or `produc tion`. If you're running staging and production Pods in the same cluster (see "Do I need multiple clusters?" on page 98) you might want to use a label like this to distinguish between the two environments. For example, your Service selector for production might be:

```
selector:
  app: demo
  environment: production
```

Without the extra `environment` selector, the Service would match any and all Pods with `app: demo`, including the staging ones, which you probably don't want.

Depending on your applications, you might want to use labels to slice and dice your resources in a number of different ways. Here are some examples:

```
metadata:
  labels:
    app: demo
    tier: frontend
    environment: production
    version: v1.12.0
    role: primary
```

This allows you to query the cluster along these various different dimensions to see what's going on.

You could also use labels as a way of doing canary deployments (see "Canary Deployments" on page 244). If you want to roll out a new version of the application to just a small percentage of Pods, you could use labels like `track: stable` and `track: can ary` for two separate Deployments.

If your Service's selector matches only the `app` label, it will send traffic to all Pods matching that selector, including both `stable` and `canary`. You can alter the number of replicas for both Deployments to gradually increase the proportion of `canary` Pods. Once all running Pods are on the canary track, you can relabel them as `stable` and begin the process again with the next version.

Labels and Annotations

You might be wondering what the difference is between labels and annotations. They're both sets of key-value pairs that provide metadata about resources.

The difference is that *labels identify resources*. They're used to select groups of related resources, like in a Service's selector. Annotations, on the other hand, are for non-identifying information, to be used by tools or services outside Kubernetes. For example, in "Helm Hooks" on page 245 there's an example of using annotations to control Helm workflows.

Because labels are often used in internal queries that are performance-critical to Kubernetes, there are some fairly tight restrictions on valid labels. For example, label names are limited to 63 characters, though they may have an optional 253-character prefix in the form of a DNS subdomain, separated from the label by a slash character. Labels can only begin with an alphanumeric character (a letter or a digit), and can only contain alphanumeric characters plus dashes, underscores, and dots. Label values are similarly restricted (*https://kubernetes.io/docs/concepts/overview/working-with-objects/labels/#syntax-and-character-set*).

In practice, we doubt you'll run out of characters for your labels, since most labels in common use are just a single word (for example, app).

Node Affinities

We mentioned node affinities briefly in "Using node affinities to control scheduling" on page 90, in relation to preemptible nodes. In that section, you learned how to use node affinities to preferentially schedule Pods on certain nodes (or not). Let's take a more detailed look at node affinities now.

In most cases, you don't need node affinities. Kubernetes is pretty smart about scheduling Pods onto the right nodes. If all your nodes are equally suitable to run a given Pod, then don't worry about it.

There are exceptions, however (like preemptible nodes in the previous example). If a Pod is expensive to restart, you probably want to avoid scheduling it on a preemptible node wherever possible; preemptible nodes can disappear from the cluster without warning. You can express this kind of preference using node affinities.

There are two types of affinity: hard and soft. Because software engineers aren't always the best at naming things, in Kubernetes these are called:

- requiredDuringSchedulingIgnoredDuringExecution (hard)
- preferredDuringSchedulingIgnoredDuringExecution (soft)

It may help you to remember that required means a hard affinity (the rule *must* be satisfied to schedule this Pod) and preferred means a soft affinity (it would be *nice* if the rule were satisfied, but it's not critical).

The long names of the hard and soft affinity types make the point that these rules apply *during scheduling*, but not *during execution*. That is, once the Pod has been scheduled to a particular node satisfying the affinity, it will stay there. If things change while the Pod is running, so that the rule is no longer satisfied, Kubernetes won't move the Pod. (This feature may be added in the future.)

Hard Affinities

An affinity is expressed by describing the kind of nodes that you want the Pod to run on. There might be several rules about how you want Kubernetes to select nodes for the Pod. Each one is expressed using the `nodeSelectorTerms` field. Here's an example:

```
apiVersion: v1
kind: Pod
...
spec:
  affinity:
    nodeAffinity:
      requiredDuringSchedulingIgnoredDuringExecution:
        nodeSelectorTerms:
        - matchExpressions:
          - key: "failure-domain.beta.kubernetes.io/zone"
            operator: In
            values: ["us-central1-a"]
```

Only nodes that are in the `us-central1-a` zone will match this rule, so the overall effect is to ensure that this Pod is only scheduled in that zone.

Soft Affinities

Soft affinities are expressed in much the same way, except that each rule is assigned a numerical *weight* from 1 to 100 that determines the effect it has on the result. Here's an example:

```
preferredDuringSchedulingIgnoredDuringExecution:
- weight: 10
  preference:
    matchExpressions:
    - key: "failure-domain.beta.kubernetes.io/zone"
      operator: In
      values: ["us-central1-a"]
- weight: 100
  preference:
    matchExpressions:
    - key: "failure-domain.beta.kubernetes.io/zone"
      operator: In
      values: ["us-central1-b"]
```

Because this is a `preferred...` rule, it's a soft affinity: Kubernetes can schedule the Pod on any node, but it will give priority to nodes that match these rules.

You can see that the two rules have different `weight` values. The first rule has weight 10, but the second has weight 100. If there are nodes that match both rules, Kubernetes will give 10 times the priority to nodes that match the second rule (being in availability zone `us-central1-b`).

Weights are a useful way of expressing the relative importance of your preferences.

Pod Affinities and Anti-Affinities

We've seen how you can use node affinities to nudge the scheduler toward or away from running a Pod on certain kinds of nodes. But is it possible to influence scheduling decisions based on what other Pods are already running on a node?

Sometimes there are pairs of Pods that work better when they're together on the same node; for example, a web server and a content cache, such as Redis. It would be useful if you could add information to the Pod spec that tells the scheduler it would prefer to be colocated with a Pod matching a particular set of labels.

Conversely, sometimes you want Pods to avoid each other. In "Keeping Your Workloads Balanced" on page 91 we saw the kind of problems that can arise if Pod replicas end up together on the same node, instead of distributed across the cluster. Can you tell the scheduler to avoid scheduling a Pod where another replica of that Pod is already running?

That's exactly what you can do with Pod affinities. Like node affinities, Pod affinities are expressed as a set of rules: either hard requirements, or soft preferences with a set of weights.

Keeping Pods Together

Let's take the first case first: scheduling Pods together. Suppose you have one Pod, labeled `app: server`, which is your web server, and another, labeled `app: cache`, which is your content cache. They can still work together even if they're on separate nodes, but it's better if they're on the same node, because they can communicate without having to go over the network. How do you ask the scheduler to colocate them?

Here's an example of the required Pod affinity, expressed as part of the `server` Pod spec. The effect would be just the same if you added it to the `cache` spec, or to both Pods:

```
apiVersion: v1
kind: Pod
metadata:
```

```
    name: server
    labels:
      app: server
  ...
  spec:
    affinity:
      podAffinity:
        requiredDuringSchedulingIgnoredDuringExecution:
          labelSelector:
          - matchExpressions:
            - key: app
              operator: In
              values: ["cache"]
            topologyKey: kubernetes.io/hostname
```

The overall effect of this affinity is to ensure that the server Pod is scheduled, if possible, on a node that is also running a Pod labeled cache. If there is no such node, or if there is no matching node that has sufficient spare resources to run the Pod, it will not be able to run.

This probably isn't the behavior you want in a real-life situation. If the two Pods absolutely must be colocated, put their containers in the same Pod. If it's just preferable for them to be colocated, use a soft Pod affinity (preferredDuringSchedulingIgnoredDuringExecution).

Keeping Pods Apart

Now let's take the anti-affinity case: keeping certain Pods apart. Instead of podAffinity, we use podAntiAffinity:

```
apiVersion: v1
kind: Pod
metadata:
  name: server
  labels:
    app: server
  ...
spec:
  affinity:
    podAntiAffinity:
      requiredDuringSchedulingIgnoredDuringExecution:
        labelSelector:
        - matchExpressions:
          - key: app
            operator: In
            values: ["server"]
          topologyKey: kubernetes.io/hostname
```

It's very similar to the previous example, except that it's a `podAntiAffinity`, so it expresses the opposite sense, and the match expression is different. This time, the expression is: "The `app` label must have the value `server`."

The effect of this affinity is to ensure that the Pod will *not* be scheduled on any node matching this rule. In other words, no Pod labeled `app: server` can be scheduled on a node that already has an `app: server` Pod running. This will enforce an even distribution of `server` Pods across the cluster, at the possible expense of the desired number of replicas.

Soft Anti-Affinities

However, we usually care more about having enough replicas available than distributing them as fairly as possible. A hard rule is not really what we want here. Let's modify it slightly to make it a soft anti-affinity:

```
affinity:
  podAntiAffinity:
    preferredDuringSchedulingIgnoredDuringExecution:
    - weight: 1
      podAffinityTerm:
        labelSelector:
        - matchExpressions:
          - key: app
            operator: In
            values: ["server"]
        topologyKey: kubernetes.io/hostname
```

Notice that now the rule is `preferred...`, not `required...`, making it a soft anti-affinity. If the rule can be satisfied, it will be, but if not, Kubernetes will schedule the Pod anyway.

Because it's a preference, we specify a `weight` value, just as we did for soft node affinities. If there were multiple affinity rules to consider, Kubernetes would prioritize them according to the weight you assign each rule.

When to Use Pod Affinities

Just as with node affinities, you should treat Pod affinities as a fine-tuning enhancement for special cases. The scheduler is already good at placing Pods to get the best performance and availability from the cluster. Pod affinities restrict the scheduler's freedom, trading off one application against another. When you use one, it should be because you've observed a problem in production, and a Pod affinity is the only way to fix it.

Taints and Tolerations

In "Node Affinities" on page 159, you learned about a property of Pods that can steer them toward (or away from) a set of nodes. Conversely, *taints* allow a node to repel a set of Pods, based on certain properties of the node.

For example, you could use taints to create dedicated nodes: nodes that are reserved only for specific kinds of Pods. Kubernetes also creates taints for you if certain problems exist on the node, such as low memory, or a lack of network connectivity.

To add a taint to a particular node, use the `kubectl taint` command:

```
kubectl taint nodes docker-for-desktop dedicated=true:NoSchedule
```

This adds a taint called `dedicated=true` to the `docker-for-desktop` node, with the effect `NoSchedule`: no Pod can now be scheduled there unless it has a matching *toleration*.

To see the taints configured on a particular node, use `kubectl describe node....`

To remove a taint from a node, repeat the `kubectl taint` command but with a trailing minus sign after the name of the taint:

```
kubectl taint nodes docker-for-desktop dedicated:NoSchedule-
```

Tolerations are properties of Pods that describe the taints that they're compatible with. For example, to make a Pod tolerate the `dedicated=true` taint, add this to the Pod's spec:

```
apiVersion: v1
kind: Pod
...
spec:
  tolerations:
  - key: "dedicated"
    operator: "Equal"
    value: "true"
    effect: "NoSchedule"
```

This is effectively saying "This Pod is allowed to run on nodes that have the `dedicated=true` taint with the effect `NoSchedule`." Because the toleration *matches* the taint, the Pod can be scheduled. Any Pod without this toleration will not be allowed to run on the tainted node.

When a Pod can't run at all because of tainted nodes, it will stay in `Pending` status, and you'll see a message like this in the Pod description:

```
Warning  FailedScheduling  4s (x10 over 2m)  default-scheduler  0/1 nodes are
available: 1 node(s) had taints that the pod didn't tolerate.
```

Other uses for taints and tolerations include marking nodes with specialized hardware (such as GPUs), and allowing certain Pods to tolerate certain kinds of node problem.

For example, if a node falls off the network, Kubernetes automatically adds the taint `node.kubernetes.io/unreachable`. Normally, this would result in its `kubelet` evicting all Pods from the node. However, you might want to keep certain Pods running, in the hope that the network will come back in a reasonable time. To do this, you could add a toleration to those Pods that matches the `unreachable` taint.

You can read more about taints and tolerations in the Kubernetes documentation (*https://kubernetes.io/docs/concepts/configuration/taint-and-toleration/*).

Pod Controllers

We've talked a lot about Pods in this chapter, and that makes sense: all Kubernetes applications run in a Pod. You might wonder, though, why we need other kinds of objects at all. Isn't it enough just to create a Pod for an application and run it?

That's effectively what you get by running a container directly with `docker con tainer run`, as we did in "Running a Container Image" on page 22. It works, but it's very limited:

- If the container exits for some reason, you have to manually restart it.
- There's only one replica of your container and no way to load-balance traffic across multiple replicas if you ran them manually.
- If you want highly available replicas, you have to decide which nodes to run them on, and take care of keeping the cluster balanced.
- When you update the container, you have to take care of stopping each running image in turn, pulling the new image and restarting it.

That's the kind of work that Kubernetes is designed to take off your hands using *controllers*. In "ReplicaSets" on page 56, we introduced the ReplicaSet controller, which manages a group of replicas of a particular Pod. It works continuously to make sure there are always the specified number of replicas, starting new ones if there aren't enough, and killing off replicas if there are too many.

You're also now familiar with Deployments, which as we saw in "Deployments" on page 53, manage ReplicaSets to control the rollout of application updates. When you update a Deployment, for example with a new container spec, it creates a new ReplicaSet to start up the new Pods, and eventually closes down the ReplicaSet that was managing the old Pods.

For most simple applications, a Deployment is all you need. But there are a few other useful kinds of Pod controllers, and we'll look briefly at a few of them in this section.

DaemonSets

Suppose you want to send logs from all your applications to a centralized log server, like an Elasticsearch-Logstash-Kibana (ELK) stack, or a SaaS monitoring product such as Datadog (see "Datadog" on page 303). There are a few ways to do that.

You could have each application include code to connect to the logging service, authenticate, write logs, and so on, but this results in a lot of duplicated code, which is inefficient.

Alternatively, you could run an extra container in every Pod that acts as a logging agent (this is called a *sidecar* pattern). This means each application doesn't have to have built-in knowledge of how to talk to the logging service, but it does means you potentially have several copies of the logging agent running on each node.

Since all it does is manage a connection to the logging service and pass on log messages to it, you really only need one copy of the logging agent on each node. This is such a common requirement that Kubernetes provides a special controller object for it: the *DaemonSet*.

The term *daemon* traditionally refers to long-running background processes on a server that handle things like logging, so by analogy, Kubernetes DaemonSets run a *daemon* container on each node in the cluster.

The manifest for a DaemonSet, as you might expect, looks very much like that for a Deployment:

```
apiVersion: apps/v1
kind: DaemonSet
metadata:
  name: fluentd-elasticsearch
  ...
spec:
  ...
  template:
    ...
    spec:
      containers:
      - name: fluentd-elasticsearch
        ...
```

Use a DaemonSet when you need to run one copy of a Pod on each of the nodes in your cluster. If you're running an application where maintaining a given number of replicas is more important than exactly which node the Pods run on, use a Deployment instead.

StatefulSets

Like a Deployment or DaemonSet, a StatefulSet is a kind of Pod controller. What a StatefulSet adds is the ability to start and stop Pods in a specific sequence.

With a Deployment, for example, all your Pods are started and stopped in a random order. This is fine for stateless services, where every replica is identical and does the same job.

Sometimes, though, you need to start Pods in a specific numbered sequence, and be able to identify them by their number. For example, distributed applications such as Redis, MongoDB, or Cassandra create their own clusters, and need to be able to identify the cluster leader by a predictable name.

A StatefulSet is ideal for this. For example, if you create a StatefulSet named `redis`, the first Pod started will be named `redis-0`, and Kubernetes will wait until that Pod is ready before starting the next one, `redis-1`.

Depending on the application, you can use this property to cluster the Pods in a reliable way. For example, each Pod can run a startup script that checks if it is running on `redis-0`. If it is, it will be the cluster leader. If not, it will attempt to join the cluster by contacting `redis-0`.

Each replica in a StatefulSet must be running and ready before Kubernetes starts the next one, and similarly when the StatefulSet is terminated, the replicas will be shut down in reverse order, waiting for each Pod to finish before moving on to the next.

Apart from these special properties, a StatefulSet looks very similar to a normal Deployment:

```
apiVersion: apps/v1
kind: StatefulSet
metadata:
  name: redis
spec:
  selector:
    matchLabels:
      app: redis
  serviceName: "redis"
  replicas: 3
  template:
    ...
```

To be able to address each of the Pods by a predictable DNS name, such as `redis-1`, you also need to create a Service with a `clusterIP` type of `None` (known as a *headless service*).

With a nonheadless Service, you get a single DNS entry (such as `redis`) that load-balances across all the backend Pods. With a headless service, you still get that single service DNS name, but you also get individual DNS entries for each numbered Pod, like `redis-0`, `redis-1`, `redis-2`, and so on.

Pods that need to join the Redis cluster can contact `redis-0` specifically, but applications that simply need a load-balanced Redis service can use the `redis` DNS name to talk to a randomly selected Redis Pod.

StatefulSets can also manage disk storage for their Pods, using a VolumeClaimTemplate object that automatically creates a PersistentVolumeClaim (see "Persistent Volumes" on page 150).

Jobs

Another useful type of Pod controller in Kubernetes is the Job. Whereas a Deployment runs a specified number of Pods and restarts them continually, a Job only runs a Pod for a specified number of times. After that, it is considered completed.

For example, a batch processing task or queue worker Pod usually starts up, does its work, and then exits. This is an ideal candidate to be managed by a Job.

There are two fields that control Job execution: `completions` and `parallelism`. The first, `completions`, determines the number of times the specified Pod needs to run successfully before the Job is considered complete. The default value is 1, meaning the Pod will run once.

The `parallelism` field specifies how many Pods should run at once. Again, the default value is 1, meaning that only one Pod will run at a time.

For example, suppose you want to run a queue worker Job whose purpose is to consume work items from a queue. You could set `parallelism` to 10, and leave `comple tions` unset. This will start 10 Pods, each of which will keep consuming work from the queue until there is no more work to do, and then exit, at which point the Job will be completed:

```
apiVersion: batch/v1
kind: Job
metadata:
  name: queue-worker
spec:
  completions: 10
  template:
    metadata:
      name: queue-worker
    spec:
      containers:
        ...
```

Alternatively, if you want to run something like a batch processing job, you could leave both completions and parallelism at 1. This will start one copy of the Pod, and wait for it to complete successfully. If it crashes, fails, or exits in any non-successful way, the Job will restart it, just like a Deployment does. Only successful exits count toward the required number of completions.

How do you start a Job? You could do it manually, by applying a Job manifest using kubectl or Helm. Alternatively, a Job might be triggered by automation; your continuous deployment pipeline, for example (see Chapter 14).

Probably the most common way to run a Job, though, is to start it periodically, at a given time of day or at a given interval. Kubernetes has a special type of Job just for this: the Cronjob.

Cronjobs

In Unix environments, scheduled jobs are run by the cron daemon (whose name comes from the Greek word χρόνος, meaning "time"). Accordingly, they're known as *cron jobs*, and the Kubernetes Cronjob object does exactly the same thing.

A Cronjob looks like this:

```
apiVersion: batch/v1beta1
kind: CronJob
metadata:
  name: demo-cron
spec:
  schedule: "*/1 * * * *"
  jobTemplate:
    spec:
      ...
```

The two important fields to look at in the CronJob manifest are spec.schedule and spec.jobTemplate. The schedule field specifies when the job will run, using the same format (*https://en.wikipedia.org/wiki/Cron*) as the Unix cron utility.

The jobTemplate specifies the template for the Job that is to be run, and is exactly the same as a normal Job manifest (see "Jobs" on page 168).

Horizontal Pod Autoscalers

Remember that a Deployment controller maintains a specified number of Pod replicas. If one replica fails, another will be started to replace it, and if there are too many Pods for some reason, the Deployment will stop excess Pods in order to achieve the target number of replicas.

The desired replica count is set in the Deployment manifest, and we've seen that you can adjust this to increase the number of Pods if there is heavy traffic, or reduce it to scale down the Deployment if there are idle Pods.

But what if Kubernetes could adjust the number of replicas for you automatically, responding to demand? This is exactly what the Horizontal Pod Autoscaler does. (*Horizontal* scaling refers to adjusting the number of replicas of a service, in contrast to *vertical* scaling, which makes individual replicas bigger or smaller.)

A Horizontal Pod Autoscaler (HPA) watches a specified Deployment, constantly monitoring a given metric to see if it needs to scale the number of replicas up or down.

One of the most common autoscaling metrics is CPU utilization. Remember from "Resource Requests" on page 70 that Pods can request a certain amount of CPU resources; for example, 500 millicpus. As the Pod runs, its CPU usage will fluctuate, meaning that at any given moment the Pod is actually using some percentage of its original CPU request.

You can autoscale the Deployment based on this value: for example, you could create an HPA that targets 80% CPU utilization for the Pods. If the mean CPU usage over all the Pods in the Deployment is only 70% of their requested amount, the HPA will scale down by decreasing the target number of replicas. If the Pods aren't working very hard, we don't need so many of them.

On the other hand, if the average CPU utilization is 90%, this exceeds the target of 80%, so we need to add more replicas until the average CPU usage comes down. The HPA will modify the Deployment to increase the target number of replicas.

Each time the HPA determines that it needs to do a scaling operation, it adjusts the replicas by a different amount, based on the ratio of the actual metric value to the target. If the Deployment is very close to the target CPU utilization, the HPA will only add or remove a small number of replicas; but if it's way out of scale, the HPA will adjust it by a larger number.

Here's an example of an HPA based on CPU utilization:

```
apiVersion: autoscaling/v2beta1
kind: HorizontalPodAutoscaler
metadata:
  name: demo-hpa
  namespace: default
spec:
  scaleTargetRef:
    apiVersion: apps/v1
    kind: Deployment
    name: demo
  minReplicas: 1
  maxReplicas: 10
```

```
  metrics:
  - type: Resource
    resource:
      name: cpu
      targetAverageUtilization: 80
```

The interesting fields here are:

- `spec.scaleTargetRef` specifies the Deployment to scale
- `spec.minReplicas` and `spec.maxReplicas` specify the limits of scaling
- `spec.metrics` determines the metrics that will be used for scaling

Although CPU utilization is the most common scaling metric, you can use any metrics available to Kubernetes, including both the built-in *system metrics* like CPU and memory usage, and app-specific *service metrics*, which you define and export from your application (see Chapter 16). For example, you could scale based on the application error rate.

You can read more about autoscalers and custom metrics in the Kubernetes documentation (*https://kubernetes.io/docs/tasks/run-application/horizontal-pod-autoscale-walkthrough/*).

PodPresets

PodPresets are an experimental alpha feature in Kubernetes that allow you to inject information into Pods when they're created. For example, you could create a PodPreset that mounts a volume on all Pods matching a given set of labels.

A PodPreset is a type of object called an *admission controller*. Admission controllers watch for Pods being created and take some action when Pods matching their selector are about to be created. For example, some admission controllers might block creation of the Pod if it violates a policy, while others, like PodPreset, inject extra configuration into the Pod.

Here's an example PodPreset that adds a `cache` volume to all Pods matching the `tier: frontend` selector:

```
apiVersion: settings.k8s.io/v1alpha1
kind: PodPreset
metadata:
  name: add-cache
spec:
  selector:
    matchLabels:
      tier: frontend
  volumeMounts:
    - mountPath: /cache
      name: cache-volume
```

```
volumes:
  - name: cache-volume
    emptyDir: {}
```

The settings defined by a PodPreset are merged with those of each Pod. If a Pod is modified by a PodPreset, you'll see an annotation like this:

```
podpreset.admission.kubernetes.io/podpreset-add-cache: "<resource version>"
```

What happens if a Pod's own settings conflict with those defined in a PodPreset, or if multiple PodPresets specify conflicting settings? In that case, Kubernetes will refuse to modify the Pod, and you'll see an event in the Pod's description with the message `Conflict on pod preset`.

Because of this, PodPresets can't be used to override a Pod's own configuration, only to fill in settings which the Pod itself doesn't specify. A Pod can opt out of being modified by PodPresets altogether, by setting the annotation:

```
podpreset.admission.kubernetes.io/exclude: "true"
```

Because PodPresets are still experimental, they may not be available on managed Kubernetes clusters, and you may have to take extra steps to enable them in your self-hosted clusters, such as supplying command-line arguments to the API server. For details, see the Kubernetes documentation (*https://kubernetes.io/docs/concepts/work loads/pods/podpreset/*).

Operators and Custom Resource Definitions (CRDs)

We saw in "StatefulSets" on page 167 that, while the standard Kubernetes objects such as Deployment and Service are fine for simple, stateless applications, they have their limitations. Some applications require multiple, collaborating Pods which have to be initialized in a particular order (for example, replicated databases or clustered services).

For applications which need more complicated management than StatefulSets can provide, Kubernetes allows you to create your own new types of object. These are called *Custom Resource Definitions* (CRDs). For example, the Velero backup tool creates custom Kubernetes objects such as Configs and Backups (see "Velero" on page 210).

Kubernetes is designed to be extensible, and you're free to define and create any type of object you want to, using the CRD mechanism. Some CRDs just exist to store data, like the Velero BackupStorageLocation object. But you can go further, and create objects that act as Pod controllers, just like a Deployment or StatefulSet.

For example, if you wanted to create a controller object that sets up replicated, high-availability MySQL database clusters in Kubernetes, how would you go about it?

The first step would be to create a CRD for your custom controller object. In order to make it do anything, you then need to write a program that communicates with the Kubernetes API. This is easy to do, as we saw in "Building Your Own Kubernetes Tools" on page 131. Such a program is called an *operator* (perhaps because it automates the kinds of actions that a human operator might perform).

You don't need any custom objects in order to write an operator; DevOps engineer Michael Treacher has written a nice example operator (*https://medium.com/@mtreacher/writing-a-kubernetes-operator-a9b86f19bfb9*) that watches for namespaces being created, and automatically adds a RoleBinding to any new namespace (see "Introducing Role-Based Access Control (RBAC)" on page 202 for more about Role-Bindings).

In general, though, operators use one or more custom objects created via CRDs, whose behavior is then implemented by a program talking to the Kubernetes API.

Ingress Resources

You can think of an Ingress as a load balancer that sits in front of a Service (see Figure 9-1). The Ingress receives requests from clients and sends them on to the Service. The Service then sends them to the right Pods, based on the label selector (see "Service Resources" on page 60).

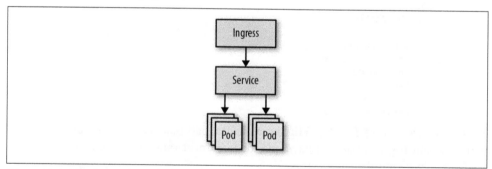

Figure 9-1. The Ingress resource

Here is a very simple example Ingress resource:

```
apiVersion: apps/v1
kind: Ingress
metadata:
  name: demo-ingress
spec:
  backend:
    serviceName: demo-service
    servicePort: 80
```

This Ingress forwards traffic to a Service named `demo-service` on port 80. (In fact, requests go directly from the Ingress to a suitable Pod, but it's helpful to think of them conceptually as going via the Service.)

By itself, this example doesn't seem very useful. Ingresses can do much more, however.

Ingress Rules

While Services are useful for routing *internal* traffic in your cluster (for example, from one microservice to another), an Ingress is useful for routing *external* traffic into your cluster and to the appropriate microservice.

An Ingress can forward traffic to different services, depending on certain rules that you specify. One common use for this is to route requests to different places, depending on the request URL (known as a *fanout*):

```
apiVersion: apps/v1
kind: Ingress
metadata:
  name: fanout-ingress
spec:
  rules:
  - http:
      paths:
      - path: /hello
        backend:
          serviceName: hello
          servicePort: 80
      - path: /goodbye
        backend:
          serviceName: goodbye
          servicePort: 80
```

There are lots of uses for this. Highly available load balancers can be expensive, so with a fanout Ingress, you can have one load balancer (and associated Ingress) route traffic to a large number of services.

You're not just limited to routing based on URLs; you can also use the HTTP `Host` header (equivalent to the practice known as *name-based virtual hosting*). Requests for websites with different domains (such as `example.com`) will be routed to the appropriate backend Service based on the domain.

Terminating TLS with Ingress

In addition, Ingress can handle secure connections using TLS (the protocol formerly known as SSL). If you have lots of different services and applications on the same domain, they can all share a TLS certificate, and a single Ingress resource can manage those connections (known as *TLS termination*):

```
apiVersion: apps/v1
kind: Ingress
metadata:
  name: demo-ingress
spec:
  tls:
  - secretName: demo-tls-secret
    backend:
      serviceName: demo-service
      servicePort: 80
```

Here we've added a new `tls` section, which instructs the Ingress to use a TLS certificate to secure traffic with clients. The certificate itself is stored as a Kubernetes Secret resource (see "Kubernetes Secrets" on page 189).

Using existing TLS certificates

If you have an existing TLS certificate, or you're going to purchase one from a certificate authority, you can use that with your Ingress. Create a Secret that looks like this:

```
apiVersion: v1
kind: Secret
type: kubernetes.io/tls
metadata:
  name: demo-tls-secret
data:
  tls.crt: LS0tLS1CRUdJTiBDRV...LS0tCg==
  tls.key: LS0tLS1CRUdJTiBSU0...LS0tCg==
```

Put the contents of the certificate in the `tls.crt` field, and the key in `tls.key`. As usual with Kubernetes Secrets, you should base64-encode the certificate and key data before adding them to the manifest (see "base64" on page 191).

Automating LetsEncrypt certificates with Cert-Manager

If you want to automatically request and renew TLS certificates using the popular LetsEncrypt authority (or another ACME certificate provider), you can use `cert-manager` (*http://docs.cert-manager.io/en/latest/*).

If you run `cert-manager` in your cluster, it will automatically detect TLS Ingresses that have no certificate, and request one from the specified provider (for example, LetsEncrypt). `cert-manager` is a more modern and capable successor to the popular `kube-lego` tool.

Exactly how TLS connections are handled depends on something called your *Ingress controller*.

Ingress Controllers

An Ingress controller is responsible for managing Ingress resources in a cluster. Depending on where you are running your clusters, the controller you use may vary.

Usually, customizing the behavior of your Ingress is done by adding specific annotations that are recognized by the Ingress controller.

Clusters running on Google's GKE have the option to use Google's Compute Load Balancer for Ingress. AWS has a similar product called an Application Load Balancer. These managed services provide a public IP address where the Ingress will listen for requests.

These are good places to start if you need to use Ingress and are running Kubernetes on Google Cloud or AWS. You can read through the documentation of each product in their respective repositories:

- Google Ingress documentation (*https://github.com/kubernetes/ingress-gce*)
- AWS Ingress documentation (*https://github.com/kubernetes-sigs/aws-alb-ingress-controller*)

You also have the option to install and run your own Ingress controller inside your cluster, or even run multiple controllers if you like. Some popular options include:

nginx-ingress (https://github.com/nginxinc/kubernetes-ingress)
> NGINX has long been a popular load balancer tool, even before Kubernetes came into the scene. This controller brings much of the functionality and features offered by NGINX to Kubernetes. There are other ingress controllers based on NGINX, but this is the official one.

Contour (https://github.com/projectcontour/contour)
> Contour actually uses another tool under the hood called Envoy to proxy requests between clients and Pods.

Traefik (https://docs.traefik.io/user-guide/kubernetes/)
> This is a lightweight proxy tool that can automatically manage TLS certificates for your Ingress.

Each of these controllers has different features, and comes with its own setup and installation instructions, as well as its own ways of handling things like routes and certificates. Read about the different options and try them out in your own cluster, with your own applications, to get a feel for how they work.

Istio

Istio is an example of what's often referred to as a *service mesh*, and becomes very useful when teams have multiple applications and services that communicate with each other. It handles routing and encrypting network traffic between services, and adds important features like metrics, logs, and load balancing.

Istio is an optional add-on component to many hosted Kubernetes clusters, including Google Kubernetes Engine (check the documentation for your provider to see how to enable Istio).

If you want to install Istio in a self-hosted cluster, use the official Istio Helm chart (*https://istio.io/docs/setup/kubernetes/helm-install/*).

If your applications rely heavily on communicating with each other, Istio may be worth researching. Istio deserves a book of its own, and will probably get one, but in the meantime a great place to start is the introductory documentation (*https://istio.io/docs/concepts/what-is-istio/*).

Envoy

Most managed Kubernetes services, such as Google Kubernetes Engine, provide some kind of cloud load balancer integration. For example, when you create a Service of type LoadBalancer on GKE, or an Ingress, a Google Cloud Load Balancer is automatically created and connected to your service.

While these standard cloud load balancers scale well, they are very simple, and don't give you much to configure. For example, the default load balancing algorithm is usually random (see "Service Resources" on page 60). This sends each connection to a different backend at random.

However, random isn't always what you want. For example, if requests to your service can be long-running and CPU-intensive, some of your backend nodes may get overloaded while others remain idle.

A smarter algorithm would route requests to the backend that is least busy. This is sometimes known as leastconn or LEAST_REQUEST.

For more sophisticated load balancing like this, you can use a product called Envoy (*https://www.envoyproxy.io/*). This is not part of Kubernetes itself, but it's commonly used with Kubernetes applications.

Envoy is a high-performance C++ distributed proxy designed for single services and applications, but can also be used as part of a service mesh architecture (see "Istio" on page 177).

Developer Mark Vincze has written a great blog post (*https://blog.markvincze.com/how-to-use-envoy-as-a-load-balancer-in-kubernetes/*) detailing how to set up and configure Envoy in Kubernetes.

Summary

Ultimately, everything in Kubernetes is about running Pods. We've gone into some detail about them, therefore, and we apologize if it's too much. You don't need to understand or remember everything we've covered in this chapter, at least for now. Later on, you may run into problems that the more advanced topics in this chapter can help you solve.

The basic ideas to remember:

- Labels are key-value pairs that identify resources, and can be used with selectors to match a specified group of resources.

- Node affinities attract or repel Pods to or from nodes with specified attributes. For example, you can specify that a Pod can only run on a node in a specified availability zone.

- While hard node affinities can block a Pod from running, soft node affinities are more like suggestions to the scheduler. You can combine multiple soft affinities with different weights.

- Pod affinities express a preference for Pods to be scheduled on the same node as other Pods. For example, Pods that benefit from running on the same node can express that using a Pod affinity for each other.

- Pod anti-affinities repel other Pods instead of attracting. For example, an anti-affinity to replicas of the same Pod can help spread your replicas evenly across the cluster.

- Taints are a way of tagging nodes with specific information; usually, about node problems or failures. By default, Pods won't be scheduled on tainted nodes.

- Tolerations allow a Pod to be scheduled on nodes with a specific taint. You can use this mechanism to run certain Pods only on dedicated nodes.

- DaemonSets allow you to schedule one copy of a Pod on every node (for example, a logging agent).

- StatefulSets start and stop Pod replicas in a specific numbered sequence, allowing you to address each by a predictable DNS name. This is ideal for clustered applications, such as databases.

- Jobs run a Pod once (or a specified number of times) before completing. Similarly, Cronjobs run a Pod periodically at specified times.

- Horizontal Pod Autoscalers watch a set of Pods, trying to optimize a given metric (such as CPU utilization). They increase or decrease the desired number of replicas to achieve the specified goal.

- PodPresets can inject bits of common configuration into all selected Pods at creation time. For example, you could use a PodPreset to mount a particular Volume on all matching Pods.

- Custom Resource Definitions (CRDs) allow you to create your own custom Kubernetes objects, to store any data you wish. Operators are Kubernetes client programs that can implement orchestration behavior for your specific application (for example, MySQL).

- Ingress resources route requests to different services, depending on a set of rules, for example, matching parts of the request URL. They can also terminate TLS connections for your application.

- Istio is a tool that provides advanced networking features for microservice applications and can be installed, like any Kubernetes application, using Helm.

- Envoy provides more sophisticated load balancing features than standard cloud load balancers, as well as a service mesh facility.

CHAPTER 10

Configuration and Secrets

If you want to keep a secret, you must also hide it from yourself.

—George Orwell, *1984*

It's very useful to be able to separate the *logic* of your Kubernetes application from its *configuration*: that is, any values or settings that might change over the life of the application. Configuration values commonly include things like environment-specific settings, DNS addresses of third-party services, and authentication credentials.

While you could simply put these values directly into your code, that's not a very flexible approach. For one thing, changing a configuration value would require a complete rebuild and redeploy of the application. It's much better to separate these values out from the code and read them in from a file, or from environment variables.

Kubernetes provides a few different ways to help you manage configuration. One is to pass values to the application via environment variables in the Pod spec (see "Environment Variables" on page 142). Another is to store configuration data directly in Kubernetes, using the ConfigMap and Secret objects.

In this chapter we'll explore ConfigMaps and Secrets in detail, and look at some practical techniques for managing configuration and secrets in applications, using the demo application as an example.

ConfigMaps

The ConfigMap is the primary object for storing configuration data in Kubernetes. You can think of it as being a named set of key-value pairs that stores configuration data. Once you have a ConfigMap, you can supply that data to an application either by creating a file in the Pod, or by injecting it into the Pod's environment.

In this section, we'll look at some different ways to get data into a ConfigMap, and then explore the various ways you can extract that data and feed it into your Kubernetes application.

Creating ConfigMaps

Suppose you want to create a YAML configuration file in your Pod's filesystem named *config.yaml*, with the following contents:

```
autoSaveInterval: 60
batchSize: 128
protocols:
  - http
  - https
```

Given this set of values, how do you turn them into a ConfigMap resource that you can apply to Kubernetes?

One way is to specify that data, as literal YAML values, in the ConfigMap manifest. This is what the manifest for a ConfigMap object looks like:

```
apiVersion: v1
data:
  config.yaml: |
    autoSaveInterval: 60
    batchSize: 128
    protocols:
      - http
      - https
kind: ConfigMap
metadata:
  name: demo-config
  namespace: demo
```

You could create a ConfigMap by writing the manifest from scratch, and adding the values from *config.yaml* into the data section, as we've done in this example.

An easier way, though, is to let kubectl do some of the work for you. You can create a ConfigMap directly from a YAML file as follows:

```
kubectl create configmap demo-config --namespace=demo --from-file=config.yaml
configmap "demo-config" created
```

To export the manifest file that corresponds to this ConfigMap, run:

```
kubectl get configmap/demo-config --namespace=demo -o yaml
    >demo-config.yaml
```

This writes a YAML manifest representation of the cluster's ConfigMap resource to the file *demo-config.yaml*, however it will contain extra info like the status section that you may want to remove before applying again (see "Exporting Resources" on page 118).

Setting Environment Variables from ConfigMaps

Now that we have the required configuration data in a ConfigMap object, how do we then get that data into a container? Let's look at a complete example using our demo application. You'll find the code in the *hello-config-env* directory of the demo repo.

It's the same demo application we've used in previous chapters that listens for HTTP requests and responds with a greeting (see "Looking at the Source Code" on page 23).

This time, though, instead of hard coding the string `Hello` into the application, we'd like to make the greeting configurable. So there's a slight modification to the `handler` function to read this value from the environment variable `GREETING`:

```
func handler(w http.ResponseWriter, r *http.Request) {
        greeting := os.Getenv("GREETING")
        fmt.Fprintf(w, "%s, 世界\n", greeting)
}
```

Don't worry about the exact details of the Go code; it's just a demo. Suffice it to say that if the `GREETING` environment variable is present when the program runs, it will use that value when responding to requests. Whatever language you're using to write applications, it's a good bet that you'll be able to read environment variables with it.

Now, let's create the ConfigMap object to hold the greeting value. You'll find the manifest file for the ConfigMap, along with the modified Go application, in the *hello-config-env* directory of the demo repo.

It looks like this:

```
apiVersion: v1
kind: ConfigMap
metadata:
  name: demo-config
data:
  greeting: Hola
```

In order to make this data visible in the container's environment, we need to modify the Deployment slightly. Here's the relevant part of the demo Deployment:

```
spec:
  containers:
    - name: demo
      image: cloudnatived/demo:hello-config-env
      ports:
        - containerPort: 8888
      env:
        - name: GREETING
          valueFrom:
            configMapKeyRef:
              name: demo-config
              key: greeting
```

Note that we're using a different container image tag to that in previous examples (see "Image Identifiers" on page 139). The `:hello-config-env` tag gets us the modified version of the demo application that reads the `GREETING` variable: `cloudnatived/demo:hello-config-env`.

The second point of interest is the `env` section. Remember from "Environment Variables" on page 142 that you can create environment variables with literal values by adding a `name`/`value` pair.

We still have `name` here, but instead of `value`, we've specified `valueFrom`. This tells Kubernetes that, rather than taking a literal value for the variable, it should look elsewhere to find the value.

`configMapKeyRef` tells it to reference a specific key in a specific ConfigMap. The name of the ConfigMap to look at is `demo-config`, and the key we want to look up is `greeting`. We created this data with the ConfigMap manifest, so it should now be available to read into the container's environment.

If the ConfigMap doesn't exist, the Deployment won't be able to run (its Pod will show a status of `CreateContainerConfigError`).

That's everything you need to make the updated application work, so go ahead and deploy the manifests to your Kubernetes cluster. From the demo repo directory, run the following command:

```
kubectl apply -f hello-config-env/k8s/
configmap "demo-config" created
deployment.extensions "demo" created
```

As before, to see the application in your web browser, you'll need to forward a local port to the Pod's port 8888:

```
kubectl port-forward deploy/demo 9999:8888
Forwarding from 127.0.0.1:9999 -> 8888
Forwarding from [::1]:9999 -> 8888
```

(We didn't bother creating a Service this time; while you'd use a Service with a real production app, for this example we've just used `kubectl` to forward the local port directly to the `demo` Deployment.)

If you point your web browser to http://localhost:9999/ you should see, if all is well:

`Hola, 世界`

Exercise

In another terminal (you'll need to leave the `kubectl` `port-forward` command running), edit the *configmap.yaml* file to change the greeting. Reapply the file with `kubectl`. Refresh the web browser. Does the greeting change? If not, why not? What do you need to do to get the application to read the updated value? ("Updating Pods on a Config Change" on page 188 may help.)

Setting the Whole Environment from a ConfigMap

While you can set one or two environment variables from individual ConfigMap keys, as we saw in the previous example, that could get tedious for a large number of variables.

Fortunately, there's an easy way to take all the keys from a ConfigMap and turn them into environment variables, using `envFrom`:

```
spec:
  containers:
    - name: demo
      image: cloudnatived/demo:hello-config-env
      ports:
        - containerPort: 8888
      envFrom:
      - configMapRef:
          name: demo-config
```

Now every setting in the `demo-config` ConfigMap will be a variable in the container's environment. Because in our example ConfigMap the key is called `greeting`, the environment variable will also be named `greeting` (in lowercase). To make your environment variable names uppercase when you're using `envFrom`, change them in the ConfigMap.

You can also set other environment variables for the container in the normal way, using `env`; either by putting the literal values in the manifest file, or using a `Config MapKeyRef` as in our previous example. Kubernetes allows you to use either `env`, `env From`, or both at once, to set environment variables.

If a variable set in `env` has the same name as one set in `envFrom`, it will take precedence. For example, if you set the variable `GREETING` in both `env` and a ConfigMap referenced in `envFrom`, the value specified in `env` will override the one from the ConfigMap.

Using Environment Variables in Command Arguments

While it's useful to be able to put configuration data into a container's environment, sometimes you need to supply it as command-line arguments for the container's entrypoint instead.

You can do this by sourcing the environment variables from the ConfigMap, as in the previous example, but using the special Kubernetes syntax $(VARIABLE) to reference them in the command-line arguments.

In the *hello-config-args* directory of the demo repo, you'll find this example in the *deployment.yaml* file:

```
spec:
  containers:
    - name: demo
      image: cloudnatived/demo:hello-config-args
      args:
        - "-greeting"
        - "$(GREETING)"
      ports:
        - containerPort: 8888
      env:
        - name: GREETING
          valueFrom:
            configMapKeyRef:
              name: demo-config
              key: greeting
```

Here we've added an `args` field for the container spec, which will pass our custom arguments to the container's default entrypoint (`/bin/demo`).

Kubernetes replaces anything of the form $(VARIABLE) in a manifest with the value of the environment variable VARIABLE. Since we've created the GREETING variable and set its value from the ConfigMap, it's available for use in the container's command line.

When you apply these manifests, the value of GREETING will be passed to the demo app in this way:

```
kubectl apply -f hello-config-args/k8s/
configmap "demo-config" configured
deployment.extensions "demo" configured
```

You should see the effect in your web browser:

```
Salut, 世界
```

Creating Config Files from ConfigMaps

We've seen a couple of different ways of getting data from Kubernetes ConfigMaps into applications: via the environment, and via the container command line. More complex applications, however, often expect to read their configuration from files on disk.

Fortunately, Kubernetes gives us a way to create such files directly from a ConfigMap. First, let's change our ConfigMap so that instead of a single key, it stores a complete YAML file (which happens to only contain one key, but it could be a hundred, if you like):

```
apiVersion: v1
kind: ConfigMap
metadata:
  name: demo-config
data:
  config: |
    greeting: Buongiorno
```

Instead of setting the key greeting, as we did in the previous example, we're creating a new key called config, and assigning it a *block* of data (the pipe symbol | in YAML indicates that what follows is a block of raw data). This is the data:

```
greeting: Buongiorno
```

It happens to be valid YAML, but don't be confused by that; it could be JSON, TOML, plain text, or any other format. Whatever it is, Kubernetes will eventually write the whole block of data, as is, to a file on our container.

Now that we've stored the necessary data, let's deploy it to Kubernetes. In the *hello-config-file* directory of the demo repo, you'll find the Deployment template, containing:

```
spec:
  containers:
    - name: demo
      image: cloudnatived/demo:hello-config-file
      ports:
        - containerPort: 8888
      volumeMounts:
      - mountPath: /config/
        name: demo-config-volume
        readOnly: true
  volumes:
  - name: demo-config-volume
    configMap:
      name: demo-config
      items:
      - key: config
        path: demo.yaml
```

Looking at the volumes section, you can see that we create a Volume named demo-config-volume, from the existing demo-config ConfigMap.

In the container's `volumeMounts` section, we mount this volume on the `mountPath: /config/`, select the key `config`, and write it to the path *demo.yaml*. The result of this will be that Kubernetes will create a file in the container at */config/demo.yaml*, containing the `demo-config` data in YAML format:

```
greeting: Buongiorno
```

The demo application will read its config from this file on startup. As before, apply the manifests using this command:

```
kubectl apply -f hello-config-file/k8s/
configmap "demo-config" configured
deployment.extensions "demo" configured
```

You should see the results in your web browser:

```
Buongiorno, 世界
```

If you want to see what the ConfigMap data looks like in the cluster, run the following command:

```
kubectl describe configmap/demo-config
Name:         demo-config
Namespace:    default
Labels:       <none>
Annotations:
kubectl.kubernetes.io/last-applied-configuration={"apiVersion":"v1",
"data":{"config":"greeting: Buongiorno\n"},"kind":"ConfigMap","metadata":
{"annotations":{},"name":"demo-config","namespace":"default...

Data
====
config:
greeting: Buongiorno

Events:  <none>
```

If you update a ConfigMap and change its values, the corresponding file (*/config/demo.yaml* in our example) will be updated automatically. Some applications may autodetect that their config file has changed and reread it; others may not.

One option is to redeploy the application to pick up the changes (see "Updating Pods on a Config Change" on page 188), but this may not be necessary if the application has a way to trigger a live reload, such as a Unix signal (for example `SIGHUP`) or running a command in the container.

Updating Pods on a Config Change

Suppose you have a Deployment running in your cluster, and you want to change some values in its ConfigMap. If you're using a Helm chart (see "Helm: A Kubernetes

---

Package Manager" on page 64) there's a neat trick to have it automatically detect a config change and reload your Pods. Add this annotation to your Deployment spec:

```
checksum/config: {{ include (print $.Template.BasePath "/configmap.yaml") .
  | sha256sum }}
```

Because the Deployment template now includes a hash sum of the config settings, if these settings change, then so will the hash. When you run `helm upgrade`, Helm will detect that the Deployment spec has changed, and restart all the Pods.

Kubernetes Secrets

We've seen that the Kubernetes ConfigMap object provides a flexible way of storing and accessing configuration data in the cluster. However, most applications have some config data that is secret and sensitive, such as passwords or API keys. While we could use ConfigMaps to store these, that's not an ideal solution.

Instead, Kubernetes provides a special type of object intended to store secret data: the Secret. Let's see an example of how to use it with the demo application.

First, here's the Kubernetes manifest for the Secret (see *hello-secret-env/k8s/secret.yaml*):

```
apiVersion: v1
kind: Secret
metadata:
  name: demo-secret
stringData:
  magicWord: xyzzy
```

In this example, the secret key is `magicWord`, and the secret value is the word `xyzzy` (*https://en.wikipedia.org/wiki/Xyzzy_(computing)*) (a very useful word in computing). As with a ConfigMap, you can put multiple keys and values into a Secret. Here, just to keep things simple, we're only using one key-value pair.

Using Secrets as Environment Variables

Just like ConfigMaps, Secrets can be made visible to containers by putting them into environment variables, or mounting them as a file on the container's filesystem. In this example, we'll set an environment variable to the value of the Secret:

```
spec:
  containers:
    - name: demo
      image: cloudnatived/demo:hello-secret-env
      ports:
        - containerPort: 8888
      env:
        - name: MAGIC_WORD
          valueFrom:
```

```
    secretKeyRef:
      name: demo-secret
      key: magicWord
```

We set the environment variable MAGIC_WORD exactly as we did when using a Config-Map, except that now it's a secretKeyRef instead of a configMapKeyRef (see "Setting Environment Variables from ConfigMaps" on page 183).

Run the following command in the demo repo directory to apply these manifests:

```
kubectl apply -f hello-secret-env/k8s/
deployment.extensions "demo" configured
secret "demo-secret" created
```

As before, forward a local port to the Deployment so you can see the results in your web browser:

```
kubectl port-forward deploy/demo 9999:8888
Forwarding from 127.0.0.1:9999 -> 8888
Forwarding from [::1]:9999 -> 8888
```

Browse to *http://localhost:9999/* and you should see:

```
The magic word is "xyzzy"
```

Writing Secrets to Files

In this example we'll mount the Secret on the container as a file. You'll find the code for this example in the *hello-secret-file* folder of the demo repo.

In order to mount the Secret in a file on the container, we use a Deployment like this:

```
spec:
  containers:
    - name: demo
      image: cloudnatived/demo:hello-secret-file
      ports:
        - containerPort: 8888
      volumeMounts:
        - name: demo-secret-volume
          mountPath: "/secrets/"
          readOnly: true
  volumes:
    - name: demo-secret-volume
      secret:
        secretName: demo-secret
```

Just as we did in "Creating Config Files from ConfigMaps" on page 186, we create a Volume (demo-secret-volume in this example), and mount it on the container in the volumeMounts section of the spec. The mountPath is /secrets, and Kubernetes will create one file in this directory for each of the key-value pairs defined in the Secret.

We've only defined one key-value pair in the example Secret, named magicWord, so this manifest will create the read-only file */secrets/magicWord* on the container, and the contents of the file will be the secret data.

If you apply this manifest in the same way as for the previous example, you should see the same results:

```
The magic word is "xyzzy"
```

Reading Secrets

In the previous section we were able to use kubectl describe to see the data inside the ConfigMap. Can we do the same with a Secret?

```
kubectl describe secret/demo-secret
Name:           demo-secret
Namespace:      default
Labels:         <none>
Annotations:
Type:           Opaque


Data
====
magicWord:   5 bytes
```

Notice that this time, the actual data is not shown. Kubernetes Secrets are Opaque, which means they're not shown in kubectl describe output, in log messages, or in the terminal. This prevents secret data being exposed accidentally.

You can see an obfuscated version of the secret data by using kubectl get with YAML output format:

```
kubectl get secret/demo-secret -o yaml
apiVersion: v1
data:
  magicWord: eHl6enk=
kind: Secret
metadata:
...
type: Opaque
```

base64

What's that eHl6enk=? That doesn't look much like our original secret data. In fact, it's a *base64* representation of the Secret. Base64 is a scheme for encoding arbitrary binary data as a character string.

Because the secret data could be nonprintable binary data (for example, a TLS encryption key), Kubernetes Secrets are always stored in base64 format.

The text `eHl6enk=` is the base64-encoded version of our secret word `xyzzy`. You can verify this using the `base64 --decode` command in the terminal:

```
echo "eHl6enk=" | base64 --decode
xyzzy
```

So although Kubernetes protects you from accidentally printing secret data to the terminal, or in log files, if you have permission to read the Secrets in a particular namespace, you can get the data in base64 format and then decode it.

If you need to base64-encode some text (for instance, to add it to a Secret), use the `base64` tool with the `-n` flag to avoid including a newline character:

```
echo -n xyzzy | base64
eHl6enk=
```

Access to Secrets

Who can read or edit Secrets? That's controlled by the Kubernetes access control mechanism, RBAC, which we'll talk about in much more detail in "Introducing Role-Based Access Control (RBAC)" on page 202. If you're using a cluster that doesn't support RBAC or doesn't have it enabled, then all Secrets are accessible to any user or any container. (You absolutely shouldn't be running any cluster in production without RBAC, as we'll explain.)

Encryption at Rest

What about someone with access to the *etcd* database where all Kubernetes information is stored? Could they access the secret data, even without API permissions to read the Secret object?

From Kubernetes version 1.7 onwards, *encryption at rest* is supported. That means that the secret data in the *etcd* database is actually stored encrypted on disk, and unreadable even to someone who can access the database directly. Only the Kubernetes API server has the key to decrypt this data. In a properly configured cluster, encryption at rest should be enabled.

You can check whether encryption at rest is enabled in your cluster by running:

```
kubectl describe pod -n kube-system -l component=kube-apiserver |grep encryption
    --experimental-encryption-provider-config=...
```

If you don't see the `experimental-encryption-provider-config` flag, then encryption at rest is not enabled. (If you're using Google Kubernetes Engine, or some other managed Kubernetes services, your data is encrypted using a different mechanism and you won't see this flag. Check with your Kubernetes provider to find out whether etcd data is encrypted or not.)

Keeping Secrets

Sometimes you'll have Kubernetes resources that you never want to be deleted from the cluster, such as a particularly important Secret. Using a Helm-specific annotation, you can prevent a resource from being removed:

```
kind: Secret
metadata:
  annotations:
    "helm.sh/resource-policy": keep
```

Secrets Management Strategies

In the example in the previous section, our secret data was protected against unauthorized access once it was stored in the cluster. But the secret data was represented in plain text in our manifest files.

You should never expose secret data like this in files that are committed to source control. So how do you manage and store secret data securely before it's applied to the Kubernetes cluster?

Whatever tool or strategy you choose for managing secrets in your applications, you'll need it to answer at least the following questions:

1. Where do you store secrets so that they are highly available?

2. How do you make secrets available to your running applications?

3. What needs to happen to your running applications when you rotate or change secrets?

In this section we'll look at three of the most popular secrets management strategies, and examine how each of them tackles these questions.

Encrypt Secrets in Version Control

The first option for secrets management is to store your secrets directly in code, in version control repositories, but in encrypted form, and decrypt them at deploy time.

This is probably the simplest choice. Secrets are put directly into source code repos, but never in plain text. Instead, they are encrypted in a form that can only be decrypted with a certain trusted key.

When you deploy the application, the secrets are decrypted just before the Kubernetes manifests are applied to the cluster. The application can then read and use the secrets just like any other configuration data.

Encrypting secrets in version control lets you review and track changes to secrets, just as you would changes to application code. And so long as your version control repositories are highly available, your secrets will be highly available as well.

To change or rotate secrets, just decrypt them in your local copy of the source, update them, re-encrypt, and commit the change to version control.

While this strategy is simple to implement and has no dependencies except the key and the encryption/decryption tool (see "Encrypting Secrets with Sops" on page 196), there's one potential drawback. If the same secret is used by multiple applications, they all need a copy of it in their source code. This means rotating the secret is more work, because you have to make sure you've found and changed all instances of it.

There is also a serious risk of accidentally committing plain-text secrets to version control. Mistakes do happen, and even with private version control repositories, any secret so committed should be considered compromised, and you should rotate it as soon as possible. You may want to restrict access to the encryption key to only certain individuals, rather than handing it out to all developers.

Nonetheless, the *encrypt secrets in source code* strategy is a good starting point for small organizations with noncritical secrets. It's relatively low-touch and easy to set up, while still being flexible enough to handle multiple apps and different types of secret data. In the final section of this chapter, we'll outline some options for encryption/decryption tools you can use to do this, but first, let's briefly describe the other secrets management strategies.

Store Secrets Remotely

Another option for secrets management is to keep them in a file (or multiple files) in a remote, secure file storage, such as an AWS S3 bucket, or Google Cloud Storage. When you deploy an individual application, the files would be downloaded, decrypted, and provided to the application. This is similar to the *encrypt secrets in version control* option, except that instead of living in the source code repo, the secrets are stored centrally. You can use the same encryption/decryption tool for both strategies.

This solves the problem of secrets being duplicated across multiple code repos, but it does need a little extra engineering and coordination to pull the relevant secrets file down at deploy time. This gives you some of the benefits of a dedicated secrets management tool, but without having to set up and manage an extra software component, or refactoring your apps to talk to it.

Because your secrets are not in version control, though, you'll need a process to handle changing secrets in an orderly way, ideally with an audit log (who changed what, when, and why), and some kind of change control procedure equivalent to a pull request review and approval.

Use a Dedicated Secrets Management Tool

While the *encrypt secrets in source code* and *keep secrets in a bucket* strategies are fine for most organizations, at very large scale you may need to think about using a dedicated secrets management tool, such as Hashicorp's Vault, Square's Keywhiz, AWS Secrets Manager, or Azure's Key Vault. These tools handle securely storing all of your application secrets in one central place in a highly available way, and can also control which users and service accounts have permissions to add, remove, change, or view secrets.

In a secrets management system, all actions are audited and reviewable, making it easier to analyze security breaches and prove regulatory compliance. Some of these tools also provide the ability to automatically rotate secrets on a regular basis, which is not only a good idea in any case, but is also required by many corporate security policies.

How do applications get their data from a secrets management tool? One common way is to use a service account with read-only access to the secrets vault, so that each application can only read the secrets it needs. Developers can have their own individual credentials, with permission to read or write secrets for only the applications that they're responsible for.

While a central secrets management system is the most powerful and flexible option available, it also adds significant complexity to your infrastructure. As well as setting up and running the secrets vault, you will need to add tooling or middleware to each application and service that consumes secrets. While applications can be refactored or redesigned to access the secrets vault directly, this may be more expensive and time-consuming than simply adding a layer in front of them that gets secrets and puts them in the application's environment or config file.

Of the various options, one of the most popular is Vault (*https://www.vaultpro ject.io/*), from Hashicorp.

Recommendations

While, at first glance, a dedicated secrets management system such as Vault might seem to be the logical choice, we don't recommend you start with this. Instead, try out a lightweight encryption tool such as Sops (see "Encrypting Secrets with Sops" on page 196), encrypting secrets directly in your source code.

Why? Well, you may not actually have that many secrets to manage. Unless your infrastructure is very complex and interdependent, which you should be avoiding anyway, any individual application should only need one or two pieces of secret data: API keys and tokens for other services, for example, or database credentials. If a given app really needs a great many different secrets, you might consider putting them all in a single file and encrypting that instead.

We take a pragmatic approach to secrets management, as we have with most issues throughout this book. If a simple, easy-to-use system solves your problem, start there. You can always switch to a more powerful or complicated setup later. It's often hard to know at the beginning of a project exactly how much secret data will be involved, and if you're not sure, choose the option that gets you up and running most quickly, without limiting your choices in the future.

That said, if you know from the outset that there are regulatory or compliance restrictions on your handling of secret data, it's best to design with that in mind, and you will probably need to look at a dedicated secrets management solution.

Encrypting Secrets with Sops

Assuming that you're going to do your own encryption, at least to start with, you'll need an encryption tool that can work with your source code and data files. Sops (short for *secrets operations*), from the Mozilla project, is an encryption/decryption tool that can work with YAML, JSON, or binary files, and supports multiple encryption backends, including PGP/GnuPG, Azure Key Vault, AWS's Key Management Service (KMS), and Google's Cloud KMS.

Introducing Sops

Let's introduce Sops by showing what it does. Rather than encrypting the whole file, Sops encrypts only the individual secret values. For example, if your plain-text file contains:

```
password: foo
```

when you encrypt it with Sops, the resulting file will look like this:

```
password: ENC[AES256_GCM,data:p673w==,iv:YY=,aad:UQ=,tag:A=]
```

This makes it easy to edit and review code, especially in pull requests, without needing to decrypt the data in order to understand what it is.

Visit the Sops project home page (*https://github.com/mozilla/sops*) for installation and usage instructions.

In the remainder of this chapter, we'll run through some examples of using Sops, see how it works with Kubernetes, and add some Sops-managed secrets to our demo app. But first, we should mention that other secrets encryption tools are available. If you're already using a different tool, that's fine: as long as you can encrypt and decrypt secrets within plain-text files in the same way as Sops does, use whichever tool works best for you.

We're fans of Helm, as you'll know if you've read this far, and if you need to manage encrypted secrets in a Helm chart, you can do that with Sops using the `helm-secrets` plug-in. When you run `helm upgrade` or `helm install`, `helm-secrets` will decrypt your secrets for deployment. For more information about helm-secrets, including installation and usage instructions, consult the GitHub repo (*https://github.com/futur esimple/helm-secrets*).

Encrypting a File with Sops

Let's try out Sops by encrypting a file. As we mentioned, Sops doesn't actually handle encryption itself; it delegates that to a backend such as GnuPG (a popular open source implementation of the Pretty Good Privacy, or PGP, protocol). We'll use Sops with GnuPG in this example to encrypt a file containing a secret. The end result will be a file that you can safely commit to version control.

We won't get into the details of how PGP encryption works, but just know that, like SSH and TLS, it's a *public key* cryptosystem. Instead of encrypting data with a single key, it actually uses a pair of keys: one public, one private. You can safely share your public key with others, but you should never give out your private key.

Let's generate your key pair now. First, install GnuPG (*https://gnupg.org/download*), if you haven't got it already.

Once that's installed, run this command to generate a new key pair:

```
gpg --gen-key
```

Once your key has been successfully generated, make a note of the `Key fingerprint` (the string of hex digits): this uniquely identifies your key, and you'll need it in the next step.

Now that you have a key pair, let's encrypt a file using Sops and your new PGP key. You will also need to have Sops installed on your machine, if you haven't already. There are binaries available for download (*https://github.com/mozilla/sops/releases*), or you can install it with Go:

```
go get -u go.mozilla.org/sops/cmd/sops
sops -v
sops 3.0.5 (latest)
```

Now let's create a test secret file to encrypt:

```
echo "password: secret123" > test.yaml
cat test.yaml
password: secret123
```

And finally, use Sops to encrypt it. Pass your key fingerprint to the `--pgp` switch, with the spaces removed, like this:

```
sops --encrypt --in-place --pgp E0A9AF924D5A0C123F32108EAF3AA2B4935EA0AB
test.yaml cat test.yaml
password: ENC[AES256_GCM,data:Ny220Ml8JoqP,iv:HMkwA8eFFmdUU1Dle6NTpVgy8vlQu/
```

```
6Zqx95Cd/+NL4=,tag:Udg9Wef8coZRbPb0fo0OSA==,type:str]
sops:
  ...
```

Success! Now the *test.yaml* file is encrypted securely, and the value of `password` is scrambled and can only be decrypted with your private key. You will also notice that Sops added some metadata to the bottom of file, so that it will know how to decrypt it in the future.

Another nice feature of Sops is that only the *value* of `password` is encrypted, so the YAML format of the file is preserved, and you can see that the encrypted data is labeled `password`. If you have a long list of key-value pairs in your YAML file, Sops will encrypt only the values, leaving the keys alone.

To make sure that we can get the encrypted data back, and to check that it matches what we put in, run:

```
sops --decrypt test.yaml
You need a passphrase to unlock the secret key for
user: "Justin Domingus <justin@example.com>"
2048-bit RSA key, ID 8200750F, created 2018-07-27 (main key ID 935EA0AB)
Enter passphrase: *highly secret passphrase*

password: secret123
```

Remember the passphrase that you chose when you generated your key pair? We hope so, because you need to type it in now! If you remembered it right, you will see the decrypted value of `password`: `secret123`.

Now you know how to use Sops, you can encrypt any sensitive data in your source code, whether that's application config files, Kubernetes YAML resources, or anything else.

When it comes time to deploy the application, use Sops in decrypt mode to produce the plain-text secrets that you need (but remember to delete the plain-text files, and don't check them in to version control!).

Later on, we'll show you how to use Sops this way with Helm charts. You can not only decrypt secrets when deploying your application with Helm, but also use different sets of secrets, depending on the deployment environment: for example, `staging` versus `production` (see "Managing Helm Chart Secrets with Sops" on page 228).

Using a KMS Backend

If you are using Amazon KMS or Google Cloud KMS for key management in the cloud, you can also use them with Sops. Using a KMS key works exactly the same as in our PGP example, but the metadata in the file will be different. Instead, the `sops:` section at the bottom might look something like this:

```
sops:
  kms:
  - created_at: 1441570389.775376
    enc: CiC....Pm1Hm
    arn: arn:aws:kms:us-east-1:656532927350:key/920aff2e...
```

Just like with our PGP example, the key ID (`arn:aws:kms...`) is embedded in the file so that Sops knows how to decrypt it later.

Summary

Configuration and secrets is one of the topics that people ask us about the most in relation to Kubernetes. We're glad to be able to devote a chapter to it, and to outline some ways you can connect your applications with the settings and data they need.

The most important things we've learned:

- Separate your configuration data from application code and deploy it using Kubernetes ConfigMaps and Secrets. That way, you don't need to redeploy your app every time you change a password.

- You can get data into ConfigMaps by writing it directly in your Kubernetes manifest file, or use `kubectl` to convert an existing YAML file into a ConfigMap spec.

- Once data is in a ConfigMap, you can insert it into a container's environment, or into the command-line arguments of its entrypoint. Alternatively, you can write the data to a file that is mounted on the container.

- Secrets work just like ConfigMaps, except that the data is encrypted at rest, and obfuscated in `kubectl` output.

- A simple, flexible way to manage secrets is to store them directly in your source code repo, but encrypt them using Sops or another text-based encryption tool.

- Don't overthink secrets management, especially at first. Start with something simple that's easy to set up for developers.

- Where secrets are shared by many applications, you can store them (encrypted) in a cloud bucket, and fetch them at deploy time.

- For enterprise-level secrets management, you'll need a dedicated service such as Vault. But don't start with Vault, because you may end up not needing it. You can always move to Vault later.

- Sops is an encryption tool that works with key-value files like YAML and JSON. It can get its encryption key from a local GnuPG keyring, or cloud key management services like Amazon KMS and Google Cloud KMS.

CHAPTER 11

Security and Backups

If you think technology can solve your security problems, then you don't understand the problems and you don't understand the technology.

—Bruce Schneier, *Applied Cryptography*

In this chapter we'll explore the security and access control machinery in Kubernetes, including Role-Based Access Control (RBAC), outline some vulnerability scanning tools and services, and explain how to back up your Kubernetes data and state (and even more importantly, how to restore it). We'll also look at some useful ways to get information about what's happening in your cluster.

Access Control and Permissions

Small tech companies tend to start out with just a few employees, and everyone has administrator access on every system.

As the organization grows, though, eventually it becomes clear that it is no longer a good idea for everyone to have administrator rights: it's too easy for someone to make a mistake and change something they shouldn't. The same applies to Kubernetes.

Managing Access by Cluster

One of the easiest and most effective things you can do to secure your Kubernetes cluster is limit who has access to it. There are generally two groups of people who need to access Kubernetes clusters: *cluster operators* and *application developers*, and they often need different permissions and privileges as part of their job function.

Also, you may well have multiple deployment environments, such as production and staging. These separate environments will need different policies, depending on your organization. Production may be restricted to only some individuals, whereas staging may be open to a broader group of engineers.

As we saw in "Do I need multiple clusters?" on page 98, it's often a good idea to have separate clusters for production and staging or testing. If someone accidentally deploys something in staging that brings down the cluster nodes, it will not impact production.

If one team should not have have access to another team's software and deployment process, each team could have their own dedicated cluster and not even have credentials on the other team's clusters.

This is certainly the most secure approach, but additional clusters come with trade-offs. Each needs to be patched and monitored, and many small clusters tend to run less efficiently than larger clusters.

Introducing Role-Based Access Control (RBAC)

Another way you can manage access is by controlling who can perform certain operations inside the cluster, using Kubernetes's Role-Based Access Control (RBAC) system.

RBAC is designed to grant specific permissions to specific users (or service accounts, which are user accounts associated with automated systems). For example, you can grant the ability to list all Pods in the cluster to a particular user if they need it.

The first and most important thing to know about RBAC is that it should be turned on. RBAC was introduced in Kubernetes 1.6 as an option when setting up clusters. However, whether this option is actually enabled in your cluster depends on your cloud provider or Kubernetes installer.

If you're running a self-hosted cluster, try this command to see whether or not RBAC is enabled on your cluster:

```
kubectl describe pod -n kube-system -l component=kube-apiserver
Name:           kube-apiserver-docker-for-desktop
Namespace:      kube-system
...
Containers:
  kube-apiserver:
    ...
    Command:
      kube-apiserver
      ...
      --authorization-mode=Node,RBAC
```

If `--authorization-mode` doesn't contain `RBAC`, then RBAC is not enabled for your cluster. Check the documentation for your service provider or installer to see how to rebuild the cluster with RBAC enabled.

Without RBAC, anyone with access to the cluster has the power to do anything, including running arbitrary code or deleting workloads. This probably isn't what you want.

Understanding Roles

So, assuming you have RBAC enabled, how does it work? The most important concepts to understand are users, roles, and role bindings.

Every time you connect to a Kubernetes cluster, you do so as a specific user. Exactly how you authenticate to the cluster depends on your provider; for example, in Google Kubernetes Engine, you use the gcloud tool to get an access token to a particular cluster.

There are other users configured in the cluster; for example, there is a default service account for each namespace. All these users can potentially have different sets of permissions.

These are governed by Kubernetes *roles*. A role describes a specific set of permissions. Kubernetes includes some predefined roles to get you started. For example, the cluster-admin role, intended for superusers, has access to read and change any resource in the cluster. By contrast, the view role can list and examine most objects in a given namespace, but not modify them.

You can define roles on the namespace level (using the Role object) or across the whole cluster (using the ClusterRole object). Here's an example of a ClusterRole manifest that grants read access to secrets in any namespace:

```
kind: ClusterRole
apiVersion: rbac.authorization.k8s.io/v1
metadata:
  name: secret-reader
rules:
- apiGroups: [""]
  resources: ["secrets"]
  verbs: ["get", "watch", "list"]
```

Binding Roles to Users

How do you associate a user with a role? You can do that using a *role binding*. Just like with roles, you can create a RoleBinding object that applies to a specific namespace, or a ClusterRoleBinding that applies at the cluster level.

Here's the RoleBinding manifest that gives the daisy user the edit role in the demo namespace only:

```
kind: RoleBinding
apiVersion: rbac.authorization.k8s.io/v1
metadata:
```

```
  name: daisy-edit
  namespace: demo
subjects:
- kind: User
  name: daisy
  apiGroup: rbac.authorization.k8s.io
roleRef:
  kind: ClusterRole
  name: edit
  apiGroup: rbac.authorization.k8s.io
```

In Kubernetes, permissions are *additive*; users start with no permissions, and you can add them using Roles and RoleBindings. You can't subtract permissions from someone who already has them.

 You can read more about the details of RBAC, and the available roles and permissions, in the Kubernetes documentation (*https:// kubernetes.io/docs/reference/access-authn-authz/rbac/*).

What Roles Do I Need?

So what roles and bindings should you set up in your cluster? The predefined roles cluster-admin, edit, and view will probably cover most requirements. To see what permissions a given role has, use the kubectl describe command:

```
kubectl describe clusterrole/edit
Name:          edit
Labels:        kubernetes.io/bootstrapping=rbac-defaults
Annotations:   rbac.authorization.kubernetes.io/autoupdate=true
PolicyRule:
  Resources    ... Verbs
  ---------    ... -----
  bindings     ... [get list watch]
  configmaps   ... [create delete deletecollection get list patch update watch]
  endpoints    ... [create delete deletecollection get list patch update watch]
  ...
```

You could create roles for specific people or jobs within your organization (for example, a developer role), or individual teams (for example, QA or security).

Guard Access to Cluster-Admin

Be very careful about who has access to the cluster-admin role. This is the cluster superuser, equivalent to the root user on Unix systems. It can do anything to anything. Never give this role to users who are not cluster operators, and especially not to service accounts for apps which might be exposed to the internet, such as the Kubernetes Dashboard (see "Kubernetes Dashboard" on page 217).

Don't fix problems by granting *cluster-admin* unnecessarily. You'll find some bad advice about this on sites like Stack Overflow. When faced with a Kubernetes permissions error, a common response is to grant the cluster-admin role to the application. *Don't do this.* Yes, it makes the errors go away, but at the expense of bypassing all security checks and potentially opening up your cluster to an attacker. Instead, grant the application a role with the fewest privileges it needs to do its job.

Applications and Deployment

Apps running in Kubernetes usually don't need any RBAC permissions. Unless you specify otherwise, all Pods will run as the default service account in their namespace, which has no roles associated with it.

If your app needs access to the Kubernetes API for some reason (for example, a monitoring tool that needs to list Pods), create a dedicated service account for the app, use a RoleBinding to associate it with the necessary role (for example, view), and limit it to specific namespaces.

What about the permissions required to deploy applications to the cluster? The most secure way is to allow only a continuous deployment tool to deploy apps (see Chapter 14). It can use a dedicated service account, with permission to create and delete Pods in a particular namespace.

The edit role is ideal for this. Users with the edit role can create and destroy resources in the namespace, but can't create new roles or grant permissions to other users.

If you don't have an automated deployment tool, and developers have to deploy directly to the cluster, they will need edit rights to the appropriate namespaces too. Grant these on an application-by-application basis; don't give anyone edit rights across the whole cluster. People who don't need to deploy apps should have only the view role by default.

Best Practice

Make sure RBAC is enabled in all your clusters. Give cluster-admin rights only to users who actually need the power to destroy everything in the cluster. If your app needs access to cluster resources, create a service account for it and bind it to a role with only the permissions it needs, in only the namespaces where it needs them.

RBAC Troubleshooting

If you're running an older third-party application that isn't RBAC-aware, or if you're still working out the required permissions for your own application, you may run into RBAC permission errors. What do these look like?

If an application makes an API request for something it doesn't have permission to do (for example, list nodes) it will see a *Forbidden* error response (HTTP status 403) from the API server:

```
Error from server (Forbidden): nodes.metrics.k8s.io is forbidden: User
"demo" cannot list nodes.metrics.k8s.io at the cluster scope.
```

If the application doesn't log this information, or you're not sure which application is failing, you can check the API server's log (see "Viewing a Container's Logs" on page 119 for more about this). It will record messages like this, containing the string RBAC DENY with a description of the error:

```
kubectl logs -n kube-system -l component=kube-apiserver | grep "RBAC DENY"
RBAC DENY: user "demo" cannot "list" resource "nodes" cluster-wide
```

(You won't be able to do this on a GKE cluster, or any other managed Kubernetes service that doesn't give you access to the control plane: see the documentation for your Kubernetes provider to find out how to access API server logs.)

RBAC has a reputation for being complicated, but it's really not. Just grant users the minimum privileges they need, keep cluster-admin safe, and you'll be fine.

Security Scanning

If you're running third-party software in your cluster, it's wise to check it for security problems and malware. But even your own containers may have software in them that you're not aware of, and that needs to be checked too.

Clair

Clair (*https://github.com/coreos/clair*) is an open source container scanner produced by the CoreOS project. It statically analyzes container images, before they are actually run, to see if they contain any software or versions that are known to be insecure.

You can run Clair manually to check specific images for problems, or integrate it into your CD pipeline to test all images before they are deployed (see Chapter 14).

Alternatively, Clair can hook into your container registry to scan any images that are pushed to it and report problems.

It's worth mentioning that you shouldn't automatically trust base images, such as `alpine`. Clair is preloaded with security checks for many popular base images, and will tell you immediately if you're using one that has a known vulnerability.

Aqua

Aqua's Container Security Platform (*https://www.aquasec.com/products/aqua-container-security-platform/*) is a full-service commercial container security offering, allowing organizations to scan containers for vulnerabilities, malware, and suspicious activity, as well as providing policy enforcement and regulatory compliance.

As you'd expect, Aqua's platform integrates with your container registry, CI/CD pipeline, and multiple orchestration systems, including Kubernetes.

Aqua also offers a free-to-use tool called MicroScanner (*https://github.com/aquasecurity/microscanner*), that you can add to your container images to scan installed packages for known vulnerabilities from the same database that the Aqua Security Platform uses.

MicroScanner is installed by adding it to a Dockerfile, like this:

```
ADD https://get.aquasec.com/microscanner /
RUN chmod +x /microscanner
RUN /microscanner <TOKEN> [--continue-on-failure]
```

MicroScanner outputs a list of detected vulnerabilities in JSON format, which you can consume and report on using other tools.

Another handy open source tool from Aqua is kube-hunter (*https://kube-hunter.aquasec.com/*), designed to find security issues in your Kubernetes cluster itself. If you run it as a container on a machine outside your cluster, as an attacker might, it will check for various kinds of problems: exposed email addresses in certificates, unsecured dashboards, open ports and endpoints, and so on.

Anchore Engine

The Anchore Engine (*https://github.com/anchore/anchore-engine*) is an open source tool for scanning container images, not only for known vulnerabilities, but to identify the *bill of materials* of everything present in the container, including libraries, configuration files, and file permissions. You can use this to verify containers against user-defined policies: for example, you can block any images that contain security credentials, or application source code.

Best Practice

Don't run containers from untrusted sources or when you're not sure what's in them. Run a scanning tool like Clair or MicroScanner over all containers, even those you build yourself, to make sure there are no known vulnerabilities in any of the base images or dependencies.

Backups

You might be wondering whether you still need backups in cloud native architectures. After all, Kubernetes is inherently reliable and can handle the loss of several nodes at once, without losing state or even degrading application performance too much.

Also, Kubernetes is a declarative infrastructure as code system. All Kubernetes resources are described by data stored in a reliable database (*etcd*). In the event of some Pods being accidentally deleted, their supervising Deployment will re-create them from the spec held in the database.

Do I Need to Back Up Kubernetes?

So do you still need backups? Well, yes. The data stored on persistent volumes, for example, is vulnerable to failure (see "Persistent Volumes" on page 150). While your cloud vendor may provide nominally high-availability volumes (replicating the data across two different availability zones, for example), that's not the same as backup.

Let's repeat that point, because it's not obvious:

Replication is not backup. While replication may protect you from the failure of the underlying storage volume, it won't protect you from accidentally deleting the volume by mis-clicking in a web console, for example.

Nor will replication prevent a misconfigured application from overwriting its data, or an operator from running a command with the wrong environment variables and accidentally dropping the production database instead of the development one. (This has happened (*https://thenewstack.io/junior-dev-deleted-production-database*), probably more often than anyone's willing to admit.)

Backing Up etcd

As we saw in "High Availability" on page 35, Kubernetes stores all its state in the *etcd* database, so any failure or data loss here could be catastrophic. That's one very good reason why we recommend that you use managed services that guarantee the availability of *etcd* and the control plane generally (see "Use Managed Kubernetes if You Can" on page 47).

If you run your own master nodes, you are responsible for managing *etcd* clustering, replication, and backup. Even with regular data snapshots, it still takes a certain amount of time to retrieve and verify the snapshot, rebuild the cluster, and restore the data. During this time your cluster will likely be unavailable or seriously degraded.

Best Practice

Use a managed or turnkey service provider to run your master nodes with *etcd* clustering and backups. If you run them yourself, be very sure you know what you're doing. Resilient *etcd* management is a specialist job, and the consequences of getting it wrong can be serious.

Backing Up Resource State

Apart from *etcd* failures, there is also the question of saving the state of your individual resources. If you delete the wrong Deployment, for example, how would you re-create it?

Throughout this book we emphasize the value of the *infrastructure as code* paradigm, and recommend that you always manage your Kubernetes resources declaratively, by applying YAML manifests or Helm charts stored in version control.

In theory, then, to re-create the total state of your cluster workloads, you should be able to check out the relevant version control repos, and apply all the resources in them. *In theory.*

Backing Up Cluster State

In practice, not everything you have in version control is running in your cluster right now. Some apps may have been taken out of service, or replaced by newer versions. Some may not be ready to deploy.

We've recommended throughout this book that you should avoid making direct changes to resources, and instead apply changes from the updated manifest files (see "When Not to Use Imperative Commands" on page 117). However, people don't always follow good advice (the consultant's lament throughout the ages).

In any case, it's likely that during initial deployment and testing of apps, engineers may be adjusting settings like replica count and node affinities on the fly, and only storing them in version control once they've arrived at the right values.

Supposing your cluster were to be shut down completely, or have all its resources deleted (hopefully an unlikely scenario, but a useful thought experiment). How would you re-create it?

Even if you have an admirably well-designed and up-to-date cluster automation system that can redeploy everything to a fresh cluster, how do you *know* that the state of this cluster matches the one that was lost?

One way to help ensure this is to make a snapshot of the running cluster, which you can refer to later in case of problems.

Large and Small Disasters

It's not very likely that you'd lose the whole cluster: thousands of Kubernetes contributors have worked hard to make sure that doesn't happen.

What's more likely is that you (or your newest team member) might delete a namespace by accident, shut down a Deployment without meaning to, or specify the wrong set of labels to a kubectl delete command, removing more than you intended.

Whatever the cause, disasters do happen, so let's look at a backup tool that can help you avoid them.

Velero

Velero (formerly known as Ark) is a free and open source tool that can back up and restore your cluster state and persistent data.

Velero runs in your cluster and connects to a cloud storage service of your choice (for example, Amazon S3, or Azure Storage).

Follow the instructions (*https://velero.io/*) to set up Velero for your platform.

Configuring Velero

Before you use Velero, you need to create a BackupStorageLocation object in your Kubernetes cluster, telling it where to store backups (for example, an AWS S3 cloud storage bucket). Here's an example that configures Velero to back up to the demo-backup bucket:

```
apiVersion: velero.io/v1
kind: BackupStorageLocation
metadata:
  name: default
  namespace: velero
spec:
  provider: aws
  objectStorage:
    bucket: demo-backup
```

```
config:
  region: us-east-1
```

You must have at least a storage location called `default`, though you can add others with any names you like.

Velero can also back up the contents of your persistent volumes. To tell it where to store them, you need to create a VolumeSnapshotLocation object:

```
apiVersion: velero.io/v1
kind: VolumeSnapshotLocation
metadata:
  name: aws-default
  namespace: velero
spec:
  provider: aws
  config:
    region: us-east-1
```

Creating a Velero backup

When you create a backup using the `velero backup` command, the Velero server queries the Kubernetes API to retrieve the resources matching the selector you provided (by default, it backs up all resources). You can back up a set of namespaces, or the whole cluster:

```
velero backup create demo-backup --include-namespaces demo
```

It will then export all these resources to a named file in your cloud storage bucket, according to your configured BackupStorageLocation. The metadata and contents of your persistent volumes will also be backed up to your configured VolumeSnapshot-Location.

Alternatively, you can back up everything in your cluster *except* specified namespaces (for example, `kube-system`). You can also schedule automatic backups: for example, you can have Velero back up your cluster nightly, or even hourly.

Each Velero backup is complete in itself, not an incremental backup. So, to restore a backup, you only need the most recent backup file.

Restoring data

You can list your available backups using the `velero backup get` command:

```
velero backup get
NAME          STATUS      CREATED                          EXPIRES   SELECTOR
demo-backup   Completed   2018-07-14 10:54:20 +0100 BST    29d       <none>
```

To see what's in a particular backup, use `velero backup download`:

```
velero backup download demo-backup
Backup demo-backup has been successfully downloaded to
$PWD/demo-backup-data.tar.gz
```

The downloaded file is a *tar.gz* archive that you can unpack and inspect using standard tools. If you only want the manifest for a specific resource, for example, you can extract it from the backup file and restore it individually with kubectl apply -f.

To restore the whole backup, the velero restore command will start the process, and Velero will re-create all the resources and volumes described in the specified snapshot, skipping anything that already exists.

If the resource *does* exist, but is different from the one in the backup, Velero will warn you, but not overwrite the existing resource. So, for example, if you want to reset the state of a running Deployment to the way it was in the most recent snapshot, delete the running Deployment first, then restore it with Velero.

Alternatively, if you're restoring a backup of a namespace, you can delete the namespace first, and then restore the backup.

Restore procedures and tests

You should write a detailed, step-by-step procedure describing how to restore data from backups, and make sure all staff know where to find this document. When a disaster happens, it's usually at an inconvenient time, the key people aren't available, everyone's in a panic, and your procedure should be so clear and precise that it can be carried out by someone who isn't familiar with Velero or even Kubernetes.

Each month, run a restore test by having a different team member execute the restore procedure against a temporary cluster. This verifies both that your backups are good and that the restore procedure is correct, and makes sure everyone is familiar with how to do it.

Scheduling Velero backups

All backups should be automated, and Velero is no exception. You can schedule a regular backup using the velero schedule create command:

```
velero schedule create demo-schedule --schedule="0 1 * * *" --include-namespaces
demo
Schedule "demo-schedule" created successfully.
```

The schedule argument specifies when to run the backup, in Unix cron format (see "Cronjobs" on page 169). In the example, 0 1 * * * runs the backup at 01:00 every day.

To see what backups you have scheduled, use velero schedule get:

```
velero schedule get
NAME          STATUS  CREATED     SCHEDULE    BACKUP TTL LAST BACKUP SELECTOR
demo-schedule Enabled 2018-07-14  * 10 * * *  720h0m0s   10h ago     <none>
```

The BACKUP TTL field shows how long the backup will be kept around before being automatically deleted (by default, 720 hours, equivalent to one month).

Other uses for Velero

While Velero is extremely useful for disaster recovery, you can also use it to migrate resources and data from one cluster to another—a process sometimes called *lift and shift*.

Making regular Velero backups can also help you understand how your Kubernetes usage is changing over time; comparing the current state to the state a month ago, six months ago, and a year ago, for example.

The snapshots can also be a useful source of audit information: for example, finding out what was running in your cluster at a given date or time, and how and when the cluster state changed.

Best Practice

Use Velero to back up your cluster state and persistent data regularly: at least nightly. Run a restore test at least monthly.

Monitoring Cluster Status

Monitoring cloud native applications is a big topic, which, as we'll see in Chapter 15, includes things like observability, metrics, logging, tracing, and traditional black-box monitoring.

However, in this chapter we'll be concerned only with monitoring the Kubernetes cluster itself: the health of the cluster, the status of individual nodes, and the utilization of the cluster and the progress of its workloads.

kubectl

We introduced the invaluable kubectl command in Chapter 2, but we haven't yet exhausted its possibilities. As well as being a general administration tool for Kubernetes resources, kubectl can also report useful information about the state of the cluster components.

Control plane status

The kubectl get componentstatuses command (or kubectl get cs for short) gives health information for the control plane components—the scheduler, the controller manager, and *etcd*:

```
kubectl get componentstatuses
NAME                   STATUS    MESSAGE              ERROR
controller-manager     Healthy   ok
scheduler              Healthy   ok
etcd-0                 Healthy   {"health": "true"}
```

If there were a serious problem with any of the control plane components, it would soon become apparent anyway, but it's still handy to be able to check and report on them, as a sort of top-level health indicator for the cluster.

If any of your control plane components is not in a Healthy state, it will need to be fixed. This should never be the case with a managed Kubernetes service, but for self-hosted clusters, you will have to take care of this yourself.

Node status

Another useful command is kubectl get nodes, which will list all the nodes in your cluster, and report their status and Kubernetes version:

```
kubectl get nodes
NAME               STATUS   ROLES    AGE   VERSION
docker-for-desktop Ready    master   5d    v1.10.0
```

Since Docker Desktop clusters only have one node, this output isn't particularly informative; let's look at the output from a small Google Kubernetes Engine cluster for something more realistic:

```
kubectl get nodes
NAME                                           STATUS   ROLES    AGE   VERSION
gke-k8s-cluster-1-n1-standard-2-pool--8l6n     Ready    <none>   9d    v1.10.2-gke.1
gke-k8s-cluster-1-n1-standard-2-pool--dwtv     Ready    <none>   19d   v1.10.2-gke.1
gke-k8s-cluster-1-n1-standard-2-pool--67ch     Ready    <none>   20d   v1.10.2-gke.1
...
```

Note that in the Docker Desktop get nodes output, the node *role* was shown as master. Naturally enough, since there's only one node, that must be the master—and the sole worker node, too.

In Google Kubernetes Engine, and some other managed Kubernetes services, you don't have direct access to the master nodes. Accordingly, kubectl get nodes lists the worker nodes only (a role of <none> indicates a worker node).

If any of the nodes shows a status of NotReady, there is a problem. A reboot of the node may fix it, but if not, it may need further debugging—or you could just delete it and create a new node instead.

For detailed troubleshooting of bad nodes, you can use the `kubectl describe node` command to get more information:

```
kubectl describe nodes/gke-k8s-cluster-1-n1-standard-2-pool--8l6n
```

This will show you, for example, the memory and CPU capacity of the node, and the resources currently in use by Pods.

Workloads

You may recall from "Querying the Cluster with kubectl" on page 63 that you can also use `kubectl` to list all Pods (or any resources) in your cluster. In that example, you listed only the Pods in the default namespace, but the `--all-namespaces` flag will allow you to see all Pods in the entire cluster:

```
kubectl get pods --all-namespaces
NAMESPACE      NAME                           READY  STATUS            RESTARTS  AGE
cert-manager   cert-manager-cert-manager-55   1/1    Running           1         10d
pa-test        permissions-auditor-15281892   0/1    CrashLoopBackOff  1720      6d
freshtracks    freshtracks-agent-779758f445   3/3    Running           5         20d
...
```

This can give you a helpful overview of what's running in your cluster, and any Pod-level problems. If any Pods are not in `Running` status, like the `permissions-auditor` Pod in the example, it may need further investigation.

The `READY` column shows how many containers in the Pod are actually running, compared to the number configured. For example, the `freshtracks-agent` Pod shows 3/3: 3 out of 3 containers are running, so all is well.

On the other hand, `permissions-auditor` shows 0/1 containers ready: 0 containers running, but 1 required. The reason is shown in the `STATUS` column: `CrashLoopBack Off`. The container is failing to start properly.

When a container crashes, Kubernetes will keep trying to restart it at increasing intervals, starting at 10 seconds and doubling each time, up to 5 minutes. This strategy is called *exponential backoff*, hence the `CrashLoopBackOff` status message.

CPU and Memory Utilization

Another useful view on your cluster is provided by the `kubectl top` command. For nodes, it will show you the CPU and memory capacity of each node, and how much of each is currently in use:

```
kubectl top nodes
NAME                        CPU(cores)  CPU%   MEMORY(bytes)  MEMORY%
gke-k8s-cluster-1-n1-...8l6n   151m      7%     2783Mi         49%
gke-k8s-cluster-1-n1-...dwtv   155m      8%     3449Mi         61%
```

```
gke-k8s-cluster-1-n1-...67ch    580m         30%       3172Mi        56%
...
```

For Pods, it will show how much CPU and memory each specified Pod is using:

```
kubectl top pods -n kube-system
NAME                                    CPU(cores)   MEMORY(bytes)
event-exporter-v0.1.9-85bb4fd64d-2zjng  0m           27Mi
fluentd-gcp-scaler-7c5db745fc-h7ntr     10m          27Mi
fluentd-gcp-v3.0.0-5m627                11m          171Mi
...
```

Cloud Provider Console

If you're using a managed Kubernetes service that is offered by your cloud provider, then you will have access to a web-based console that can show you useful information about your cluster, its nodes, and workloads.

For example, the Google Kubernetes Engine (GKE) console lists all your clusters, details for each cluster, node pools, and so on (See Figure 11-1).

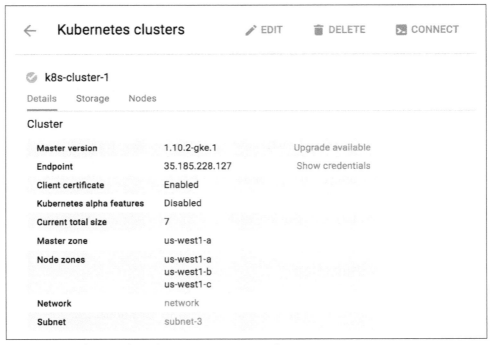

Figure 11-1. The Google Kubernetes Engine console

You can also list workloads, services, and configuration details for the cluster. This is much the same information as you can get from using the kubectl tool, but the GKE console also allows you to perform administration tasks: create clusters, upgrade nodes, and everything you'll need to manage your cluster on a day-to-day basis.

The Azure Kubernetes Service, AWS Elastic Container Service for Kubernetes, and other managed Kubernetes providers have similar facilities. It's a good idea to make yourself familiar with the management console for your particular Kubernetes service, as you'll be using it a lot.

Kubernetes Dashboard

The Kubernetes Dashboard (*https://kubernetes.io/docs/tasks/access-application-cluster/ web-ui-dashboard/*) is a web-based user interface for Kubernetes clusters (Figure 11-2). If you're running your own Kubernetes cluster, rather than using a managed service, you can run the Kubernetes Dashboard to get more or less the same information as a managed service console would provide.

Figure 11-2. The Kubernetes Dashboard displays useful information about your cluster

As you'd expect, the Dashboard lets you see the status of your clusters, nodes, and workloads, in much the same way as the kubectl tool, but with a graphical interface. You can also create and destroy resources using the Dashboard.

Because the Dashboard exposes a great deal of information about your cluster and workloads, it's very important to secure it properly, and never expose it to the public internet. The Dashboard lets you view the contents of ConfigMaps and Secrets, which could contain credentials and crypto keys, so you need to control access to the Dashboard as tightly as you would to those secrets themselves.

In 2018, security firm RedLock found hundreds of Kubernetes Dashboard consoles (*https://redlock.io/blog/cryptojacking-tesla*) accessible over the internet without any password protection, including one owned by Tesla, Inc. From these they were able to extract cloud security credentials and use them to access further sensitive information.

Best Practice

If you don't have to run the Kubernetes Dashboard (for example, if you already have a Kubernetes console provided by a managed service such as GKE), don't run it. If you do run it, make sure it has minimum privileges (*https://blog.heptio.com/on-securing-the-kubernetes-dashboard-16b09b1b7aca*), and never expose it to the internet. Instead, access it via `kubectl proxy`.

Weave Scope

Weave Scope (*https://github.com/weaveworks/scope*) is a great visualization and monitoring tool for your cluster, showing you a real-time map of your nodes, containers, and processes. You can also see metrics and metadata, and even start or stop containers using Scope.

kube-ops-view

Unlike the Kubernetes Dashboard, kube-ops-view (*https://github.com/hjacobs/kube-ops-view*) doesn't aim to be a general-purpose cluster management tool. Instead, it gives you a visualization of what's happening in your cluster: what nodes there are, the CPU and memory utilization on each, how many Pods each one is running, and the status of those Pods (Figure 11-3).

node-problem-detector

node-problem-detector (*https://github.com/kubernetes/node-problem-detector*) is a Kubernetes add-on that can detect and report several kinds of node-level issues: hardware problems, such as CPU or memory errors, filesystem corruption, and wedged container runtimes.

Currently, node-problem-detector reports problems by sending events to the Kubernetes API, and comes with a Go client library that you can use to integrate with your own tools.

Although Kubernetes currently does not take any action in response to events from the node-problem-detector, there may be further integration in the future that will allow the scheduler to avoid running Pods on problem nodes, for example.

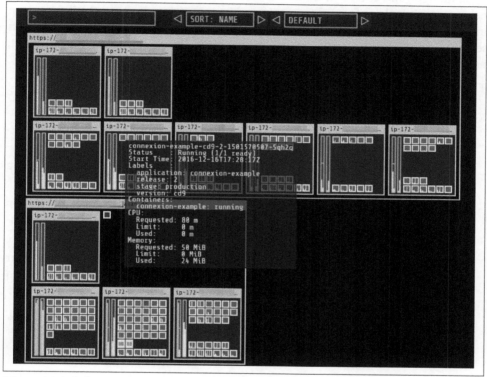

Figure 11-3. kube-ops-view gives an operational picture of your Kubernetes cluster

This is a great way to get a general overview of your cluster and what it's doing. While it's not a replacement for the Dashboard or for specialist monitoring tools, it's a good complement to them.

Further Reading

Kubernetes security is a complex and specialized topic, and we've only scratched the surface of it here. It really deserves a book of its own... and now there is one. Security experts Liz Rice and Michael Hausenblas have written the excellent *Kubernetes Secu-*

rity (O'Reilly), covering secure cluster setup, container security, secrets management, and more. We recommend it highly.

Summary

Security is not a product or an end goal, but an ongoing process that requires knowledge, thought, and attention. Container security is no different, and the machinery to help ensure it is there for you to use. If you've read and understood the information in this chapter, you know everything you need to know to configure your containers securely in Kubernetes—but we're sure you get the point that this should be the start, not the end, of your security process.

The main things to keep in mind:

- Role-Based Access Control (RBAC) gives you fine-grained management of permissions in Kubernetes. Make sure it's enabled, and use RBAC roles to grant specific users and apps only the minimum privileges they need to do their jobs.

- Containers aren't magically exempt from security and malware problems. Use a scanning tool to check any containers you run in production.

- Kubernetes is great and all, but you still need backups. Use Velero to back up your data and the state of the cluster. It's handy for moving things between clusters, too.

- kubectl is a powerful tool for inspecting and reporting on all aspects of your cluster and its workloads. Get friendly with kubectl. You'll be spending a lot of time together.

- Use your Kubernetes provider's web console and kube-ops-view for a graphical overview of what's going on. If you use the Kubernetes Dashboard, secure it as tightly as you would your cloud credentials and crypto keys.

CHAPTER 12

Deploying Kubernetes Applications

I lay on my back, surprised at how calm and focused I felt, strapped to four and a half million pounds of explosives.

—Ron Garan, astronaut

In this chapter we'll deal with the question of how to turn your manifest files into running applications. We'll learn how to build Helm charts for your applications, and look at some alternative tools for manifest management: tanka, kustomize, kapitan, and kompose.

Building Manifests with Helm

We saw in Chapter 2 how to deploy and manage applications with Kubernetes resources created from YAML manifests. There's nothing stopping you from managing all your Kubernetes applications using just the raw YAML files in this way, but it's not ideal. Not only is it difficult to maintain these files, but there is also a problem of distribution.

Suppose you want to make your application available to other people to run in their own clusters. You can distribute the manifest files to them, but they will inevitably need to customize some of the settings for their own environment.

To do this, they will have to make their own copy of the Kubernetes configs, find where the various settings are defined (perhaps duplicated in several places), and edit them.

Over time, they will need to maintain their own copies of the files, and when you make updates available, they will have to pull and reconcile them manually with their local changes.

This eventually starts to become painful. What we want is the ability to separate the raw manifest files from the particular settings and variables that you or any user of the application might need to adjust. Ideally we could then make these available in a standard format, which anyone can download and install to a Kubernetes cluster.

Once we have this, then each application can expose not only configuration values, but also any dependencies it has on other apps or services. An intelligent package management tool could then install and run an application, along with all its dependencies, in a single command.

In "Helm: A Kubernetes Package Manager" on page 64, we introduced the Helm tool and showed you how to use it to install public charts. Let's look at Helm charts in a little more detail now, and see how to create our own.

What's Inside a Helm Chart?

In the demo repo, open up the *hello-helm3/k8s* directory to see what's inside our Helm chart.

Every Helm chart has a standard structure. First, the chart is contained in a directory with the same name as the chart (demo in this case):

```
demo
├── Chart.yaml
├── production-values.yaml
├── staging-values.yaml
├── templates
│   ├── deployment.yaml
│   └── service.yaml
└── values.yaml
```

The Chart.yaml file

Next, it contains a file named *Chart.yaml*, which specifies the chart name and version:

```
name: demo
sources:
  - https://github.com/cloudnativedevops/demo
version: 1.0.1
```

There are lots of optional fields you can supply in *Chart.yaml*, including a link to the project source code, as here, but the only required information is the name and version.

The values.yaml file

There is also a file named *values.yaml*, which contains user-modifiable settings that the chart author has exposed:

```
environment: development
container:
  name: demo
  port: 8888
  image: cloudnatived/demo
  tag: hello
replicas: 1
```

This looks a bit like a Kubernetes YAML manifest, but there's an important difference. The *values.yaml* file is completely free-form YAML, with no predefined schema: it's up to you to choose what variables are defined, their names, and their values.

There don't have to be any variables at all in your Helm chart, but if there are, you can put them in *values.yaml* and then refer to them elsewhere in the chart.

Ignore the *production-values.yaml* and *staging-values.yaml* files for the moment; we'll explain what they're for shortly.

Helm Templates

So where are these variables referenced? If you look in the *templates* subdirectory, you'll see a couple of familiar-looking files:

```
ls k8s/demo/templates
deployment.yaml service.yaml
```

These are just the same as the Deployment and Service manifest files from the previous example, except that now they are *templates*: instead of referring to things like the container name directly, they contain a placeholder that Helm will replace with the actual value from *values.yaml*.

Here's what the template Deployment looks like:

```
apiVersion: apps/v1
kind: Deployment
metadata:
  name: {{ .Values.container.name }}-{{ .Values.environment }}
spec:
  replicas: {{ .Values.replicas }}
  selector:
    matchLabels:
      app: {{ .Values.container.name }}
  template:
    metadata:
      labels:
        app: {{ .Values.container.name }}
        environment: {{ .Values.environment }}
    spec:
      containers:
        - name: {{ .Values.container.name }}
          image: {{ .Values.container.image }}:{{ .Values.container.tag }}
          ports:
```

```
      - containerPort: {{ .Values.container.port }}
    env:
      - name: ENVIRONMENT
        value: {{ .Values.environment }}
```

 The curly braces indicate a place where Helm should substitute the value of a variable, but they're actually part of *Go template syntax*.

(Yes, Go is everywhere. Kubernetes and Helm themselves are written in Go, so it's no surprise that Helm charts use Go templates.)

Interpolating Variables

There are several variables referenced in this template:

```
...
metadata:
  name: {{ .Values.container.name }}-{{ .Values.environment }}
```

This whole section of text, including the curly braces, will be *interpolated* (that is, replaced) with the values of container.name and environment, taken from *values.yaml*. The generated result will look like this:

```
...
metadata:
  name: demo-development
```

This is powerful, because values like container.name are referenced more than once in the template. Naturally, it's referenced in the Service template, too:

```
apiVersion: v1
kind: Service
metadata:
  name: {{ .Values.container.name }}-service-{{ .Values.environment }}
  labels:
    app: {{ .Values.container.name }}
spec:
  ports:
  - port: {{ .Values.container.port }}
    protocol: TCP
    targetPort: {{ .Values.container.port }}
  selector:
    app: {{ .Values.container.name }}
  type: ClusterIP
```

You can see how many times .Values.container.name is referenced, for example. Even in a simple chart like this, you need to repeat the same bits of information many times. Using Helm variables eliminates this duplication. All you need to do to change the container name, for example, is to edit *values.yaml* and reinstall the chart, and the change will be propagated throughout all the templates.

The Go template format is very powerful, and you can use it to do much more than simple variable substitutions: it supports loops, expressions, conditionals, and even calling functions. Helm charts can use these features to generate fairly complex configuration from input values, unlike the simple substitutions in our example.

You can read more about how to write Helm templates in the Helm documentation (*https://docs.helm.sh/chart_template_guide*).

Quoting Values in Templates

You can use the `quote` function in Helm to automatically quote values in your templates:

```
name: {{.Values.MyName | quote }}
```

Only string values should be quoted; don't use the `quote` function with numeric values like port numbers.

Specifying Dependencies

What if your chart relies on other charts? For example, if your app uses Redis, the Helm chart for your app might need to specify the `redis` chart as a dependency.

You can do this using the *requirements.yaml* file:

```
dependencies:
  - name: redis
    version: 1.2.3
  - name: nginx
    version: 3.2.1
```

Now run the `helm dependency update` command, and Helm will download those charts, ready to install along with your own application.

Deploying Helm Charts

Let's look at what's involved in actually using a Helm chart to deploy an application. One of the most valuable features of Helm is the ability to specify, change, update, and override configuration settings. In this section we'll see how that works.

Setting Variables

We've seen that the author of a Helm chart can put all the user-modifiable settings in *values.yaml*, along with the default values for those settings. So how does the *user* of a chart change or override those settings to suit her local site or environment? The `helm install` command lets you specify additional values files on the command line, which will override any defaults in *values.yaml*. Let's look at an example.

Creating a environment variable

Suppose you want to deploy a version of the application in a staging environment. For the purposes of our example, it doesn't really matter what that means in practice, but let's say the application knows whether it's in staging or production based on the value of an environment variable named ENVIRONMENT, and changes its behavior accordingly. How does that environment variable get created?

Looking again at the *deployment.yaml* template, this environment variable is supplied to the container using this code:

```
...
env:
  - name: ENVIRONMENT
    value: {{ .Values.environment }}
```

The value of environment comes from *values.yaml*, as you'd expect:

```
environment: development
...
```

So installing the chart with the default values will result in the container's ENVIRON MENT variable containing development. Suppose you want to change that to staging. You could edit the *values.yaml* file, as we've seen, but a better way is to create an additional YAML file containing a value for just that one variable:

```
environment: staging
```

You'll find this value in the file *k8s/demo/staging-values.yaml*, which isn't part of the Helm chart—we've just supplied it to save you a little typing.

Specifying Values in a Helm Release

To specify an extra values file with the helm install command, use the --values flag, like this:

```
helm install --name demo-staging --values=./k8s/demo/staging-values.yaml
./k8s/demo ...
```

This will create a new release, with a new name (demo-staging), and the running container's ENVIRONMENT variable will be set to staging instead of development. The variables listed in the extra values file we specified with --values are combined with those in the default values file (*values.yaml*). In this case, there's only one variable (environment) and the value from *staging-values.yaml* overrides that from the default values file.

You can also specify values to helm install directly on the command line, using the --set flag, but this isn't in the spirit of infrastructure as code. Instead, to customize the settings for a Helm chart, create a YAML file that overrides the default, like the *staging-values.yaml* file in the example, and apply it on the command line using the `--values` flag.

While you'll naturally want to set configuration values this way for installing your own Helm charts, you can do it with public charts too. To see the list of values a chart makes available for you to set, run `helm inspect values` with a chart name:

```
helm inspect values stable/prometheus
```

Updating an App with Helm

You've learned how to install a Helm chart with the default values, and with a custom values file, but what about changing some values for an application that's already running?

The `helm upgrade` command will do this for you. Suppose you want to change the number of replicas (the number of copies of the Pod that Kubernetes should run) for the demo application. By default it's 1, as you can see from the *values.yaml* file:

```
replicas: 1
```

You know how to override this using a custom values file, so edit the *staging-values.yaml* file to add a suitable setting:

```
environment: staging
replicas: 2
```

Run the following command to apply your changes to the *existing* `demo-staging` Deployment, rather than creating a new one:

```
helm upgrade demo-staging --values=./k8s/demo/staging-values.yaml ./k8s/demo
Release "demo-staging" has been upgraded. Happy Helming!
```

You can run `helm upgrade` as many times as you like to update a running Deployment, and Helm will cheerfully oblige.

Rolling Back to Previous Versions

If you decide you don't like the version you've just deployed, or there turns out to be a problem, it's easy to roll back to a previous version, using the `helm rollback` command, and specifying the number of a previous release (as shown in `helm history` output):

```
helm rollback demo-staging 1
Rollback was a success! Happy Helming!
```

In fact, the rollback doesn't have to be to a previous release; let's say you roll back to revision 1, and then decide you want to roll *forward* to revision 2. If you run `helm rollback demo-staging 2`, that's exactly what will happen.

Automatic rollback with helm-monitor

You can even have Helm roll back a release automatically based on metrics (see Chapter 16). For example, suppose you're running Helm in a continuous deployment pipeline (see Chapter 14). You might want to automatically undo the release if the number of errors recorded by your monitoring system exceeds a certain amount.

To do this, you can use the `helm-monitor` plug-in, which can query a Prometheus server (see "Prometheus" on page 300) for any metrics expression you like, and trigger a rollback if the query succeeds. `helm-monitor` will watch the metric for five minutes and roll the release back if it detects a problem during that time. For more about `helm-monitor`, see this blog post (*https://container-solutions.com/automated-rollback-helm-releases-based-logs-metrics/*).

Creating a Helm Chart Repo

So far we've used Helm to install charts from a local directory, or from the `stable` repo. You don't need your own chart repo to use Helm, as it's common to store an application's Helm chart in the application's own repo.

But if you do want to maintain your own Helm chart repo, it's very straightforward. The charts need to be available over HTTP, and there's a variety of ways you can do this: put them in a cloud storage bucket, use GitHub Pages, or an existing web server if you have one.

Once all your charts are collected together under a single directory, run `helm repo index` on that directly to create the *index.yaml* file that contains the repo metadata.

Your chart repo is ready to use! See the Helm documentation (*https://docs.helm.sh/developing_charts/#the-chart-repository-guide*) for more details on managing chart repos.

To install charts from your repo, you'll first of all need to add the repo to Helm's list:

```
helm repo add myrepo http://myrepo.example.com
helm install myrepo/myapp
```

Managing Helm Chart Secrets with Sops

We saw in "Kubernetes Secrets" on page 189 how to store secret data in Kubernetes, and how to pass it to applications via environment variables or mounted files. If you have more than one or two secrets to manage, you may find it easier to create a single file containing all the secrets, rather than individual files each containing one secret. And if you're using Helm to deploy your app, you can make that file a values file, and encrypt it with Sops (see "Encrypting Secrets with Sops" on page 196).

We've built an example for you to try in the demo repo, in the *hello-sops* directory:

```
cd hello-sops
tree
.
├── k8s
│   └── demo
│       ├── Chart.yaml
│       ├── production-secrets.yaml
│       ├── production-values.yaml
│       ├── staging-secrets.yaml
│       ├── staging-values.yaml
│       ├── templates
│       │   ├── deployment.yaml
│       │   └── secrets.yaml
│       └── values.yaml
└── temp.yaml

3 directories, 9 files
```

This is a similar Helm chart layout to our earlier example (see "What's Inside a Helm Chart?" on page 222). Here, we've defined a `Deployment` and a `Secret`. But in this example, we have added a twist to make it easier to manage multiple secrets for different environments.

Let's see the secrets our application will need:

```
cat k8s/demo/production-secrets.yaml
secret_one: ENC[AES256_GCM,data:ekH3xIdCFiS4j1I2ja8=,iv:C95KilXL...1g==,type:str]
secret_two: ENC[AES256_GCM,data:0Xcmm1cdv3TbfM3mIkA=,iv:PQOcI9vX...XQ==,type:str]
...
```

Here we have used Sops to encrypt the values of multiple secrets for our application to use.

Now take a look at the Kubernetes *secrets.yaml* file:

```
cat k8s/demo/templates/secrets.yaml
apiVersion: v1
kind: Secret
metadata:
  name: {{ .Values.container.name }}-secrets
type: Opaque
data:
    {{ $environment := .Values.environment }}
    app_secrets.yaml: {{ .Files.Get (nospace (cat $environment "-secrets.yaml"))
        | b64enc }}
```

On the last two lines, we've added some Go templating into the Helm chart to read secrets from either the *production-secrets.yaml* or the *staging-secrets.yaml* files, depending on which environment is set in the *values.yaml* file.

The end result will be a single Kubernetes Secret named *demo-secrets, containing _all* of the key-value pairs defined in either secret file. This Secret will get mounted in the Deployment as a single file named *secrets.yaml* for the application to use.

We've also added . . . | b64enc to the end of the last line. This is another handy shortcut using Helm's Go templating to automatically convert the secret data from plain text to base64, which, by default, is what Kubernetes expects secrets to be (see "base64" on page 191).

We need to first temporarily decrypt the files using Sops, and then apply the changes to a Kubernetes cluster. Here is a command pipeline to deploy a staging version of the demo application, with its staging secrets:

```
sops -d k8s/demo/staging-secrets.yaml > temp-staging-secrets.yaml && \
helm upgrade --install staging-demo --values staging-values.yaml \
--values temp-staging-secrets.yaml ./k8s/demo && rm temp-staging-secrets.yaml
```

Here's how that works:

1. Sops decrypts the *staging-secrets* file and writes the decrypted output to *temp-staging-secrets*.

2. Helm installs the demo chart using values from *staging-values* and *temp-staging-secrets*.

3. The *temp-staging-secrets* file is deleted.

Because all this happens in one step, we don't leave a file containing plain-text secrets lying around for the wrong people to find.

Managing Multiple Charts with Helmfile

When we introduced Helm in "Helm: A Kubernetes Package Manager" on page 64, we showed you how to deploy the demo application Helm chart to a Kubernetes cluster. As useful as Helm is, it only operates on one chart at a time. How do you know what applications should be running in your cluster, together with the custom settings you applied when you installed them with Helm?

There's a neat tool called Helmfile (*https://github.com/roboll/helmfile*) that can help you do this. Much as Helm makes it possible for you to deploy a single application using templating and variables, Helmfile enables you to deploy everything that should be installed on your cluster, with a single command.

What's in a Helmfile?

There's an example of how to use Helmfile in the demo repository. In the *hello-helmfile* folder, you'll find *helmfile.yaml*:

```
repositories:
  - name: stable
    url: https://kubernetes-charts.storage.googleapis.com/

releases:
  - name: demo
    namespace: demo
    chart: ../hello-helm3/k8s/demo
    values:
      - "../hello-helm3/k8s/demo/production-values.yaml"

  - name: kube-state-metrics
    namespace: kube-state-metrics
    chart: stable/kube-state-metrics

  - name: prometheus
    namespace: prometheus
    chart: stable/prometheus
    set:
      - name: rbac.create
        value: true
```

The `repositories` section defines the Helm chart repositories we are going to reference. In this case, the only repository is `stable`, the official stable Kubernetes chart repository. If you're using your own Helm chart repo (see "Creating a Helm Chart Repo" on page 228), add it here.

Next, we define a set of `releases`: applications we would like to deploy to the cluster. Each release specifies some of the following metadata:

- `name` of the Helm chart to deploy
- `namespace` to deploy it to
- `chart` is the URL or path to the chart itself
- `values` gives the path to a *values.yaml* file to use with the Deployment
- `set` sets any extra values in addition to those in the values file

We've defined three releases here: the demo app, plus Prometheus (see "Prometheus" on page 300) and `kube-state-metrics` (see "Kubernetes Metrics" on page 285).

Chart Metadata

Note that we've specified a relative path to the `demo` chart and values files:

```
- name: demo
  namespace: demo
  chart: ../hello-helm3/k8s/demo
  values:
    - "../hello-helm3/k8s/demo/production-values.yaml"
```

So your charts don't need to be in a chart repository for Helmfile to manage them; you could keep them all in the same source code repo, for example.

For the `prometheus` chart, we've specified simply `stable/prometheus`. Since this isn't a filesystem path, Helmfile knows to look for the chart in the `stable` repo, which we defined earlier in the `repositories` section:

```
- name: stable
  url: https://kubernetes-charts.storage.googleapis.com/
```

All charts have various default values set in their respective *values.yaml* files. In the `set:` sections of Helmfile, you can specify any values that you would like to overwrite when installing the application.

In this example, for the `prometheus` release, we changed the default value for `rbac.create` from `false` to `true`:

```
- name: prometheus
  namespace: prometheus
  chart: stable/prometheus
  set:
    - name: rbac.create
      value: true
```

Applying the Helmfile

The *helmfile.yaml*, then, specifies everything that should be running in the cluster (or at least, a subset of it) in a declarative way, just like Kubernetes manifests. When you apply this declarative manifest, Helmfile will bring the cluster into line with your specification.

To do this, run:

```
helmfile sync
exec: helm repo add stable https://kubernetes-charts.storage.googleapis.com/
"stable" has been added to your repositories
exec: helm repo update
Hang tight while we grab the latest from your chart repositories...
...Skip local chart repository
...Successfully got an update from the "cloudnativedevops" chart repository
...Successfully got an update from the "stable" chart repository
Update Complete. ❁ Happy Helming!❁
exec: helm dependency update .../demo/hello-helm3/k8s/demo
...
```

It's just as though you had run `helm install` / `helm upgrade` in turn for each of the Helm charts you've defined.

You might like to run `helm sync` automatically as part of your continuous deployment pipeline, for example (see Chapter 14). Instead of manually running `helm` `install` to add a new application to the cluster, you could just edit your Helmfile, check it into source control, and wait for the automation to roll out your changes.

 Use a single source of truth. Don't mix deploying individual charts manually with Helm, and declaratively managing all your charts across the cluster with Helmfile. Pick one or the other. If you apply a Helmfile, and then use Helm to deploy or modify applications out of band, the Helmfile will no longer be the single source of truth for your cluster. This is bound to lead to problems, so if you use Helmfile, make all your deployments using only Helmfile.

If Helmfile isn't quite to your liking, there are a few other tools that do more or less the same thing:

- Landscaper (*https://github.com/Eneco/landscaper*)
- Helmsman (*https://github.com/Praqma/helmsman*)

As with any new tool, we recommend reading through the docs, comparing the various options, trying them out, and then deciding which suits you.

Advanced Manifest Management Tools

While Helm is a great tool, and widely used, it does have a few limitations. Writing and editing Helm templates isn't a lot of fun. Kubernetes YAML files are complicated, verbose, and repetitive. Therefore, so are Helm templates.

Several new tools are under development that try to address these problems, and make it easier to work with Kubernetes manifests: either by describing them in a more powerful language than YAML, such as Jsonnet, or by grouping the YAML files into basic patterns and customizing them with overlay files.

Tanka

Sometimes declarative YAML isn't enough, especially for large and complex deployments where you need to be able to use computation and logic. For example, you might want to set the number of replicas dynamically based on the size of the cluster. For this, you need a real programming language.

tanka (*https://github.com/grafana/tanka/*) lets you author Kubernetes manifests using a language called Jsonnet, which is an extended version of JSON (which is a declarative data format equivalent to YAML, and Kubernetes can understand JSON format manifests too). Jsonnet adds important capabilities to JSON—variables, loops, arithmetic, conditional statements, error handling, and so on:

Kapitan

Kapitan (*https://github.com/deepmind/kapitan*) is another Jsonnet-based manifest tool, focused on sharing configuration values across multiple applications or even clusters. Kapitan has a hierarchical database of config values (called the *inventory*) that lets you re-use manifest patterns by plugging in different values, depending on the environment or application:

```
local kube = import "lib/kube.libjsonnet";
local kap = import "lib/kapitan.libjsonnet";
local inventory = kap.inventory();
local p = inventory.parameters;

{
    "00_namespace": kube.Namespace(p.namespace),
    "10_serviceaccount": kube.ServiceAccount("default")
}
```

kustomize

kustomize (*https://github.com/kubernetes-sigs/kustomize*) is another manifest management tool that uses plain YAML, instead of templates or an alternate language like Jsonnet. You start with a base YAML manifest, and use *overlays* to patch the manifest for different environments or configurations. The kustomize command-line tool will generate the final manifests from the base files plus the overlays:

```
namePrefix: staging-
commonLabels:
  environment: staging
  org: acmeCorporation
commonAnnotations:
  note: Hello, I am staging!
bases:
- ../../base
patchesStrategicMerge:
- map.yaml
EOF
```

This means deploying manifests can be as simple as running:

```
kustomize build /myApp/overlays/stagingq | kubectl apply -f -
```

If templates or Jsonnet don't appeal to you, and you want the ability to work with plain Kubernetes manifests, this tool is worth checking out.

kompose

If you've been running production services in Docker containers, but not using Kubernetes, you may be familiar with Docker Compose.

Compose lets you define and deploy sets of containers that work together: for example, a web server, a backend application, and a database such as Redis. A single *docker-compose.yml* file could be used to define how these containers talk to each other.

kompose (*https://github.com/kubernetes/kompose*) is a tool to convert *docker-compose.yml* files into Kubernetes manifests, to help you migrate from Docker Compose to Kubernetes, without having to write your own Kubernetes manifests or Helm charts from scratch.

Ansible

You may already be familiar with Ansible, a popular infrastructure automation tool. It's not Kubernetes-specific, but it can manage many different kinds of resources, using extension modules, much like Puppet (see "Puppet Kubernetes Module" on page 46).

As well as installing and configuring Kubernetes clusters, Ansible can manage Kubernetes resources like Deployments and Services directly, using the k8s module (*https://docs.ansible.com/ansible/latest/modules/k8s_module.html*).

Like Helm, Ansible can template Kubernetes manifests using its standard templating language (Jinja), and it has a more sophisticated notion of variable lookup, using a hierarchical system. For example, you can set common values for a group of applications, or a deployment environment such as staging.

If you're already using Ansible in your organization, it's definitely worth evaluating whether you should use it for managing Kubernetes resources too. If your infrastructure is based solely on Kubernetes, then Ansible may be more power than you need, but for mixed infrastructures it can be very helpful to use just one tool to manage everything:

```
kube_resource_configmaps:
  my-resource-env: "{{ lookup('template', template_dir +
'/my-resource-env.j2') }}"
kube_resource_manifest_files: "{{ lookup('fileglob', template_dir +
'/*manifest.yml') }}"
- hosts: "{{ application }}-{{ env }}-runner"
  roles:
    - kube-resource
```

A talk by Ansible expert Will Thames shows some of the possibilities of managing Kubernetes with Ansible (*http://willthames.github.io/ansiblefest2018*).

kubeval

Unlike the other tools we've discussed in this section, kubeval (*https://github.com/garethr/kubeval*) isn't for generating or templating Kubernetes manifests, but for validating them.

Each version of Kubernetes has a different schema for its YAML or JSON manifests, and it's important to be able to check automatically that your manifests match the schema. For example, kubeval will check that you've specified all the required fields for a particular object, and that the values are of the right type.

kubectl also validates manifests when they're applied, and will give you an error when you try to apply an invalid manifest. But it's also very useful to be able to validate them beforehand. kubeval doesn't need access to a cluster, and it can also validate against any version of Kubernetes.

It's a good idea to add kubeval to your continuous deployment pipeline, so that manifests are automatically validated whenever you make changes to them. You can also use kubeval to test, for example, whether your manifests need any adjustments to work on the latest version of Kubernetes before you actually upgrade.

Summary

While you can deploy applications to Kubernetes using just raw YAML manifests, it's inconvenient. Helm is a powerful tool that can help with this, provided you understand how to get the best out of it.

There are lots of new tools being developed right now that will make Kubernetes Deployment much easier in the future. Some of their features may be incorporated into Helm, too. Either way, it's important to be familiar with the basics of using Helm:

- A chart is a Helm package specification, including metadata about the package, some configuration values for it, and template Kubernetes objects that reference those values.

- Installing a chart creates a Helm release. Each time you install an instance of a chart, a new release is created. When you update a release with different config values, Helm increments the release revision number.

- To customize a Helm chart for your own requirements, create a custom values file overriding just the settings you care about, and add it to the helm install or helm upgrade command line.

- You can use a variable (environment, for example) to select different sets of values or secrets depending on the deployment environment: staging, production, and so on.

- With Helmfile, you can declaratively specify a set of Helm charts and values to be applied to your cluster, and install or update all of them with a single command.

- Helm can be used along with Sops for handling secret configuration in your charts. It can also use a function to automatically base64-encode your secrets, which Kubernetes expects them to be.

- Helm is not the only available tool for managing Kubernetes manifests. Tanka and Kapitan use Jsonnet, a different templating language. kustomize takes a different approach and rather than interpolating variables, it just uses YAML overlays to configure manifests.

- A quick way to test and validate manifests is to use kubeval, which will check for valid syntax and common errors in manifests.

CHAPTER 13

Development Workflow

Surfing is such an amazing concept. You're taking on Nature with a little stick and say-ing, *I'm gonna ride you!* And a lot of times Nature says, *No you're not!* and crashes you to the bottom.

—Jolene Blalock

In this chapter we'll expand on the discussion in Chapter 12, turning our attention to the whole application life cycle, from local development to deploying updates to a Kubernetes cluster, including the tricky topic of database migrations. We'll cover some tools that help you develop, test, and deploy your applications: Skaffold, Draft, Telepresence, and Knative. Once you're ready to deploy your application to the clus-ter, you'll learn about more complex deployments with Helm using hooks.

Development Tools

In Chapter 12 we looked at some tools to help you write, build, and deploy your Kubernetes resource manifests. That's fine as far as it goes, but often when you're developing an application that runs in Kubernetes, you want to be able to try things out and see changes instantly, without going through a full build-push-deploy-update loop.

Skaffold

Skaffold (*https://github.com/GoogleContainerTools/skaffold*) is an open source tool from Google designed to provide a fast local development workflow. It automatically rebuilds your containers as you develop locally, and deploys those changes to either a local or remote cluster.

You define your desired workflow in a *skaffold.yaml* file in your repository and run the skaffold command-line tool to start the pipeline. As you make changes to files in your local directory, Skaffold wakes up, builds a new container with the changes, and then deploys it for you automatically, saving you a round trip to the container registry.

Draft

Draft (*https://github.com/Azure/draft*) is an open source tool maintained by the Azure team at Microsoft. Like Skaffold, it can use Helm to automatically deploy updates to a cluster when code changes.

Draft also introduces the concept of Draft Packs: prewritten Dockerfiles and Helm charts for whatever language your app is using. Currently there are packs available for .NET, Go, Node, Erlang, Clojure, C#, PHP, Java, Python, Rust, Swift, and Ruby.

If you are just starting out with a new application, and you don't yet have a Dockerfile or Helm chart, Draft may be the perfect tool for you to get up and running quickly. When you run `draft init && draft create`, Draft will examine the files in your local application directory and try to determine which language your code uses. It will then create a Dockerfile for your specific language, as well as a Helm chart.

To apply these, run the `draft up` command. Draft will build a local Docker container using the Dockerfile it created and deploy it to your Kubernetes cluster.

Telepresence

Telepresence (*https://www.telepresence.io/*) takes a slightly different approach from Skaffold and Draft. You don't need a local Kubernetes cluster; a Telepresence Pod runs in your real cluster as a placeholder for your application. Traffic for the application Pod is then intercepted and routed to the container running on your local machine.

This enables the developer to make her local machine participate in the remote cluster. As she makes changes to application code, they will be reflected in the live cluster, without a new container having to be deployed to it.

Knative

While the other tools we've looked at are focused on speeding up the local development loop, Knative (*https://github.com/knative/docs*) is more ambitious. It aims to provide a standard mechanism for deploying all kinds of workloads to Kubernetes: not just containerized applications, but *serverless*-style functions too.

Knative integrates with both Kubernetes and Istio (see "Istio" on page 177) to provide a complete application/function deployment platform, including setting up a build process, automated deployment, and an *eventing* mechanism that standardizes the

---

way applications use messaging and queueing systems (for example, Pub/Sub, Kafka, or RabbitMQ).

The Knative project is at an early stage, but it's one to watch.

Deployment Strategies

If you were upgrading a running application by hand, without Kubernetes, one way to do it would be to just shut down the application, install the new version, and restart it. But that means downtime.

If you had multiple replicas, a better way would be to upgrade each replica in turn, so that there's no interruption in service: a so-called *zero-downtime deployment*.

Not all applications need zero downtime; internal services that consume message queues, for example, are idempotent, so they can be upgraded all at once. This means the upgrade happens faster, but for user-facing applications, we are usually more concerned with avoiding downtime than achieving quick upgrades.

In Kubernetes, you can choose whichever of these strategies is most appropriate. Roll ingUpdate is the zero-downtime, Pod-by-Pod option, while Recreate is the fast, all-Pods-at-once option. There are also some fields that you can tweak to get the exact behavior that you need for your application.

In Kubernetes, an application's deployment strategy is defined in the Deployment manifest. The default is RollingUpdate, so if you don't specify a strategy, this is what you'll get. To change the strategy to Recreate, set it like this:

```
apiVersion: apps/v1
kind: Deployment
spec:
  replicas: 1
  strategy:
    type: Recreate
```

Now let's look more closely at these deployment strategies and see how they work.

Rolling Updates

In a rolling update, Pods are upgraded one at a time, until all replicas have been replaced with the new version.

For example, let's imagine an application with three replicas, each running v1. The developer starts an upgrade to v2 with a kubectl apply... or helm upgrade... command. What happens?

First, one of the three v1 Pods will be terminated. Kubernetes will flag it as unready, and stop sending it traffic. A new v2 Pod will be spun up to take its place. Meanwhile, the remaining v1 Pods continue receiving incoming requests. While we're waiting for the first v2 Pod to become ready, we're down to two Pods, but we're still serving users.

When the v2 Pod becomes ready, Kubernetes will start sending it user traffic, alongside the other two v1 Pods. Now we're back to our full complement of three Pods.

This process will continue, Pod by Pod, until all of the v1 Pods have been replaced with v2 Pods. While there are times when fewer Pods than usual are available to handle traffic, the application as a whole is never actually down. That's zero-downtime deployment.

 During a rolling update, both old and new versions of your application will be in service at the same time. While this usually isn't a problem, you may need to take steps to ensure that this is safe; if your changes involve a database migration, for example (see "Handling Migrations with Helm" on page 245), a normal rolling update won't be possible.

If your Pods can sometimes crash or fail after a short time in a ready state, use the minReadySeconds field to have the rollout wait until each Pod is stable (see "minReadySeconds" on page 75).

Recreate

In Recreate mode, all running replicas are terminated at once, and then new ones are created.

For applications that do not directly handle requests, this should be acceptable. One advantage of Recreate is that it avoids the situation where two different versions of the application are running simultaneously (see "Rolling Updates" on page 241).

maxSurge and maxUnavailable

As a rolling update progresses, sometimes you will have more Pods running than the nominal replicas value, and sometimes less. Two important settings govern this behavior: maxSurge and maxUnavailable:

- maxSurge sets the maximum number of excess Pods. For example, if you have 10 replicas and you set maxSurge to 30%, then no more than 13 Pods will be allowed to run at any one time.

- maxUnavailable sets the maximum number of unavailable Pods. With a nominal 10 replicas and maxUnavailable of 20%, Kubernetes will never let the number of available Pods drop below 8.

These can be set as either a whole number, or as a percentage:

```
apiVersion: apps/v1
kind: Deployment
spec:
  replicas: 10
  strategy:
    type: RollingUpdate
    rollingUpdate:
      maxSurge: 20%
      maxUnavailable: 3
```

Usually, the default values for both (25%, or 1, depending on your Kubernetes version) are fine, and you won't need to adjust these. In some situations, you may need to tweak them to make sure your application can maintain acceptable capacity during an upgrade. At very large scale, you may find that running at 75% availability is not sufficient, and you'll need to reduce maxUnavailable slightly.

The bigger the value of maxSurge, the faster your rollout, but the more extra load it places on your cluster's resources. Large values of maxUnavailable also speed up rollouts, at the expense of your application's capacity.

On the other hand, small values of maxSurge and maxUnavailable reduce the impact on your cluster and your users, but can make your rollouts take much longer. Only you can decide what the right trade-off is for your application.

Blue/Green Deployments

In a *blue/green* deployment, rather than killing and replacing Pods one at a time, a whole new Deployment is created, and a new separate stack of Pods running v2 is launched beside the existing v1 Deployment.

One advantage of this is that you don't have to deal with both old and new versions of the application processing requests simultaneously. On the other hand, your cluster will need to be big enough to run twice the number of replicas required for your application, which can be expensive, and means a lot of unused capacity sitting around most of the time (unless you scale the cluster up and down as needed).

Recall from "Service Resources" on page 60 that Kubernetes uses labels to decide which Pods should receive traffic from a Service. One way to implement a blue/green deployment is to set different labels on your old and new Pods (see "Labels" on page 155).

With a small tweak to the Service definition for our example application, you can send traffic to only Pods labeled deployment: blue:

```
apiVersion: v1
kind: Service
metadata:
```

```
    name: demo
spec:
  ports:
  - port: 8080
    protocol: TCP
    targetPort: 8080
  selector:
    app: demo
    deployment: blue
  type: ClusterIP
```

When deploying a new version, you can label it `deployment: green`. It won't receive any traffic, even when it's fully up and running, because the Service only sends traffic to `blue` Pods. You can test it and make sure it's ready before making the cutover.

To switch over to the new Deployment, edit the Service to change the selector to `deployment: green`. Now the new `green` Pods will start receiving traffic, and once all the old `blue` Pods are idle, you can shut them down.

Rainbow Deployments

In some rare cases, particularly when Pods have very long-lived connections (websockets, for example), just blue and green may not be enough. You may need to maintain three or more versions of your application in flight at the same time.

This is sometimes referred to as a *rainbow deployment*. Every time you deploy an update, you get a new color set of Pods. As connections finally drain from your oldest set of Pods, they can be shut down.

Brandon Dimcheff describes a rainbow deployment example (*https://github.com/bdimcheff/rainbow-deploys*) in detail.

Canary Deployments

The advantage of blue/green (or rainbow) deployments is that if you decide you don't like the new version, or it isn't behaving correctly, you can simply switch back to the old version, which is still running. However, it is expensive because you need the capacity to run both versions simultaneously.

One alternative approach that avoids this problem is a *canary deployment*. Like a canary in a coal mine, a small handful of new Pods are exposed to the dangerous world of production to see what happens to them. If they survive, the rollout can continue to completion. If there *is* a problem, the blast radius is strictly limited.

Just as with blue/green deployments, you can do this using labels (see "Labels" on page 155). There is a detailed example of running a canary deployment in the Kubernetes documentation (*https://kubernetes.io/docs/concepts/cluster-administration/manage-deployment/#canary-deployments*).

A more sophisticated way to do this is to use Istio (see "Istio" on page 177), which allows you to randomly route a variable proportion of traffic to one or more service versions. This also makes it easy to do things like A/B testing.

Handling Migrations with Helm

Stateless applications are easy to deploy and upgrade, but when a database is involved, the situation can be more complicated. Changes to the schema of a database usually require a *migration* task to be run at a specific point in the rollout. For example, with Rails apps, you need to run `rake db:migrate` before starting the new Pods.

On Kubernetes, you can use a Job resource to do this (see "Jobs" on page 168). You could script this using `kubectl` commands as part of your upgrade process, or if you are using Helm, then you can use a built-in feature called *hooks*.

Helm Hooks

Helm hooks allow you to control the order in which things happen during a deployment. They also let you bail out of an upgrade if things go wrong.

Here is an example of a database migration Job for a Rails application deployed with Helm:

```
apiVersion: batch/v1
kind: Job
metadata:
  name: {{ .Values.appName }}-db-migrate
  annotations:
    "helm.sh/hook": pre-upgrade
    "helm.sh/hook-delete-policy": hook-succeeded
spec:
  activeDeadlineSeconds: 60
  template:
    name: {{ .Values.appName }}-db-migrate
    spec:
      restartPolicy: Never
      containers:
      - name: {{ .Values.appName }}-migration-job
        image: {{ .Values.image.repository }}:{{ .Values.image.tag }}
        command:
          - bundle
          - exec
          - rails
          - db:migrate
```

The `helm.sh/hook` properties are defined in the `annotations` section:

```
annotations:
  "helm.sh/hook": pre-upgrade
  "helm.sh/hook-delete-policy": hook-succeeded
```

The `pre-upgrade` setting tells Helm to apply this Job manifest before doing an upgrade. The Job will run the standard Rails migration command.

The `"helm.sh/hook-delete-policy": hook-succeeded` tells Helm to delete the Job if it completes successfully (that is, exits with status 0).

Handling Failed Hooks

If the Job returns a nonzero exit code, this is a sign that there was an error and the migration did not complete successfully. Helm will leave the Job in place in its failed state, so that you can debug what went wrong.

If this happens, the release process will stop, and the application will not be upgraded. Running `kubectl get pods` will show you the failed Pod, allowing you to inspect the logs and see what happened.

Once the issue has been resolved, you can delete the failed job (`kubectl delete job <job-name>`) and then try the upgrade again.

Other Hooks

Hooks have phases other than just `pre-upgrade`. You can use a hook at any of the following stages of a release:

- `pre-install` executes after templates are rendered, but before any resources are created.
- `post-install` executes after all resources are loaded.
- `pre-delete` executes on a deletion request before any resources are deleted.
- `post-delete` executes on a deletion request after all of the release's resources have been deleted.
- `pre-upgrade` executes on an upgrade request after templates are rendered, but before any resources are loaded (for example, before a `kubectl apply` operation).
- `post-upgrade` executes on an upgrade after all resources have been upgraded.
- `pre-rollback` executes on a rollback request after templates are rendered, but before any resources have been rolled back.
- `post-rollback` executes on a rollback request after all resources have been modified.

Chaining Hooks

Helm hooks also come with the ability to chain them together in a specific order, using the `helm.sh/hook-weight` property. The hooks will be run in order from lowest to highest, so a Job with a `hook-weight` of 0 will run before one with a `hook-weight` of 1:

```
apiVersion: batch/v1
kind: Job
metadata:
  name: {{ .Values.appName }}-stage-0
  annotations:
    "helm.sh/hook": pre-upgrade
    "helm.sh/hook-delete-policy": hook-succeeded
    "helm.sh/hook-weight": "0
```

You can find everything you need to know about hooks in the Helm documentation (*https://docs.helm.sh/developing_charts/#hooks*).

Summary

Developing Kubernetes applications can be tedious if you have to build, push, and deploy a container image to test every little code change. Tools like Draft, Skaffold, and Telepresence make this loop much faster, speeding up development.

In particular, rolling out changes to production is far easier with Kubernetes than with traditional servers, provided you understand the basic concepts, and how you can customize them to suit your application:

- The default `RollingUpdate` deployment strategy in Kubernetes upgrades a few Pods at a time, waiting for each replacement Pod to become ready before shutting down the old one.

- Rolling updates avoid downtime, at the expense of making the rollout take longer. It also means that both old and new versions of your application will be running simultaneously during the rollout period.

- You can adjust the `maxSurge` and `maxUnavailable` fields to fine-tune rolling updates. Depending on the versions of the Kubernetes API you are using, the defaults may or may not be appropriate for your situation.

- The `Recreate` strategy just blows away all the old Pods and starts up new ones all at once. This is fast, but results in downtime, so it's not suitable for user-facing applications.

- In a blue/green deployment, all the new Pods are started up and made ready without receiving any user traffic. Then all traffic is switched over to the new Pods in one go, before retiring the old Pods.

- Rainbow deployments are similar to blue/green deployments, but with more than two versions in service simultaneously.

- You can implement blue/green and rainbow deployments in Kubernetes by adjusting the labels on your Pods and changing the selector on the front-end Service to direct traffic to the appropriate set of Pods.

- Helm hooks provide a way to apply certain Kubernetes resources (usually Jobs) at a particular stage of a deployment, for example, to run a database migration. Hooks can define the order in which resources should be applied during a deployment, and cause the deployment to halt if something does not succeed.

CHAPTER 14

Continuous Deployment in Kubernetes

Tao does not do, but nothing is not done.

—Lao Tzu

In this chapter we'll look at a key DevOps principle—*continuous deployment*—and see how we can achieve this in a cloud native, Kubernetes-based environment. We outline some of the options for setting up continuous deployment (CD) pipelines to work with Kubernetes, and show you a fully worked example using Google's Cloud Build.

What Is Continuous Deployment?

Continuous deployment (CD) is the automatic deployment of successful builds to production. Like the test suite, deployment should also be managed centrally and automated. Developers should be able to deploy new versions by either pushing a button, or merging a merge request, or pushing a Git release tag.

CD is often associated with *continuous integration* (CI): the automatic integration and testing of developers' changes against the mainline branch. The idea is that if you're making changes on a branch that would break the build when merged to the mainline, continuous integration will let you know that right away, rather than waiting until you finish your branch and do the final merge. The combination of continuous integration and deployment is often referred to as *CI/CD*.

The machinery of continuous deployment is often referred to as a *pipeline*: a series of automated actions that take code from the developer's workstation to production, via a sequence of test and acceptance stages.

A typical pipeline for containerized applications might look like the following:

1. A developer pushes her code changes to Git.
2. The build system automatically builds the current version of the code and runs tests.
3. If all tests pass, the container image will be published into the central container registry.
4. The newly built container is deployed automatically to a staging environment.
5. The staging environment undergoes some automated acceptance tests.
6. The verified container image is deployed to production.

A key point is that the artifact that is tested and deployed through your various environments is not the *source code*, but the *container*. There are many ways for errors to creep in between source code and a running binary, and testing the container instead of the code can help catch a lot of these.

The great benefit of CD is *no surprises in production*; nothing gets deployed unless the exact binary image has already been successfully tested in staging.

You can see a detailed example of a CD pipeline like this in "A CD Pipeline with Cloud Build" on page 253.

Which CD Tool Should I Use?

As usual, the problem is not a shortage of available tools, but the sheer range of choices. There are several CD tools designed specifically for cloud native applications, and long-established traditional build tools such as Jenkins now have plug-ins to allow them to work with Kubernetes and containers.

As a result, if you already use CD, you probably don't need to switch to a whole new system. If you are migrating existing applications to Kubernetes, you can almost certainly do this with a few changes to your existing build system.

If you haven't yet adopted a CD system, then we'll outline some of your options in this section.

Jenkins

Jenkins (*https://jenkins.io/*) is a very widely adopted CD tool and has been around for years. It has plugins for just about everything you could want to use in a CD workflow, including Docker, kubectl, and Helm.

There is also a newer dedicated side project for running Jenkins in your Kubernetes cluster, JenkinsX (*https://jenkins-x.io/*).

Drone

Drone (*https://github.com/drone/drone*) is a newer CD tool built with, and for, containers. It is simple and lightweight, with the pipeline defined by a single YAML file. Since each build step consists of running a container, it means that anything you can run in a container you can run on Drone.[1]

Google Cloud Build

If you run your infrastructure on Google Cloud Platform, then Google Cloud Build (*https://cloud.google.com/cloud-build*) should be your first choice for CD. Like Drone, Cloud Build runs containers as the various build steps and the configuration YAML lives in your code repository.

You can configure Cloud Build to watch your Git repository (GitHub integration is available). When a preset condition is triggered, such as pushing to a certain branch or tag, Cloud Build will run your specified pipeline, building a new container, running your test suite, publishing the image, and perhaps deploying the new version to Kubernetes.

For a complete working example of a CD pipeline in Cloud Build, see "A CD Pipeline with Cloud Build" on page 253.

Concourse

Concourse (*https://concourse-ci.org/*) is an open source CD tool written in Go. It also adopts the declarative pipeline approach, much like Drone and Cloud Build, using a YAML file to define and execute build steps. Concourse already has an official stable Helm chart to deploy it on Kubernetes, making it easy to get a containerized pipeline up and running quickly.

Spinnaker

Spinnaker is very powerful and flexible, but can be a little daunting at first glance. Developed by Netflix, it excels at large-scale and complex deployments, such as blue/green deployments (see "Blue/Green Deployments" on page 243). There is a free ebook (*https://www.spinnaker.io/ebook*) about Spinnaker that should give you some idea whether Spinnaker fits your needs.

---

1 The *New York Times* dev team wrote a useful blog post on deploying to GKE with Drone (*https://nyti.ms/2E636iB*).

GitLab CI

GitLab is a popular alternative to GitHub for hosting Git repositories. It also comes with a powerful built-in CD tool, GitLab CI (*https://about.gitlab.com/features/gitlab-ci-cd*), that can be used for testing and deploying your code.

If you are already using GitLab, it makes sense to look at GitLab CI for implementing your continuous deployment pipeline.

Codefresh

Codefresh (*https://codefresh.io/*) is a managed CD service for testing and deploying applications to Kubernetes. One interesting feature is the ability to deploy temporary staging environments for every feature branch.

Using containers, CodeFresh can build, test, and deploy on-demand environments, and then you can configure how you would like to deploy your containers into various environments in your clusters.

Azure Pipelines

Microsoft's Azure DevOps service (formerly known as Visual Studio Team Services) includes a continuous delivery pipeline facility, called Azure Pipelines (*https://azure.microsoft.com/services/devops/pipelines*), similar to Google Cloud Build.

CD Components

If you already have a well-established CD system, and just need to add a component for building containers, or for deploying containers once they have been built, here are some options that you may be able to integrate with your existing system.

Docker Hub

One of the easiest ways to automatically build new containers on code changes is to use Docker Hub (*https://docs.docker.com/docker-hub/builds/*). If you have a Docker Hub account (see "Container Registries" on page 28), you can create a trigger against a GitHub or BitBucket repository which will automatically build and publish new containers to Docker Hub.

Gitkube

Gitkube (*https://gitkube.sh/*) is a self-hosted tool that runs in your Kubernetes cluster, watches a Git repo, and automatically builds and pushes a new container when one of your triggers is executed. It's very simple and portable, and easy to set up.

Flux

The pattern of triggering a CD pipeline (or other automated processes) on Git branches or tags is sometimes called *GitOps* (*https://www.weave.works/blog/gitops-operations-by-pull-request*). Flux (*https://github.com/weaveworks/flux*) extends this idea by watching for changes to a container registry, instead of a Git repo. When a new container is pushed, Flux will deploy it automatically to your Kubernetes cluster.

Keel

Keel (*https://keel.sh/*), like Flux, is concerned with deploying new container images from a registry. It can be configured to respond to webhooks, send and receive Slack messages, wait for approvals before deploying, and do other useful workflows.

A CD Pipeline with Cloud Build

Now that you know the general principles of CD, and have learned about some of the tooling options, let's look at a complete, end-to-end example of a CD pipeline.

The idea is not that you should necessarily use exactly the same tools and configuration as we have here; rather, we hope you'll get a sense of how everything fits together, and can adapt some parts of this example to suit your own environment.

In this example we'll be using Google Cloud Platform (GCP), Google Kubernetes Engine clusters (GKE), and Google Cloud Build, but we don't rely on any specific features of those products. You can replicate this kind of pipeline using whatever tools you prefer.

If you'd like to work through this example using your own GCP account, please bear in mind that it uses some chargeable resources. It won't cost a fortune, but you'll want to delete and clean up any cloud resources afterwards to make sure you don't get billed more than necessary.

Setting Up Google Cloud and GKE

If you're signing up to Google Cloud for the first time, you'll be eligible for a fairly substantial free credit, which should enable you to run Kubernetes clusters and other resources for quite a while without being charged. You can find out more and create an account at the Google Cloud Platform site (*https://cloud.google.com/free*).

Once you are signed up and logged in to your own Google Cloud project, follow these instructions (*https://cloud.google.com/kubernetes-engine/docs/how-to/creating-a-cluster*) to create a GKE cluster.

Next, initialize Helm in the cluster (see "Helm: A Kubernetes Package Manager" on page 64).

Now, to set up the pipeline, we'll walk you through the following steps:

1. Fork the demo repository into your own personal GitHub account.
2. Create a Cloud Build trigger for building and testing on a push to any Git branch.
3. Create a trigger for deploying to GKE based on Git tags.

Forking the Demo Repository

If you have a GitHub account, use the GitHub interface to fork the demo repo (*https://github.com/cloudnativedevops/demo*).

If you're not using GitHub, make a copy of our repo and push it to your own Git server.

Introducing Cloud Build

In Cloud Build, like Drone and many other modern CD platforms, each step of your build pipeline consists of running a container. The build steps are defined using a YAML file that lives in your Git repo.

When the pipeline is triggered by a commit, Cloud Build makes a copy of the repo at that specific commit SHA, and executes each pipeline step in order.

Inside the demo repository there is a folder called *hello-cloudbuild*. In that folder you'll find the *cloudbuild.yaml* file that defines our Cloud Build pipeline.

Let's look at each of the build steps in this file in turn.

Building the Test Container

Here's the first step:

```
- id: build-test-image
  dir: hello-cloudbuild
  name: gcr.io/cloud-builders/docker
  entrypoint: bash
  args:
    - -c
    - |
      docker image build --target build --tag demo:test .
```

Like all Cloud Build steps, this consists of a set of YAML key-value pairs:

- id gives a human-friendly label to the build step.
- dir specifies the subdirectory of the Git repo to work in.
- name identifies the container to run for this step.

- entrypoint specifies the command to run in the container, if not the default.

- args gives the necessary arguments to the entrypoint command.

And that's it!

The purpose of this step is to build a container that we can use to run our application's tests. Since we are using a multi-stage build (see "Understanding Dockerfiles" on page 25), we want to build only the first stage for now. So we run this command:

```
docker image build --target build --tag demo:test .
```

The `--target build` argument tells Docker to only build the part in the Dockerfile under FROM `golang:1.14-alpine AS build` and stop before moving on to the next step.

This means that the resulting container will still have Go installed, along with any of the packages or files used in the step labeled `...AS build`. This will essentially be a throwaway container, only used for running the test suite of our application, and then it will be discarded.

Running the Tests

Here's the next step:

```
- id: run-tests
  dir: hello-cloudbuild
  name: gcr.io/cloud-builders/docker
  entrypoint: bash
  args:
    - -c
    - |
      docker container run demo:test go test
```

Since we tagged our throwaway container as `demo:test`, that temporary image will still be available for the rest of this build inside Cloud Build, and this step will run `go test` against that container. If any tests fail, the build will exit and report the failure. Otherwise, it will continue to the next step.

Building the Application Container

Here we run `docker build` again, but without the `--target` flag, so that we run the whole multistage build, ending up with the final application container:

```
- id: build-app
  dir: hello-cloudbuild
  name: gcr.io/cloud-builders/docker
  entrypoint: bash
  args:
    - -c
```

```
        - |
          docker build --tag gcr.io/${PROJECT_ID}/demo:${COMMIT_SHA} .
```

Validating the Kubernetes Manifests

At this point we have a container that has passed tests and is ready to run in Kubernetes. To actually deploy it, though, we are using a Helm chart, and in this step we'll run `helm template` to generate the Kubernetes manifests, and then pipe them through the `kubeval` tool to check them (see "kubeval" on page 236):

```
    - id: kubeval
      dir: hello-cloudbuild
      name: cloudnatived/helm-cloudbuilder
      entrypoint: bash
      args:
        - -c
        - |
          helm template ./k8s/demo/ | kubeval
```

 Note that we're using our own Helm container image here (cloud natived/helm-cloudbuilder). Oddly for a tool aimed specifically at deploying containers, Helm does not have an official container image. You can use ours for the example, but in production you'll probably want to build your own.

Publishing the Image

Assuming the pipeline completes successfully, Cloud Build will automatically publish the resulting container image to the registry. To specify which images you want to publish, list them under `images` in the Cloud Build file:

```
    images:
      - gcr.io/${PROJECT_ID}/demo:${COMMIT_SHA}
```

Git SHA Tags

What's with the `COMMIT_SHA` tag? In Git, every commit has a unique identifier, called a SHA (named for the Secure Hash Algorithm that generates it). A SHA is a long string of hex digits, like `5ba6bfd64a31eb4013ccaba27d95cddd15d50ba3`.

If you use this SHA to tag your image, it provides a link to the Git commit that generated it, which is also a snapshot of the exact code that is in the container. The nice thing about tagging build artifacts with the originating Git SHA is that you can build and test lots of feature branches simultaneously, without any conflicts.

Now that you've seen how the pipeline works, let's turn our attention to the build triggers that will actually execute the pipeline, based on our specified conditions.

Creating the First Build Trigger

A Cloud Build trigger specifies a Git repo to watch, a condition on which to activate (such as pushing to a particular branch or tag), and a pipeline file to execute.

Go ahead and create a new trigger now. Log in to your Google Cloud project and browse to *https://console.cloud.google.com/cloud-build/triggers?pli=1*.

Click the Add Trigger button to make a new build trigger, and select GitHub as the source repository.

You'll be asked to grant permission for Google Cloud to access your GitHub repo. Select YOUR_GITHUB_USERNAME/demo and Google Cloud will link to your repository.

Next, configure the trigger as shown in Figure 14-1:

You can name the trigger whatever you like. Under the branch section, keep the default .*; this will match any branch.

Change the Build configuration section from Dockerfile to cloudbuild.yaml.

The cloudbuild.yaml Location field tells Cloud Build where to find our pipeline file containing the build steps. In this case, it will be *hello-cloudbuild/cloudbuild.yaml*.

Click the Create trigger button when you are done. You're now ready to test the trigger and see what happens!

Testing the Trigger

Go ahead and make a change to your copy of demo repository. For example, let's create a new branch and modify the greeting from Hello to Hola:

```
cd hello-cloudbuild
git checkout -b hola
Switched to a new branch hola
```

Edit both *main.go* and *main_test.go*, replace Hello with Hola, or whatever greeting you like, and save both files.

Run the tests yourself to make sure everything works:

```
go test
PASS
ok    github.com/cloudnativedevops/demo/hello-cloudbuild 0.011s
```

Now commit the changes and push them to your forked repository. If all is well, this should trigger Cloud Build to start a new build. Browse to *https://console.cloud.google.com/cloud-build/builds*.

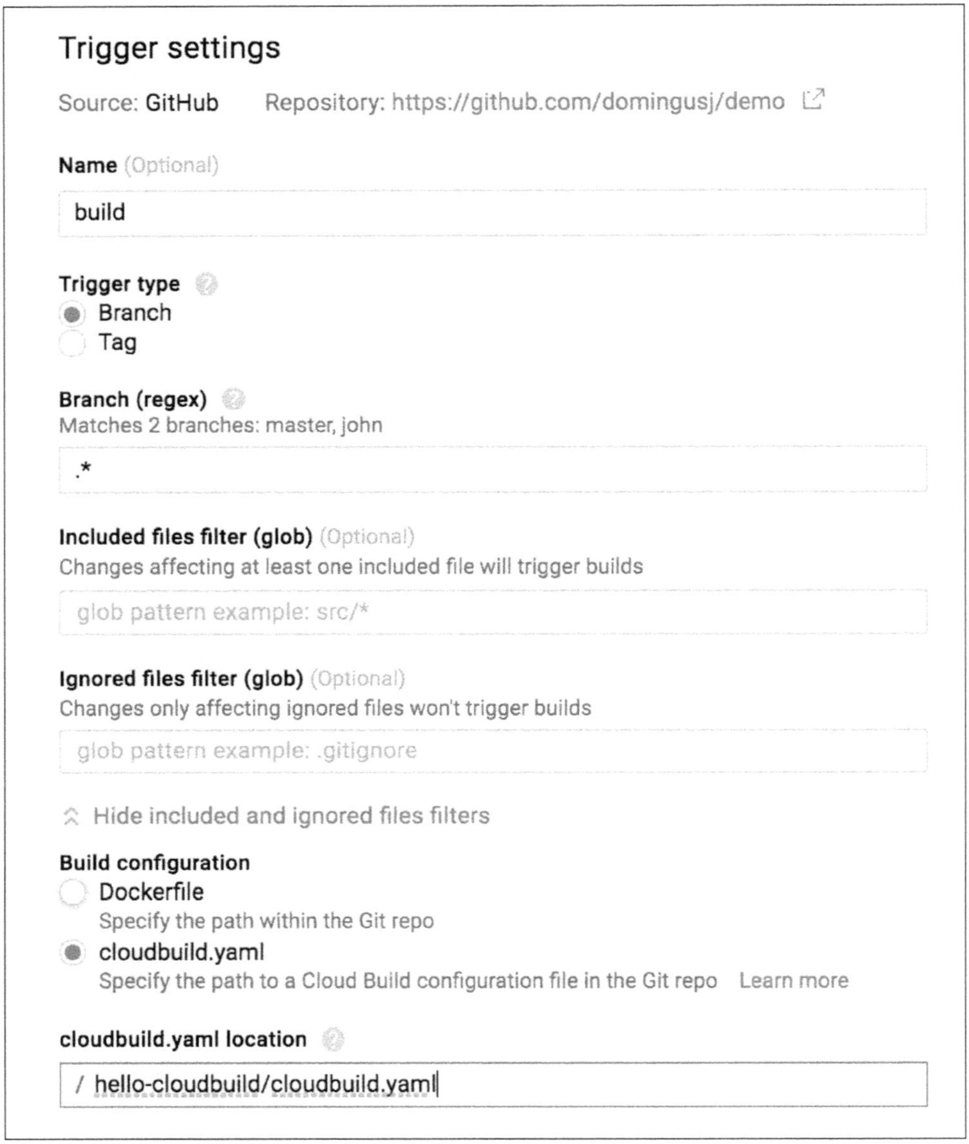

Trigger settings

Source: **GitHub**   Repository: https://github.com/domingusj/demo ↗

Name (Optional)

> build

Trigger type ⓘ
- ● Branch
- ○ Tag

Branch (regex) ⓘ
Matches 2 branches: master, john

> .*

Included files filter (glob) (Optional)
Changes affecting at least one included file will trigger builds

> glob pattern example: src/*

Ignored files filter (glob) (Optional)
Changes only affecting ignored files won't trigger builds

> glob pattern example: .gitignore

≳ Hide included and ignored files filters

Build configuration
- ○ Dockerfile
  Specify the path within the Git repo
- ● cloudbuild.yaml
  Specify the path to a Cloud Build configuration file in the Git repo   Learn more

cloudbuild.yaml location ⓘ

> / hello-cloudbuild/cloudbuild.yaml|

Figure 14-1. Create Trigger

You'll see the list of recent builds in your project. You should see one at the top of the list for the current change you just pushed. It may be still running, or it may have already finished.

Hopefully you will see a green check indicating that all steps passed. If not, check the log output in the build and see what failed.

Assuming it passed, a container should have been published into your private Google Container Registry tagged with the Git commit SHA of your change.

Deploying from a CD Pipeline

So now you can trigger a build with a Git push, run tests, and publish the final container to the registry. At this stage, you're ready to deploy that container to Kubernetes.

For this example we will imagine there are two environments, one for production, and one for staging, and we will deploy them into separate namespaces: staging-demo and production-demo.

We will configure Cloud Build to deploy to staging when it sees a Git tag containing staging, and to production when it sees production. This requires a new pipeline, in a separate YAML file, *cloudbuild-deploy.yaml*. Here are the steps.

Getting credentials for the Kubernetes cluster

To deploy to Kubernetes with Helm, we'll need to configure kubectl to talk to our cluster:

```
- id: get-kube-config
  dir: hello-cloudbuild
  name: gcr.io/cloud-builders/kubectl
  env:
  - CLOUDSDK_CORE_PROJECT=${_CLOUDSDK_CORE_PROJECT}
  - CLOUDSDK_COMPUTE_ZONE=${_CLOUDSDK_COMPUTE_ZONE}
  - CLOUDSDK_CONTAINER_CLUSTER=${_CLOUDSDK_CONTAINER_CLUSTER}
  - KUBECONFIG=/workspace/.kube/config
  args:
    - cluster-info
```

In this step we reference some variables like ${_CLOUDSDK_CORE_PROJECT}. We can define these variables either in the build trigger, as we will in this example, or in the pipeline file itself, under the substitutions heading:

```
substitutions:
  _CLOUDSDK_CORE_PROJECT=demo_project
```

User-defined substitutions must begin with an underscore character (_) and use only uppercase letters and numbers. Cloud Build also gives us some predefined substitutions, such as $PROJECT_ID and $COMMIT_SHA (full list here (*https://cloud.google.com/cloud-build/docs/configuring-builds/substitute-variable-values*)).

You will also need to authorize the Cloud Build service account to have permission to make changes to your Kubernetes Engine cluster. Under the IAM section in GCP, grant the service account for Cloud Build the *Kubernetes Engine Developer* IAM role in your project.

Adding an environment tag

In this step we'll tag the container with the same Git tag that triggered the deploy:

```
- id: update-deploy-tag
  dir: hello-cloudbuild
  name: gcr.io/cloud-builders/gcloud
  args:
    - container
    - images
    - add-tag
    - gcr.io/${PROJECT_ID}/demo:${COMMIT_SHA}
    - gcr.io/${PROJECT_ID}/demo:${TAG_NAME}
```

Deploying to the cluster

Here we run Helm to actually upgrade the application in the cluster, using the Kubernetes credentials that we acquired earlier:

```
- id: deploy
  dir: hello-cloudbuild
  name: cloudnatived/helm-cloudbuilder
  env:
    - KUBECONFIG=/workspace/.kube/config
  args:
    - helm
    - upgrade
    - --install
    - ${TAG_NAME}-demo
    - --namespace=${TAG_NAME}-demo
    - --values
    - k8s/demo/${TAG_NAME}-values.yaml
    - --set
    - container.image=gcr.io/${PROJECT_ID}/demo
    - --set
    - container.tag=${COMMIT_SHA}
    - ./k8s/demo
```

We are passing a few additional flags to the `helm upgrade` command:

namespace
: The namespace where the application should be deployed

values
: The Helm values file to use for this environment

set container.image
: Sets the container name to deploy

set container.tag
: Deploys the image with this specific tag (the originating Git SHA)

Creating a Deploy Trigger

Now let's add triggers for deploying to staging and production.

Create a new trigger in Cloud Build as you did in "Creating the First Build Trigger" on page 257, but this time configure it to trigger a build when a tag is pushed instead of a branch.

Also, instead of using the *hello-cloudbuild/cloudbuild.yaml* file, for this build we will use *hello-cloudbuild/cloudbuild-deploy.yaml*.

In the Substitution variables section, we'll set values specific to the staging build:

- _CLOUDSDK_CORE_PROJECT needs to be set to the value of your Google Cloud project ID where your GKE cluster is running.

- _CLOUDSDK_COMPUTE_ZONE should match the availability zone of your cluster (or region, if it's a regional cluster).

- _CLOUDSDK_CONTAINER_CLUSTER is the actual name of your GKE cluster.

These variables mean we can use the same YAML file for deploying both staging and production, even if we wanted to run these environments in separate clusters, or even separate GCP projects.

Once you have created the trigger for the staging tag, go ahead and try it out by pushing a staging tag to the repo:

```
git tag -f staging
git push -f origin refs/tags/staging
Total 0 (delta 0), reused 0 (delta 0)
To github.com:domingusj/demo.git
 * [new tag]              staging -> staging
```

As before, you can watch the build progress (*https://console.cloud.google.com/projectse lector/cloud-build/builds?supportedpurview=project*).

If all goes as planned, Cloud Build should successfully authenticate to your GKE cluster and deploy the staging version of your application into the staging-demo namespace.

You can verify this by checking the GKE dashboard (*https://console.cloud.google.com/ kubernetes/workload*) (or use helm status).

Finally, follow the same steps to create a trigger that deploys to production on a push to the production tag.

Optimizing Your Build Pipeline

If you're using a container-based CD pipeline tool like Cloud Build, it's important to make each step's container as small as possible (see "Minimal Container Images" on page 26). When you're running tens or hundreds of builds a day, the increased pull time of obese containers really adds up.

For example, if you're using Sops to decrypt secrets (see "Encrypting Secrets with Sops" on page 196), the official `mozilla/sops` container image is about 800 MiB. By building your own custom image with a multi-stage build, you can reduce the image size to around 20 MiB. Since this image will be pulled on every build, making it 40 times smaller is worth it.

A version of Sops with a modified Dockerfile to build a minimal container image is available (*https://github.com/bitfield/sops*).

Adapting the Example Pipeline

We hope this example demonstrates the key concepts of a CD pipeline. If you're using Cloud Build, you can use the example code as a starting point for setting up your own pipeline. If you're using other tools, it should be relatively easy to adapt the steps we've shown here to work in your own environment.

Summary

Setting up a continuous deployment pipeline for your applications allows you to deploy software consistently, reliably, and quickly. Ideally developers should be able to push code to the source control repository and all of the build, test, and deploy phases will happen automatically in a centralized pipeline.

Because there are so many options for CD software and techniques, we can't give you a single recipe that'll work for everybody. Instead, we've aimed to show you how and why CD is beneficial, and give you a few important things to think about when you come to implement it in your own organization:

- Deciding which CD tools to use is an important process when building a new pipeline. All of the tools we mention throughout this book could likely be incorporated into almost any existing CD tool.

- Jenkins, GitLab, Drone, Cloud Build, and Spinnaker are just a few of the popular CD tools that work well with Kubernetes. There are also many newer tools such as Gitkube, Flux, and Keel that are specifically built for automating deployments to Kubernetes clusters.

- Defining the build pipeline steps with code allows you to track and modify these steps alongside application code.

- Containers enable developers to promote build artifacts up through environments, such as testing, staging, and eventually production, ideally without having to rebuild a new container.

- Our example pipeline using Cloud Build should be easily adaptable for other tools and types of applications. The overall build, test, and deploy steps are largely the same in any CD pipeline, regardless of the tools used or type of software.

CHAPTER 15

Observability and Monitoring

Nothing is ever completely right aboard a ship.

—William Langewiesche, *The Outlaw Sea*

In this chapter we'll consider the question of observability and monitoring for cloud native applications. What is observability? How does it relate to monitoring? How do you do monitoring, logging, metrics, and tracing in Kubernetes?

What Is Observability?

Observability may not be a familiar term to you, though it's becoming increasingly popular as a way to express the larger world beyond traditional monitoring. Let's tackle *monitoring* first before we see how observability extends it.

What Is Monitoring?

Is your website working right now? Go check; we'll wait. The most basic way to know whether all your applications and services are working as they should is to look at them yourself. But when we talk about monitoring in a DevOps context, we mostly mean *automated monitoring*.

Automated monitoring is checking the availability or behavior of a website or service, in some programmatic way, usually on a regular schedule, and usually with some automated way of alerting human engineers if there's a problem. But what defines a problem?

Black-Box Monitoring

Let's take the simple case of a static website; say, the blog (*https://cloudnativedevops blog.com/*) that accompanies this book.

If it's not working at all, it just won't respond, or you'll see an error message in the browser (we hope not, but nobody's perfect). So the simplest possible monitoring check for this site is to fetch the home page and check the HTTP status code (200 indicates a successful request). You could do this with a command-line HTTP client such as `httpie` or `curl`. If the exit status from the client is nonzero, there was a problem fetching the website.

But suppose something went wrong with the web server configuration, and although the server is working and responding with HTTP 200 OK status, it is actually serving a blank page (or some sort of default or welcome page, or maybe the wrong site altogether). Our simple-minded monitoring check won't complain at all, because the HTTP request succeeds. However, the site is actually down for users: they can't read our fascinating and informative blog posts.

A more sophisticated monitoring check might look for some specific text on the page, such as *Cloud Native DevOps*. This would catch the problem of a misconfigured, but working, web server.

Beyond static pages

You can imagine that more complex websites might need more complex monitoring. For example, if the site had a facility for users to log in, the monitoring check might also try to log in with a precreated user account and alert if the login fails. Or if the site had a search function, the check might fill in a text field with some search text, simulate clicking the search button, and verify that the results contain some expected text.

For simple websites, a *yes/no* answer to the question "Is it working?" may be sufficient. For cloud native applications, which tend to be more complex distributed systems, the question may turn into multiple questions:

- Is my application available everywhere in the world? Or only in some regions?
- How long does it take to load for most of my users?
- What about users who may have slow download speeds?
- Are all of the features of my website working as intended?
- Are certain features working slowly or not at all, and how many users are affected?
- If it relies on a third-party service, what happens to my application when that external service is faulty or unavailable?
- What happens when my cloud provider has an outage?

It starts to become clear that in the world of monitoring cloud native distributed systems, not very much is clear at all.

The limits of black-box monitoring

However, no matter how complicated these checks get, they all fall into the same category of monitoring: *black-box monitoring*. Black-box checks, as the name suggests, observe only the external behavior of a system, without any attempt to observe what's going on inside it.

Until a few years ago, black-box monitoring, as performed by popular tools such as Nagios, Icinga, Zabbix, Sensu, and Check_MK, was pretty much the state of the art. To be sure, having *any* kind of automated monitoring of your systems is a huge improvement on having none. But there are a few limitations of black-box checks:

- They can only detect predictable failures (for example, a website not responding).
- They only check the behavior of the parts of the system that are exposed to the outside.
- They are passive and reactive; they only tell you about a problem *after* it's happened.
- They can answer the question "What's broken?", but not the more important question "Why?"

To answer the *why?* question, we need to move beyond black-box monitoring.

There's a further issue with this kind of *up/down* test; what does *up* even mean?

What Does "Up" Mean?

In operations we're used to measuring the resilience and availability of our applications in *uptime*, usually measured as a percentage. For example, an application with 99% uptime was unavailable for no more than 1% of the relevant time period. 99.9% uptime, referred to as *three nines*, translates to about nine hours downtime a year, which would be a good figure for the average web application. Four nines (99.99%) is less than an hour's downtime per year, and five nines (99.999%) is about five minutes.

So, the more nines the better, you might think. But looking at things this way misses an important point:

> Nines don't matter if users aren't happy.
>
> —Charity Majors (*https://red.ht/2FMZcMZ*)

Nines don't matter if users aren't happy

As the saying goes, what gets measured gets maximized. So you'd better be very careful what you measure. If your service isn't working for users, it doesn't matter what your internal metrics say: *the service is down*. There are lots of ways a service can be making users unhappy, even if it's nominally *up*.

To take an obvious one, what if your website takes 10 seconds to load? It might work fine after that, but if it's too slow to respond, it might as well be down completely. Users will just go elsewhere.

Traditional black-box monitoring might attempt to deal with this problem by defining a load time of, say, five seconds as *up*, and anything over that is considered *down* and an alert generated. But what if users are experiencing all sorts of different load times, from 2 seconds to 10 seconds? With a hard threshold like this, you could consider the service *down* for some users, but *up* for others. What if load times are fine for users in North America, but unusable from Europe or Asia?

Cloud native applications are never up

While you could go on refining more complex rules and thresholds to enable us to give an *up/down* answer about the status of the service, the truth is that the question is irredeemably flawed. Distributed systems like cloud native applications are never *up* (*http://red.ht/2hMHwSL*); they exist in a constant state of partially degraded service.

This is an example of a class of problems called *gray failures* (*https://blog.acolyer.org/2017/06/15/gray-failure-the-achilles-heel-of-cloud-scale-systems/*). Gray failures are, by definition, hard to detect, especially from a single point of view or with a single observation.

So while black-box monitoring may be a good place to start your observability journey, it's important to recognize that you shouldn't stop there. Let's see if we can do better.

Logging

Most applications produce *logs* of some kind. Logs are a series of records, usually with some kind of timestamps to indicate when records were written, and in what order. For example, a web server records each request in its logs, including information such as:

- The URI requested
- The IP address of the client
- The HTTP status of the response

If the application encounters an error, it usually logs this fact, along with some information that may or may not be helpful for operators to figure out what caused the problem.

Often, logs from a wide range of applications and services will be *aggregated* into a central database (Elasticsearch, for example), where they can be queried and graphed to help with troubleshooting. Tools like Logstash and Kibana, or hosted services such as Splunk and Loggly, are designed to help you gather and analyze large volumes of log data.

The limits of logging

Logs can be useful, but they have their limitations too. The decision about what to log or not to log is taken by the programmer at the time the application is written. Therefore, like black-box checks, logs can only answer questions or detect problems that can be predicted in advance.

It can also be hard to extract information from logs, because every application writes logs in a different format, and operators often need to write customized parsers for each type of log record to turn it into usable numerical or event data.

Because logs have to record enough information to diagnose any conceivable kind of problem, they usually have a poor signal-to-noise ratio. If you log everything, it's difficult and time-consuming to wade through hundreds of pages of logs to find the one error message you need. If you log only occasional errors, it's hard to know what *normal* looks like.

Logs are hard to scale

Logs also don't scale very well with traffic. If every user request generates a log line that has to be sent to the aggregator, you can end up using a lot of network bandwidth (which is thus unavailable to serve users), and your log aggregator can become a bottleneck.

Many hosted logging providers also charge by the volume of logs you generate, which is understandable, but unfortunate: it incentivizes you financially to log less information, and to have fewer users and serve less traffic!

The same applies to self-hosted logging solutions: the more data you store, the more hardware, storage, and network resources you have to pay for, and the more engineering time goes into merely keeping log aggregation working.

Is logging useful in Kubernetes?

We talked a little about how containers generate logs and how you can inspect them directly in Kubernetes, in "Viewing a Container's Logs" on page 119. This is a useful debugging technique for individual containers.

If you do use logging, you should use some form of structured data, like JSON, which can be automatically parsed (see "The Observability Pipeline" on page 273) rather than plain-text records.

While centralized log aggregation (to services like ELK) can be useful with Kubernetes applications, it's certainly not the whole story. While there are some business use cases for centralized logging (audit and security requirements, for example, or customer analytics), logs can't give us all the information we need for true observability.

For that, we need to look beyond logs, to something much more powerful.

Introducing Metrics

A more sophisticated way of gathering information about your services is to use *metrics*. As the name suggests, a metric is a numerical measure of something. Depending on the application, relevant metrics might include:

- The number of requests currently being processed
- The number of requests handled per minute (or per second, or per hour)
- The number of errors encountered when handling requests
- The average time it took to serve requests (or the peak time, or the 99th percentile)

It's also useful to gather metrics about your infrastructure as well as your applications:

- The CPU usage of individual processes or containers
- The disk I/O activity of nodes and servers
- The inbound and outbound network traffic of machines, clusters, or load balancers

Metrics help answer the why? question

Metrics open up a new dimension of monitoring beyond simply *working/not working*. Like the speedometer in your car, or the temperature scale on your thermometer, they give you numerical information about what's happening. Unlike logs, metrics can easily be processed in all sorts of useful ways: drawing graphs, taking statistics, or alerting on predefined thresholds. For example, your monitoring system might alert you if the error rate for an application exceeds 10% for a given time period.

Metrics can also help answer the *why?* question about problems. For example, suppose users are experiencing long response times (high *latency*) from your app. You check your metrics, and you see that the spike in the *latency* metric coincides with a similar spike in the *CPU usage* metric for a particular machine or component. That immediately gives you a clue about where to start looking for the problem. The component may be wedged, or repeatedly retrying some failed operation, or its host node may have a hardware problem.

Metrics help predict problems

Also, metrics can be *predictive*: when things go wrong, it usually doesn't happen all at once. Before a problem is noticeable to you or your users, an increase in some metric may indicate that trouble is on the way.

For example, the disk usage metric for a server may creep up, and up over time eventually reach the point where the disk actually runs out of space and things start failing. If you alerted on that metric before it got into failure territory, you could prevent the failure from happening at all.

Some systems even use machine learning techniques to analyze metrics, detect anomalies, and reason about the cause. This can be helpful, especially in complex distributed systems, but for most purposes, simply having a way to gather, graph, and alert on metrics is plenty good enough.

Metrics monitor applications from the inside

With black-box checks, operators have to make guesses about the internal implementation of the app or service, and predict what kind of failures might happen and what effect this would have on external behavior. By contrast, metrics allow application developers to export key information about the hidden aspects of the system, based on their knowledge of how it actually works (and fails):

> Stop reverse engineering applications and start monitoring from the inside.
> —Kelsey Hightower, Monitorama 2016 (*https://vimeo.com/173610242*)

Tools like Prometheus, statsd, and Graphite, or hosted services such as Datadog, New Relic, and Dynatrace, are widely used to gather and manage metrics data.

We'll talk much more in Chapter 16 about metrics, including what kinds you should focus on, and what you should do with them. For now, let's complete our survey of observability with a look at tracing.

Tracing

Another useful technique in the monitoring toolbox is *tracing*. It's especially important in distributed systems. While metrics and logs tell you what's going on with each individual component of your system, tracing follows a single user request through its whole life cycle.

Suppose you're trying to figure out why some users are experiencing very high latency for requests. You check the metrics for each of your system components: load balancer, ingress, web server, application server, database, message bus, and so on, and everything appears normal. So what's going on?

When you trace an individual (hopefully representative) request from the moment the user's connection is opened to the moment it's closed, you'll get a picture of how that overall latency breaks down for each stage of the request's journey through the system.

For example, you may find that the time spent handling the request in each stage of the pipeline is normal, except for the database hop, which is 100 times longer than normal. Although the database is working fine and its metrics show no problems, for some reason the application server is having to wait a very long time for requests to the database to complete.

Eventually you track down the problem to excessive packet loss over one particular network link between the application servers and the database server. Without the *request's eye view* provided by distributed tracing, it's hard to find problems like this.

Some popular distributed tracing tools include Zipkin, Jaeger, and LightStep. Engineer Masroor Hasan has written a useful blog post (*https://medium.com/@mas roor.hasan/tracing-infrastructure-with-jaeger-on-kubernetes-6800132a677*) describing how to use Jaeger for distributed tracing in Kubernetes.

The OpenTracing framework (*https://opentracing.io/*) (part of the Cloud Native Computing Foundation) aims to provide a standard set of APIs and libraries for distributed tracing.

Observability

Because the term *monitoring* means different things to different people, from plain old black-box checks to a combination of metrics, logging, and tracing, it's becoming common to use *observability* as a catch-all term that covers all these techniques. The observability of your system is a measure of how well-instrumented it is, and how easily you can find out what's going on inside it. Some people say that observability is a superset of monitoring, others that observability reflects a completely different mindset from traditional monitoring.

Perhaps the most useful way to distinguish these terms is to say that monitoring tells you *whether the system is working*, while observability prompts you to ask *why it's not working*.

Observability is about understanding

More generally, observability is about *understanding*: understanding what your system does and how it does it. For example, if you roll out a code change that is designed to improve the performance of a particular feature by 10%, then observability can tell you whether or not it worked. If performance only went up a tiny bit, or worse, went down slightly, you need to revisit the code.

On the other hand, if performance went up 20%, the change succeeded beyond your expectations, and maybe you need to think about why your predictions fell short. Observability helps you build and refine your mental model of how the different parts of your system interact.

Observability is also about *data*. We need to know what data to generate, what to collect, how to aggregate it (if appropriate), what results to focus on, and how to query and display them.

Software is opaque

In traditional monitoring we have lots of data about the *machinery*; CPU loads, disk activity, network packets, and so on. But it's hard to reason backwards from that about what our *software* is doing. To do that, we need to instrument the software itself:

> Software is opaque by default; it must generate data in order to clue humans in on what it is doing. Observable systems allow humans to answer the question, "Is it working properly?", and if the answer is no, to diagnose the scope of impact and identify what is going wrong.
>
> —Christine Spang (*https://twitter.com/jetarrant/status/1025122034735435776*) (Nylas)

Building an observability culture

Even more generally, observability is about *culture*. It's a key tenet of the DevOps philosophy to close the loop between developing code, and running it at scale in production. Observability is the primary tool for closing that loop. Developers and operations staff need to work closely together to instrument services for observability, and then figure out the best way to consume and act on the information it provides:

> The goal of an observability team is not to collect logs, metrics or traces. It is to build a culture of engineering based on facts and feedback, and then spread that culture within the broader organization.
>
> —Brian Knox (*https://twitter.com/taotetek/status/974989022115323904*) (DigitalOcean)

The Observability Pipeline

How does observability work, from a practical point of view? It's common to have multiple data sources (logs, metrics, and so on) connected to various different data stores in a fairly ad hoc way.

For example, your logs might go to an ELK server, while metrics go to three or four different managed services, and traditional monitoring checks report to yet another service. This isn't ideal.

For one thing, it's hard to scale. The more data sources and stores you have, the more interconnections there are, and the more traffic over those connections. It doesn't make sense to put engineering time into making all of those different kinds of connections stable and reliable.

Also, the more tightly integrated your systems become with specific solutions or providers, the harder it is to change them or to try out alternatives.

An increasingly popular way to address this problem is the *observability pipeline* (*https://dzone.com/articles/the-observability-pipeline*):

> With an observability pipeline, we decouple the data sources from the destinations and provide a buffer. This makes the observability data easily consumable. We no longer have to figure out what data to send from containers, VMs, and infrastructure, where to send it, and how to send it. Rather, all the data is sent to the pipeline, which handles filtering it and getting it to the right places. This also gives us greater flexibility in terms of adding or removing data sinks, and it provides a buffer between data producers and consumers.
>
> —Tyler Treat

An observability pipeline brings great advantages. Now, adding a new data source is just a matter of connecting it to your pipeline. Similarly, a new visualization or alerting service just becomes another consumer of the pipeline.

Because the pipeline buffers data, nothing gets lost. If there's a sudden surge in traffic and an overload of metrics data, the pipeline will buffer it rather than drop samples.

Using an observability pipeline requires a standard metrics format (see "Prometheus" on page 300) and, ideally, structured logging from applications using JSON or some other sensible serialized data format. Instead of emitting raw text logs, and parsing them later with fragile regular expressions, start with structured data from the very beginning.

Monitoring in Kubernetes

So now that we understand a little more about what black-box monitoring is and how it relates to observability in general, let's see how it applies to Kubernetes applications.

External Black-Box Checks

As we've seen, black-box monitoring can only tell you that your application is down. But that's still very useful information. All kinds of things could be wrong with a cloud native application, and it might still be able to serve some requests acceptably. Engineers can work on fixing internal problems like slow queries and elevated error rates, without users really being aware of an issue.

However, a more serious class of problems results in a full-scale *outage*; the application is unavailable or not working for the majority of users. This is bad for the users, and depending on the application, it may be bad for your business as well. In order to detect an outage, your monitoring needs to consume the service in the same way that a user would.

Monitoring mimics user behavior

For example, if it's an HTTP service, the monitoring system needs to make HTTP requests to it, not just TCP connections. If the service just returns static text, monitoring can check the text matches some expected string. Usually, it's a little bit more complicated than that, and as we saw in "Black-Box Monitoring" on page 265, your checks can be more complicated too.

In an outage situation, though, it's quite likely that a simple text match will be sufficient to tell you the application is down. But making these black-box checks from inside your infrastructure (for example, in Kubernetes) isn't enough. An outage can result from all sorts of problems and failures between the user and the outside edge of your infrastructure, including:

- Bad DNS records
- Network partitions
- Packet loss
- Misconfigured routers
- Missing or bad firewall rules
- Cloud provider outage

In all these situations, your internal metrics and monitoring might show no problems at all. Therefore, your top-priority observability task should be to monitor the availability of your services from some point external to your own infrastructure. There are many third-party services that can do this kind of monitoring for you (sometimes called *monitoring as a service*, or MaaS), including Uptime Robot, Pingdom, and Wormly.

Don't build your own monitoring infrastructure

Most of these services have either a free tier, or fairly inexpensive subscriptions, and whatever you pay for them you should regard as an essential operating expense. Don't bother trying to build your own external monitoring infrastructure; it's not worth it. The cost of a year's Pro subscription to Uptime Robot likely would not pay for a single hour of your engineers' time.

Look for the following critical features in an external monitoring provider:

- HTTP/HTTPS checks
- Detect if your TLS certificate is invalid or expired
- Keyword matching (alert when the keyword is missing *or* when it's present)
- Automatically create or update checks via an API
- Alerts by email, SMS, webhook, or some other straightforward mechanism

Throughout this book we champion the idea of infrastructure as code, so it should be possible to automate your external monitoring checks with code as well. For example, Uptime Robot has a simple REST API for creating new checks, and you can automate it using a client library or command-line tool like uptimerobot (*https://github.com/bitfield/uptimerobot*).

It doesn't matter which external monitoring service you use, so long as you use one. But don't stop there. In the next section we'll see what we can do to monitor the health of applications inside the Kubernetes cluster itself.

Internal Health Checks

Cloud native applications fail in complex, unpredictable, and hard-to-detect ways. Applications have to be designed to be resilient and degrade gracefully in the face of unexpected failures, but ironically, the more resilient they are, the harder it is to detect these failures by black-box monitoring.

To solve this problem, applications can, and should, do their own health checking. The developer of a particular feature or service is best placed to know what it needs to be *healthy*, and she can write code to check this that exposes the results in a way that can be monitored from outside the container (like an HTTP endpoint).

Are users happy?

Kubernetes gives us a simple mechanism for applications to advertise their liveness or readiness, as we saw in "Liveness Probes" on page 72, so this is a good place to start. Usually, Kubernetes liveness or readiness probes are pretty simple; the application always responds "OK" to any requests. If it doesn't respond, therefore, Kubernetes considers it to be down or unready.

However, as many programmers know from bitter experience, just because a program runs, doesn't necessarily mean it works correctly. A more sophisticated readiness probe should ask "What does this application need to do its job?"

For example, if it needs to talk to a database, it can check that it has a valid and responsive database connection. If it depends on other services, it can check the services' availability. (Because health checks are run frequently, though, they shouldn't do anything too expensive that might affect serving requests from real users.)

Note that we're still giving a binary yes/no response to the readiness probe. It's just a more informed answer. What we're trying to do is answer the question "Are users happy?" as accurately as possible.

Services and circuit breakers

As you know, if a container's *liveness* check fails, Kubernetes will restart it automatically, in an exponential backoff loop. This isn't really that helpful in the situation where there's nothing wrong with the container, but one of its dependencies is failing. The semantics of a failed *readiness* check, on the other hand, are "I'm fine, but I can't serve user requests at the moment."

In this situation, the container will be removed from any Services it's a backend for, and Kubernetes will stop sending it requests until it becomes ready again. This is a better way to deal with a failed dependency.

Suppose you have a chain of 10 microservices, each of which depends on the next for some critical part of its work. The last service in the chain fails. The next-to-last service will detect this and start failing its readiness probe. Kubernetes will disconnect it, and the next service in line detects this, and so on up the chain. Eventually the front-end service will fail, and (hopefully) a black-box monitoring alert will be tripped.

Once the problem with the base service is fixed, or maybe cured by an automatic restart, all the other services in the chain will automatically become ready again in turn, without being restarted or losing any state. This is an example of what's called a *circuit breaker pattern* (*https://martinfowler.com/bliki/CircuitBreaker.html*). When an application detects a downstream failure, it takes itself out of service (via the readiness check) to prevent any more requests being sent to it until the problem is fixed.

Graceful degradation

While a circuit breaker is useful for surfacing problems as soon as possible, you should design your services to avoid having the whole system fail when one or more component services are unavailable. Instead, try to make your services *degrade gracefully*: even if they can't do everything they're supposed to, maybe they can still do some things.

In distributed systems, we have to assume that services, components, and connections will fail mysteriously and intermittently more or less all the time. A resilient system can handle this without failing completely.

Summary

There's a lot to say about monitoring. We didn't have space to say as much as we wanted to, but we hope this chapter has given you some useful information about traditional monitoring techniques, what they can do and what they can't do, and how things need to change in a cloud native environment.

The notion of *observability* introduces us to a bigger picture than traditional log files and black-box checks. Metrics form an important part of this picture, and in the next and final chapter, we'll take you on a deep dive into the world of metrics in Kubernetes.

Before turning the page, though, you might like to recall these key points:

- Black-box monitoring checks observe the external behavior of a system, to detect predictable failures.

- Distributed systems expose the limitations of traditional monitoring, because they're not in either *up* or *down* states: they exist in a constant state of partially degraded service. In other words, nothing is ever completely right aboard a ship.

- Logs can be useful for post-incident troubleshooting, but they're hard to scale.

- Metrics open up a new dimension beyond simply *working/not working*, and give you continuous numerical time-series data on hundreds or thousands of aspects of your system.

- Metrics can help you answer the *why* question, as well as identify problematic trends before they lead to outages.

- Tracing records events with precise timing through the life cycle of an individual request, to help you debug performance problems.

- Observability is the union of traditional monitoring, logging, metrics, and tracing, and all the other ways you can understand your system.

- Observability also represents a shift toward a team culture of engineering based on facts and feedback.

- It's still important to check that your user-facing services are up, with external black-box checks, but don't try to build your own: use a third-party monitoring service like Uptime Robot.

- Nines don't matter if users aren't happy.

CHAPTER 16

Metrics in Kubernetes

It is possible to know so much about a subject that you become totally ignorant.

—Frank Herbert, *Chapterhouse: Dune*

In this chapter we'll take the concept of metrics that we introduced in Chapter 15 and dive into the details: what kind of metrics are there, which ones are important for cloud native services, how do you choose which metrics to focus on, how do you analyze metrics data to get actionable information, and how do you turn raw metrics data into useful dashboards and alerts? Finally, we'll outline some of the options for metrics tools and platforms.

What Are Metrics, Really?

Since a metrics-centered approach to observability is relatively new to the DevOps world, let's take a moment to talk about exactly what metrics are, and how best to use them.

As we saw in "Introducing Metrics" on page 270, metrics are numerical measures of specific things. A familiar example from the world of traditional servers is the memory usage of a particular machine. If only 10% of physical memory is currently allocated to user processes, the machine has spare capacity. But if 90% of the memory is in use, the machine is probably pretty busy.

So one valuable kind of information that metrics can give us is a snapshot of what's going on at a particular instant. But we can do more. Memory usage goes up and down all the time as workloads start and stop, but sometimes what we're interested in is the *change* in memory usage over time.

Time Series Data

If you sample memory usage regularly, you can create a *time series* of that data. Figure 16-1 shows a graph of the time series data for memory usage on a Google Kubernetes Engine node, over one week. This gives a much more intelligible picture of what's happening than a handful of instantaneous values.

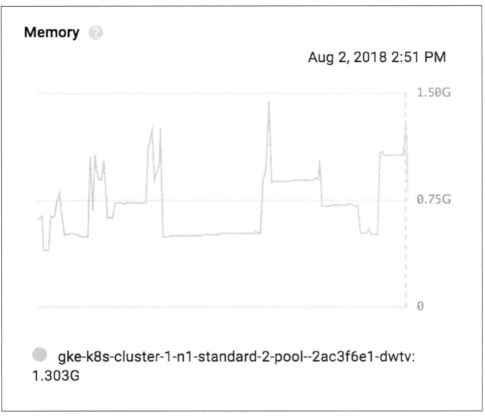

Figure 16-1. Time series graph of memory usage for a GKE node

Most metrics that we're interested in for cloud native observability purposes are expressed as time series. They are also all numeric. Unlike log data, for example, metrics are values that you can do math and statistics on.

Counters and Gauges

What kind of numbers are they? While some quantities can be represented by integers (the number of physical CPUs in a machine, for example), most require a decimal part, and to save having to handle two different types of numbers, metrics are almost always represented as floating-point decimal values.

Given that, there are two main types of metric values: *counters* and *gauges*. Counters can only go up (or reset to zero); they're suitable for measuring things like number of requests served and number of errors received. Gauges, on the other hand, can vary up and down; they're useful for continuously varying quantities like memory usage, or for expressing ratios of other quantities.

The answers to some questions are just *yes* or *no*: whether a particular endpoint is responding to HTTP connections, for example. In this case the appropriate metric will be a gauge with a limited range of values: 0 and 1, perhaps.

For example, an HTTP check of an endpoint might be named something like `http.can_connect`, and its value might be 1 when the endpoint is responding, and 0 otherwise.

What Can Metrics Tell Us?

What use are metrics? Well, as we've seen earlier in this chapter, metrics can tell you when things are broken. For example, if your error rate suddenly goes up (or requests to your support page suddenly spike), that may indicate a problem. You can generate alerts automatically for certain metrics based on a threshold.

But metrics can also tell you how well things are working, for example, how many simultaneous users your application is currently supporting. Long-term trends in these numbers can be useful for both operations decision making, and for business intelligence.

Choosing Good Metrics

At first, you might think "If metrics are good, then lots of metrics must be even better!" But it doesn't work that way. You can't monitor everything. Google Stackdriver, for example, exposes literally hundreds of metrics about your cloud resources, including:

`instance/network/sent_packets_count`
    The number of network packets sent by each compute instance

`storage/object_count`
    The total number of objects in each storage bucket

`container/cpu/utilization`
    The percentage of its CPU allocation that a container is currently using

The list goes on (*https://cloud.google.com/monitoring/api/metrics*) (and on, and on). Even if you could display graphs of all these metrics at once, which would need a monitor screen the size of a house, you'd never be able to take in all that information and deduce anything useful from it. To do that, we need to *focus* on the subset of metrics that we care about.

So what should you focus on when observing your own applications? Only you can answer that, but we have a few suggestions that may be helpful. In the rest of this section, we'll outline some common metrics patterns for observability, aimed at different audiences and designed to meet different requirements.

It's worth saying that this is a perfect opportunity for some DevOps collaboration, and you should start thinking and talking about what metrics you'll need at the beginning of development, not at the end (see "Learning Together" on page 6).

Services: The RED Pattern

Most people using Kubernetes are running some kind of web service: users make requests, and the application sends responses. The *users* could be programs or other services; in a distributed system based on microservices, each service makes requests to other services and uses the results to serve information back to yet more services. Either way, it's a request-driven system.

What's useful to know about a request-driven system?

- One obvious thing is the number of *requests* you're getting.
- Another is the number of requests that failed in various ways; that is to say, the number of *errors*.
- A third useful metric is the *duration* of each request. This gives you an idea how well your service is performing and how unhappy your users might be getting.

The *Requests-Errors-Duration* pattern (RED for short) is a classic observability tool that goes back to the earliest days of online services. Google's *Site Reliability Engineering* book talks about the Four Golden Signals, which are essentially requests, errors, duration, and *saturation* (we'll talk about saturation in a moment).

Engineer Tom Wilkie, who coined the *RED* acronym, has outlined the rationale behind this pattern in a blog post:

> Why should you measure the same metrics for every service? Surely each service is special? The benefits of treating each service the same, from a monitoring perspective, is scalability in your operations teams. By making every service look, feel and taste the same, this reduces the cognitive load on those responding to an incident. As an aside, if you treat all your services the same, many repetitive tasks become automatable.
>
> —Tom Wilkie

So how exactly do we measure these numbers? Since the total number of requests only ever goes up, it's more useful to look at request *rate*: the number of requests per second, for example. This gives us a meaningful idea of how much traffic the system is handling over a given time interval.

Because error rate is related to request rate, it's a good idea to measure errors as a percentage of requests. So, for example, a typical service dashboard might show:

- Requests received per second
- Percentage of requests that returned an error
- Duration of requests (also known as *latency*)

Resources: The USE Pattern

You've seen that the RED pattern gives you useful information about how your services are performing, and how your users are experiencing them. You could think of this as a top-down way of looking at observability data.

On the other hand, the USE pattern (*http://www.brendangregg.com/usemethod.html*), developed by Netflix performance engineer Brendan Gregg, is a bottom-up approach that is intended to help analyze performance issues and find bottlenecks. USE stands for Utilization, Saturation, and Errors.

Rather than services, with USE we're interested in *resources*: physical server components such as CPU and disks, or network interfaces and links. Any of these could be a bottleneck in system performance, and the USE metrics will help us find out which:

Utilization
> The average time that the resource was busy serving requests, or the amount of resource capacity that's currently in use. For example, a disk that is 90% full would have a utilization of 90%.

Saturation
> The extent to which the resource is overloaded, or the length of the queue of requests waiting for this resource to become available. For example, if there are 10 processes waiting to run on a CPU, it has a saturation value of 10.

Errors
> The number of times an operation on that resource failed. For example, a disk with some bad sectors might have an error count of 25 failed reads.

Measuring this data for the key resources in your system is a good way to spot bottlenecks. Resources with low utilization, no saturation, and no errors are probably fine. Anything that deviates from this is worth looking into. For example, if one of your network links is saturated, or has a high number of errors, it may be contributing to overall performance problems:

The USE Method is a simple strategy you can use to perform a complete a check of system health, identifying common bottlenecks and errors. It can be deployed early in the investigation and quickly identify problem areas, which then can be studied in more detail other methodologies, if need be.

The strength of USE is its speed and visibility: by considering all resources, you are unlikely to overlook any issues. It will, however, only find certain types of issues – bottlenecks and errors – and should be considered as one tool in a larger toolbox.

—Brendan Gregg

Business Metrics

We've looked at application and service metrics ("Services: The RED Pattern" on page 282), which are likely to be of most interest to developers, and hardware metrics ("Resources: The USE Pattern" on page 283), which are helpful to ops and infrastructure engineers. But what about the business? Can observability help managers and executives understand how the business is performing, and give them useful input to business decisions? And what metrics would contribute to this?

Most businesses already track the key performance indicators (KPIs) that matter to them, such as sales revenue, profit margin, and cost of customer acquisition. These metrics usually come from the finance department and don't need support from developers and infrastructure staff.

But there are other useful business metrics that can be generated by applications and services. For example, a subscription business, such as a software-as-a-service (SaaS) product, needs to know data about its subscribers:

- Funnel analytics (how many people hit the landing page, how many click through to the sign-up page, how many complete the transaction, and so on)

- Rate of sign-ups and cancellations (churn)

- Revenue per customer (useful for calculating monthly recurring revenue, average revenue per customer, and lifetime value of a customer)

- Effectiveness of help and support pages (for example, percentage of people who answered yes to the question "Did this page solve your problem?")

- Traffic to the *system status* announcement page (which often spikes when there are outages or degraded services)

Much of this information is easier to gather by generating real-time metrics data from your applications, rather than to try and analyze after the fact by processing logs and querying databases. When you're instrumenting your applications to produce metrics, don't neglect information that is important to the business.

There isn't necessarily a clear line between the observability information the business and customer engagement experts need, and what the technical experts need. In fact, there's a lot of overlap. It's wise to discuss metrics at an early stage with all the stakeholders involved, and agree on what data needs to be collected, how often, how it's aggregated, and so on.

Nonetheless, these two (or more) groups have different questions to ask of the observability data that you're gathering, so each will need its own view on that data. You can use the common *data lake* to create dashboards (see "Graphing Metrics with Dashboards" on page 293) and reports for each of the different groups involved.

Kubernetes Metrics

We've talked about observability and metrics in general terms, and looked at different types of data and ways to analyze it. So how does all this apply to Kubernetes? What metrics is it worth tracking for Kubernetes clusters, and what kinds of decisions can they help us make?

At the lowest level, a tool called cAdvisor monitors the resource usage and performance statistics for the containers running on each cluster node—for example, how much CPU, memory, and disk space each container is using. cAdvisor is part of the Kubelet.

Kubernetes itself consumes this cAdvisor data, by querying the Kubelet, and uses the information to make decisions about scheduling, autoscaling, and so on. But you can also export this data to a third-party metrics service, where you can graph it and alert on it. For example, it would be useful to track how much CPU and memory each container is using.

You can also monitor Kubernetes itself, using a tool called kube-state-metrics. This listens to the Kubernetes API and reports information about logical objects such as nodes, Pods, and Deployments. This data can also be very useful for cluster observability. For example, if there are replicas configured for a Deployment that can't currently be scheduled for some reason (perhaps the cluster doesn't have enough capacity), you probably want to know about it.

As usual, the problem is not a shortage of metrics data, but deciding which key metrics to focus on, track, and visualize. Here are some suggestions.

Cluster health metrics

To monitor the health and performance of your cluster at the top level, you should be looking at least at the following:

- Number of nodes
- Node health status
- Number of Pods per node, and overall
- Resource usage/allocation per node, and overall

These overview metrics will help you understand how your cluster is performing, whether it has enough capacity, how its usage is changing over time, and whether you need to expand or reduce the cluster.

If you're using a managed Kubernetes service such as GKE, unhealthy nodes will be detected automatically and autorepaired (providing autorepair is enabled for your cluster and node pool). It's still useful to know if you're getting an unusual number of failures, which may indicate an underlying problem.

Deployment metrics

For all your deployments, it's worth knowing:

- Number of deployments
- Number of configured replicas per deployment
- Number of unavailable replicas per deployment

It's especially useful to be able to track this information over time if you have enabled some of the various autoscaling options available in Kubernetes (see "Autoscaling" on page 102). Data on unavailable replicas in particular will help alert you about capacity issues.

Container metrics

At the container level, the most useful things to know are:

- Number of containers/Pods per node, and overall
- Resource usage for each container against its requests/limits (see "Resource Requests" on page 70)
- Liveness/readiness of containers
- Number of container/Pod restarts
- Network in/out traffic and errors for each container

Because Kubernetes automatically restarts containers that have failed or exceeded their resource limits, you need to know how often this is happening. An excessive number of restarts may tell you there's a problem with a particular container. If a container is regularly busting its resource limits, that could be a sign of a program bug, or maybe just that you need to increase the limits slightly.

Application metrics

Whichever language or software platform your application uses, there's probably a library or tool available to allow you to export custom metrics from it. These are primarily useful for developers and operations teams to be able to see what the application is doing, how often it's doing it, and how long it takes. These are key indicators of performance problems or availability issues.

The choice of application metrics to capture and export depends on exactly what your application does. But there are some common patterns. For example, if your service consumes messages from a queue, processes them, and takes some action based on the message, you might want to report the following metrics:

- Number of messages received
- Number of successfully processed messages
- Number of invalid or erroneous messages
- Time to process and act on each message
- Number of successful actions generated
- Number of failed actions

Similarly, if your application is primarily request-driven, you can use the RED pattern (see "Services: The RED Pattern" on page 282):

- Requests received
- Errors returned
- Duration (time to handle each request)

It can be difficult to know what metrics are going to be useful when you're at an early stage of development. If in doubt, record everything. Metrics are cheap; you may discover an unforeseen production issue a long way down the line, thanks to metrics data that didn't seem important at the time.

> If it moves, graph it. Even it doesn't move, graph it anyway, because it might someday.
>
> —Laurie Denness (*https://twitter.com/lozzd/status/604064191603834880*) (Bloomberg)

If you are going to have your application generate business metrics (see "Business Metrics" on page 284), you can calculate and export these as custom metrics too.

Another thing that may be useful to the business is to see how your applications are performing against any Service Level Objectives (SLO) or Service Level Agreements (SLA) that you may have with customers, or how vendor services are performing against SLOs. You could create a custom metric to show the target request duration (for example, 200 ms), and create a dashboard that overlays this on the actual current performance.

Runtime metrics

At the runtime level, most metrics libraries will also report useful data about what the program is doing, such as:

- Number of processes/threads/goroutines
- Heap and stack usage
- Nonheap memory usage
- Network/I/O buffer pools
- Garbage collector runs and pause durations (for garbage-collected languages)
- File descriptors/network sockets in use

This kind of information can be very valuable for diagnosing poor performance, or even crashes. For example, it's quite common for long-running applications to gradually use more and more memory until they are killed and restarted due to exceeding Kubernetes resource limits. Application runtime metrics may help you work out exactly where this memory is going, especially in combination with custom metrics about what the application is doing.

Now that you have some idea what metrics data is worth capturing, we'll turn in the next section to what to *do* with this data: in other words, how to analyze it.

Analyzing Metrics

Data is not the same thing as information. In order to get useful information out of the raw data we've captured, we need to aggregate, process, and analyze it, which means doing *statistics* on it. Statistics can be a slippery business, especially in the abstract, so let's illustrate this discussion with a concrete example: request duration.

In "Services: The RED Pattern" on page 282 we mentioned that you should track the duration metric for service requests, but we didn't say exactly how to do that. What precisely do we mean by duration? Usually, we're interested in the time the user has to wait to get a response to some request.

With a website, for example, we might define duration as the time between when the user connects to the server, and when the server first starts sending data in response.

(The user's total waiting time is actually longer than that, because making the connection takes some time, and so does reading the response data and rendering it in a browser. We usually don't have access to that data, though, so we just capture what we can.)

And every request has a different duration, so how do we aggregate the data for hundreds or even thousands of requests into a single number?

What's Wrong with a Simple Average?

The obvious answer is to take the average. But on closer inspection, what *average* means isn't necessarily straightforward. An old joke in statistics is that the average person has slightly less than two legs. To put it another way, most people have more than the average number of legs. How can this be?

Most people have two legs, but some have one or none, bringing down the overall average. (Possibly some people have more than two, but many more people have fewer than two.) A simple average doesn't give us much useful information about leg distribution in the population, or about most people's experience of leg ownership.

There is also more than one kind of average. You probably know that the commonplace notion of *average* refers to the *mean*. The mean of a set of values is the total of all the values, divided by the number of values. For example, the mean age of a group of three people is the total of their ages divided by 3.

The *median*, on the other hand, refers to the value that would divide the set into two equal halves, one containing values larger than the median, and the other containing smaller values. For example, in any group of people, half of them are taller than the median height, by definition, and half of them are shorter.

Means, Medians, and Outliers

What's the problem with taking a straightforward average (mean) of request duration? One important problem is that the mean is easily skewed by *outliers*: one or two extreme values can distort the average quite a bit.

Therefore, the median, which is less affected by outliers, is a more helpful way of averaging metrics than the mean. If the median latency for a service is 1 second, half your users experience a latency less than 1 second, and half experience more.

Figure 16-2 shows how averages can be misleading. All four sets of data have the same mean value, but look very different when shown graphically (statisticians know this example as *Anscombe's quartet*). Incidentally, this is also a good way to demonstrate the importance of graphing data, rather than just looking at raw numbers.

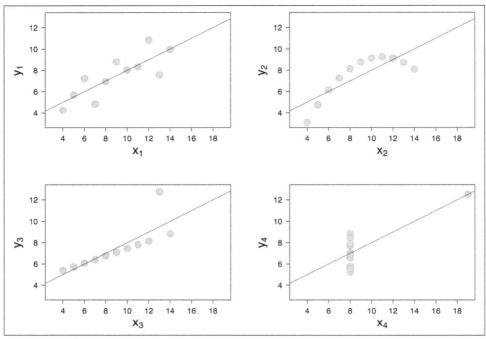

Figure 16-2. These four datasets all have the same average (mean) value, (image (https://en.wikipedia.org/wiki/Anscombe's_quartet#/media/File:Anscombe's_quartet_3.svg) by Schutz, CC BY-SA 3.0).

Discovering Percentiles

When we talk about metrics for observing request-driven systems, we're usually interested in knowing what the *worst* latency experience is for users, rather than the average. After all, having a median latency of 1 second for all users is no comfort to the small group who may be experiencing latencies of 10 seconds or more.

The way to get this information is to break down the data into *percentiles*. The 90th percentile latency (often referred to as *P90*) is the value that is greater than that experienced by 90% of your users. To put it another way, 10% of users will experience a latency higher than the P90 value.

Expressed in this language, the median is the 50th percentile, or P50. Other percentiles that are often measured in observability are P95 and P99, the 95th and 99th percentile, respectively.

Applying Percentiles to Metrics Data

Igor Wiedler of Travis CI has produced a nice demonstration (*https://igor.io/latency*) of what this means in concrete terms, starting from a dataset of 135,000 requests to a production service over 10 minutes (Figure 16-3). As you can see, this data is noisy and spiky, and it's not easy to draw any useful conclusions from it in a raw state.

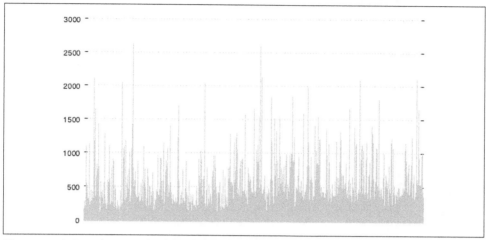

Figure 16-3. Raw latency data for 135,000 requests, in ms

Now let's see what happens if we average that data over 10-second intervals (Figure 16-4). This looks wonderful: all the data points are below 50 ms. So it looks as though most of our users are experiencing latencies of less than 50 ms. But is that really true?

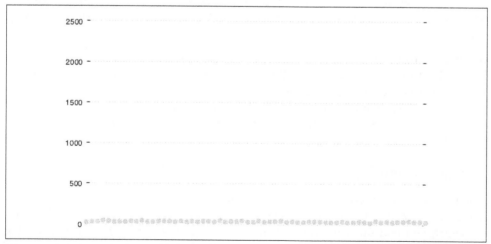

Figure 16-4. Average (mean) latency for the same data, over 10-second intervals

Let's graph the P99 latency instead. This is the maximum latency observed, if we discard the highest 1% of samples. It looks very different (Figure 16-5). Now we see a jagged pattern with most of the values clustering between 0 and 500 ms, with several requests spiking close to 1,000 ms.

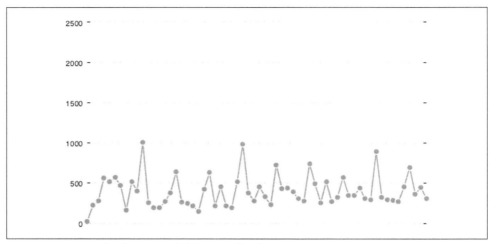

Figure 16-5. P99 (99th percentile) latency for the same data

We Usually Want to Know the Worst

Since we disproportionately notice slow web requests, the P99 data is likely to give us a more realistic picture of the latency experienced by users. For example, consider a high-traffic website with 1 million page views per day. If the P99 latency is 10 seconds, then 10,000 page views take longer than 10 seconds. That's a lot of unhappy users.

But it gets worse: in distributed systems, each page view may require tens or even hundreds of internal requests to fulfill. If the P99 latency of each internal service is 10s, and 1 page view makes 10 internal requests, then the number of slow page views rises to 100,000 per day. Now around 10% of users are unhappy, which is a big problem (*https://engineering.linkedin.com/performance/who-moved-my-99th-percentile-latency*).

Beyond Percentiles

One problem with percentile latencies, as implemented by many metrics services, is that requests tend to be sampled locally, and statistics then aggregated centrally. Consequently, you end up with your P99 latency being an average of the P99 latencies reported by each agent, potentially across hundreds of agents.

Well, a percentile is already an average, and trying to average averages is a well-known statistical trap (*https://en.wikipedia.org/wiki/Simpson%27s_paradox*). The result is not necessarily the same as the real average.

Depending how we choose to aggregate the data, the final P99 latency figure can vary by as much as a factor of 10. That doesn't bode well for a meaningful result. Unless your metrics service ingests every single raw event and produces a true average, this figure will be unreliable.

Engineer Yan Cui (*https://medium.com/theburningmonk-com/we-can-do-better-than-percentile-latencies-2257d20c3b39*) suggests that a better approach is to monitor what's *wrong*, not what's *right*:

> What could we use instead of percentiles as the primary metric to monitor our application's performance with and alert us when it starts to deteriorate?
>
> If you go back to your SLOs or SLAs, you probably have something along the lines of "99% of requests should complete in 1s or less". In other words, less than 1% of requests is allowed to take more than 1s to complete.
>
> So what if we monitor the percentage of requests that are over the threshold instead? To alert us when our SLAs are violated, we can trigger alarms when that percentage is greater than 1% over some predefined time window.
>
> —Yan Cui

If each agent submits a metric of total requests and the number of requests that were over threshold, we *can* usefully average that data to produce a percentage of requests that exceeded SLO—and alert on it.

Graphing Metrics with Dashboards

So far in this chapter we've learned about why metrics are useful, what metrics we should record, and some useful statistical techniques for analyzing them in bulk. All well and good, but what are we actually going to *do* with all these metrics?

The answer is simple: we're going to graph them, group them into dashboards, and possibly alert on them. We'll talk about alerting in the next section, but for now, let's look at some tools and techniques for graphing and dashboarding.

Use a Standard Layout for All Services

When you have more than a handful of services, it makes sense to always lay out your dashboards in the same way for each service. Someone responding to an on-call page can glance at the dashboard for the affected service and know how to interpret it immediately, without having to be familiar with that specific service.

Tom Wilkie, in a Weaveworks blog post (*https://www.weave.works/blog/the-red-method-key-metrics-for-microservices-architecture/*), suggests the following standard format (see Figure 16-6:

- One row per service

- Request and error rate on the left, with errors as a percentage of requests
- Latency on the right

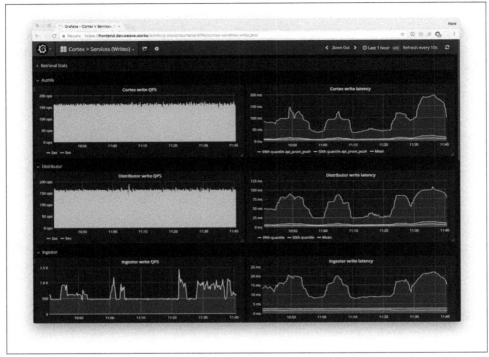

Figure 16-6. Weaveworks suggested dashboard layout for services

You don't have to use this exact layout; the important thing is that you always use the same layout for every dashboard, and that everyone is familiar with it. You should review your key dashboards regularly (at least once a week), looking at the previous week's data, so that everyone knows what *normal* looks like.

The *requests, errors, duration* dashboard works well for services (see "Services: The RED Pattern" on page 282). For resources, such as cluster nodes, disks, and network, the most useful things to know are usually *utilization, saturation, errors* (see "Resources: The USE Pattern" on page 283).

Build an Information Radiator with Master Dashboards

If you have a hundred services, you have a hundred dashboards, but you probably won't look at them very often. It's still important to have that information available (to help spot which service is failing, for example), but at this scale you need a more general overview.

To do this, make a master dashboard that shows requests, errors, and duration across *all* your services, in aggregate. Don't do anything fancy like stacked area charts; stick to simple line graphs of total requests, total error percentage, and total latency. These are easier to interpret and more accurate visualizations than complex charts.

Ideally, you'll be using an *information radiator* (also known as a wallboard, or Big Visible Chart). This is a large screen showing key observability data that is visible to everybody in the relevant team or office. The purpose of an information radiator is:

- To show the current system status at a glance
- To send a clear message about which metrics the team considers important
- To make people familiar with what *normal* looks like

What should you include on this radiator screen? Only vital information. *Vital*, in the sense of *really important*, but also in the sense of *vital signs*: information that tells you about the life of the system.

The vital signs monitors you'll see next to a hospital bed are a good example. They show the key metrics for human beings: heart rate, blood pressure, oxygen saturation, temperature, and breathing rate. There are many other metrics you could track for a patient, and they have medically important uses, but at the master dashboard level, these are the key ones. Any serious medical problem will show up in one or more of these metrics; everything else is a matter of diagnostics.

Similarly, your information radiator should show the vital signs of your business or service. If it has numbers, it should probably have no more than four or five numbers. If it has graphs, it should have no more than four or five graphs.

It's tempting to cram too much information into a dashboard, so it looks complicated and technical. That's not the goal. The goal is to focus on a few key things and make them easily visible from across a room (see Figure 16-7).

Dashboard Things That Break

Apart from your main information radiator, and dashboards for individual services and resources, you may want to create dashboards for specific metrics that tell you important things about the system. You might be able to think of some of these things already, based on the system architecture. But another useful source of information is *things that break*.

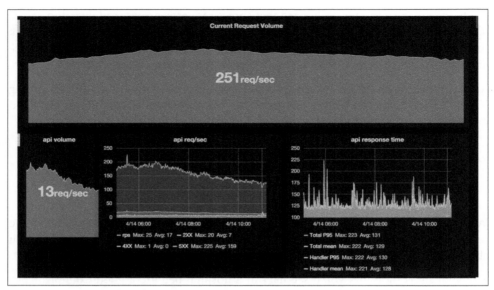

Figure 16-7. Example information radiator produced by Grafana Dash Gen (https://github.com/uber/grafana-dash-gen)

Every time you have an incident or outage, look for a metric, or combination of metrics, which would have alerted you to this problem in advance. For example, if you have a production outage caused by a server running out of disk space, it's possible that a graph of disk space on that server would have warned you beforehand that the available space was trending downward and heading into outage territory.

We're not talking here about problems that happen over a period of minutes or even hours; those are usually caught by automated alerts (see "Alerting on Metrics" on page 297). Rather, we're interested in the slow-moving icebergs that draw closer over days or weeks, and if you don't spot them and take avoiding action, will sink your system at the worst possible time.

After an incident, always ask "What would have warned us about this problem in advance, if only we'd been aware of it?" If the answer is a piece of data you already had, but didn't pay attention to, take action to highlight that data. A dashboard is one possible way to do this.

While alerts can tell you that some value has exceeded a preset threshold, you may not always know in advance what the danger level is. A graph lets you visualize how that value is behaving over long periods of time, and helps you detect problematic trends before they actually affect the system.

Alerting on Metrics

You might be surprised that we've spent most of this chapter talking about observability and monitoring without mentioning alerts. For some people, alerts are what monitoring is all about. We think that philosophy needs to change, for a number of reasons.

What's Wrong with Alerts?

Alerts indicate some unexpected deviation from a stable, working state. Well, distributed systems don't have those states!

As we've mentioned, large-scale distributed systems are never *up*; they're almost always in a state of partially degraded service (see "Cloud native applications are never up" on page 268). They have so many metrics that if you alert every time some metric goes outside normal limits, you'd be sending hundreds of pages a day to no good purpose:

> People are over-paging themselves because their observability blows and they don't trust their tools to let them reliably debug and diagnose the problem. So they get tens or hundreds of alerts, which they pattern-match for clues about what the root cause might be. They're flying blind. In the chaotic future we're all hurtling toward, you actually have to have the discipline to have radically **fewer** paging alerts, not more. Request rate, latency, error rate, saturation.
>
> —Charity Majors (*https://www.infoq.com/articles/charity-majors-observability-failure*)

For some unfortunate people, on-call alert pages are a way of life. This is a bad thing, not just for the obvious human reasons. Alert fatigue is a well-known issue in medicine, where clinicians can rapidly become desensitized by constant alarms, making them more likely to overlook a serious issue when it does arise.

For a monitoring system to be useful, it has to have a very high signal-to-noise ratio. False alarms are not only annoying, but dangerous: they reduce trust in the system, and condition people that alerts can be safely ignored.

Excessive, incessant, and irrelevant alarms were a major factor in the Three Mile Island disaster (*https://humanisticsystems.com/2015/10/16/fit-for-purpose-questions-about-alarm-system-design-from-theory-and-practice/*), and even when individual alarms are well-designed, operators can be overwhelmed by too many of them going off simultaneously.

An alert should mean one very simple thing: *Action needs to be taken now, by a person* (*https://www.infoworld.com/article/3268126/devops/beware-the-danger-of-alarm-fatigue-in-it-monitoring.html*).

If no action is needed, no alert is needed. If action needs to happen *sometime*, but not right now, the alert can be downgraded to an email or chat message. If the action can be taken by an automated system, then automate it: don't wake up a valuable human being.

On-call Should Not Be Hell

While the idea of being on-call for your own services is key to the DevOps philosophy, it's equally important that being on-call should be as painless an experience as possible.

Alert pages should be a rare and exceptional occurrence. When they do happen, there should be a well-established and effective procedure for handling them, which puts as little strain as possible on the responder.

Nobody should be on-call all the time. If this is the case, add more people to the rotation. You don't need to be a subject matter expert to be on-call: your main task is to triage the problem, decide if it needs action, and escalate it to the right people.

While the burden of on-call should be fairly distributed, people's personal circumstances differ. If you have a family, or other commitments outside work, it may not be so easy for you to take on-call shifts. It takes careful and sensitive management to arrange on-call in a way that's fair to everybody.

If the job involves being on-call, that should be made clear to the person when they're hired. Expectations about the frequency and circumstances of on-call shifts should be written into their contract. It's not fair to hire someone for a strictly 9–5 job, and then decide you also want them to be on-call nights and weekends.

On-call should be properly compensated with cash, time off in lieu, or some other meaningful benefit. This applies whether or not you actually receive any alerts; when you're on-call, to some extent you're at work.

There should also be a hard limit on the amount of time someone can spend on-call. People with more spare time or energy may want to volunteer to help reduce the stress on their coworkers, and that's great, but don't let anyone take on too much.

Recognize that when you put people on-call, you are spending human capital. Spend it wisely.

Urgent, Important, and Actionable Alerts

If alerts are so terrible, why are we talking about them at all? Well, you still need alerts. Things go wrong, blow up, fall over, and grind to a halt—usually at the most inconvenient time.

Observability is wonderful, but you can't find a problem when you're not looking for one. Dashboards are great, but you don't pay somebody to sit looking at a dashboard all day. For detecting an outage or issue that's happening right now, and drawing a human's attention to it, you can't beat automated alerts based on thresholds.

For example, you might want the system to alert you if error rates for a given service exceed 10% for some period of time, like 5 minutes. You might generate an alert when P99 latency for a service goes above some fixed value, like 1000 ms.

In general, if a problem has real or potential business impact, and action needs to be taken now, by a person, it's a possible candidate for an alert page.

Don't alert on every metric. Out of hundreds or possibly thousands of metrics, you should have only a handful of metrics that can generate alerts. Even when they do generate alerts, that doesn't necessarily mean you need to page somebody.

Pages should be restricted to only *urgent*, *important*, and *actionable* alerts:

- Alerts that are important, but not urgent, can be dealt with during normal working hours. Only things that can't wait till morning should be paged.
- Alerts that are urgent, but not important, don't justify waking someone up. For example, the failure of a little-used internal service that doesn't affect customers.
- If there's no immediate action that can be taken to fix it, there's no point paging about it.

For everything else, you can send asynchronous notifications: emails, Slack messages, support tickets, project issues, and so on. They will be seen and dealt with in a timely fashion, if your system is working properly. You don't need to send someone's cortisol levels skyrocketing by waking them up in the middle of the night with a blaring alarm.

Track Your Alerts, Out-of-Hours Pages, and Wake-ups

Your people are just as critical to your infrastructure as your cloud servers and Kubernetes clusters, if not more so. They're probably more expensive, and certainly more difficult to replace. It makes sense, then, to monitor what's happening to your people in just the same way as you monitor what's happening with your services.

The number of alerts sent in a given week is a good indicator of the overall health and stability of your system. The number of urgent pages, especially the number of pages sent out-of-hours, on weekends, and during normal sleep times, is a good indicator of your team's overall health and morale.

You should set a budget for the number of urgent pages, especially out of hours, and it should be very low. One or two out-of-hours pages per on-call engineer per week should probably be the limit. If you're regularly exceeding this, you need to fix the alerts, fix the system, or hire more engineers.

Review all urgent pages, at least weekly, and fix or eliminate any false alarms or unnecessary alerts. If you don't take this seriously, people won't take your alerts seriously. And if you regularly interrupt people's sleep and private life with unnecessary alerts, they will start looking for better jobs.

Metrics Tools and Services

Let's get into some specifics, then. What tools or services should you use to collect, analyze, and communicate metrics? In "Don't build your own monitoring infrastructure" on page 275, we made the point that, when faced with a commodity problem, you should use a commodity solution. Does that mean you should necessarily use a third-party, hosted metrics service like Datadog or New Relic?

The answer here isn't quite so clear-cut. While these services offer lots of powerful features, they can be expensive, especially at scale. There isn't such a compelling business case against running your own metrics server, because there is an excellent free and open source product available.

Prometheus

The de facto standard metrics solution in the cloud native world is Prometheus. It's very widely used, especially with Kubernetes, and almost everything can interoperate with Prometheus in some way, so it's the first thing you should consider when you're thinking about metrics monitoring options.

Prometheus is an open source systems monitoring and alerting toolkit, based on time series metrics data. The core of Prometheus is a server that collects and stores metrics. It also has various other optional components, such as an alerting tool (Alertmanager), and client libraries for programming languages such as Go, which you can use to instrument your applications.

It all sounds rather complicated, but in practice it's very simple. You can install Prometheus in your Kubernetes cluster with one command, using a standard Helm chart (see "Helm: A Kubernetes Package Manager" on page 64). It will then gather metrics automatically from the cluster, and also from any applications you tell it to, using a process called *scraping*.

Prometheus scrapes metrics by making an HTTP connection to your application on a prearranged port, and downloading whatever metrics data is available. It then stores the data in its database, where it will be available for you to query, graph, or alert on.

Prometheus's approach to collecting metrics is called *pull* monitoring. In this scheme, the monitoring server contacts the application and requests metrics data. The opposite approach, called *push*, and used by some other monitoring tools such as StatsD, works the other way: applications contact the monitoring server to send it metrics.

Like Kubernetes itself, Prometheus is inspired by Google's own infrastructure. It was developed at SoundCloud, but it takes many of its ideas from a tool called Borgmon. Borgmon, as the name suggests, was designed to monitor Google's Borg container orchestration system (see "From Borg to Kubernetes" on page 11):

> Kubernetes directly builds on Google's decade-long experience with their own cluster scheduling system, Borg. Prometheus's bonds to Google are way looser but it draws a lot of inspiration from Borgmon, the internal monitoring system Google came up with at about the same time as Borg. In a very sloppy comparison, you could say that Kubernetes is Borg for mere mortals, while Prometheus is Borgmon for mere mortals. Both are "second systems" trying to iterate on the good parts while avoiding the mistakes and dead ends of their ancestors.
>
> —Björn Rabenstein (SoundCloud)

You can read more about Prometheus on its site (*https://prometheus.io/*), including instructions on how to install and configure it for your environment.

While Prometheus itself is focused on the job of collecting and storing metrics, there are other high-quality open source options for graphing, dashboarding, and alerting. Grafana (*https://grafana.com/*) is a powerful and capable graphing engine for time series data (Figure 16-8).

The Prometheus project includes a tool called Alertmanager (*https://prometheus.io/docs/alerting/alertmanager/*), which works well with Prometheus but can also operate independently of it. Alertmanager's job is to receive alerts from various sources, including Prometheus servers, and process them (see "Alerting on Metrics" on page 297).

The first step in processing alerts is to deduplicate them. Alertmanager can then group alerts it detects to be related; for example, a major network outage might result in hundreds of individual alerts, but Alertmanager can group all of these into a single message, so that responders aren't overwhelmed with pages.

Finally, Alertmanager will route the processed alerts to an appropriate notification service, such as PagerDuty, Slack, or email.

Conveniently, the Prometheus metrics format is supported by a very wide range of tools and services, and this de facto standard is now the basis for OpenMetrics (*https://openmetrics.io/*), a Cloud Native Computing Foundation project to produce a neutral standard format for metrics data. But you don't have to wait for OpenMetrics to become a reality; right now, almost every metrics service, including Stackdriver, Cloudwatch, Datadog, and New Relic, can import and understand Prometheus data.

Figure 16-8. Grafana dashboard showing Prometheus data

Google Stackdriver

Although Stackdriver comes from Google, it's not limited to Google Cloud: it also works with AWS. Stackdriver can collect, graph, and alert on metrics and log data from a variety of sources. It will autodiscover and monitor your cloud resources, including VMs, databases, and Kubernetes clusters. Stackdriver brings all this data into a central web console where you can create custom dashboards and alerts.

Stackdriver understands how to get operational metrics from such popular software tools as Apache, Nginx, Cassandra, and Elasticsearch. If you want to include your own custom metrics from your applications, you can use Stackdriver's client library to export whatever data you want.

If you're in Google Cloud, Stackdriver is free for all GCP-related metrics; for custom metrics, or metrics from other cloud platforms, you pay per megabyte of monitoring data per month.

While not as flexible as Prometheus, or as sophisticated as more expensive tools such as Datadog, Stackdriver (*https://cloud.google.com/monitoring*) is a great way to get started with metrics without having to install or configure anything.

AWS Cloudwatch

Amazon's own cloud monitoring product, Cloudwatch, has a similar feature set to Stackdriver. It integrates with all AWS services, and you can export custom metrics using the Cloudwatch SDK or command-line tool.

Cloudwatch has a free tier that allows you to gather *basic* metrics (such as CPU utilization for VMs) at five-minute intervals, a certain number of dashboards and alarms, and so on. Over and above those you pay per metric, per dashboard, or per-alarm, and you can also pay for high-resolution metrics (one-minute intervals) on a per-instance basis.

Like Stackdriver, Cloudwatch (*https://aws.amazon.com/cloudwatch*) is basic, but effective. If your primary cloud infrastructure is AWS, Cloudwatch is a good place to start working with metrics, and for small deployments it may be all you ever need.

Azure Monitor

Monitor (*https://docs.microsoft.com/en-us/azure/azure-monitor/overview*) is the Azure equivalent of Google's Stackdriver or AWS Cloudwatch. It collects logs and metrics data from all your Azure resources, including Kubernetes clusters, and allows you to visualize and alert on it.

Datadog

In comparison to the cloud providers' built-in tools like Stackdriver and Cloudwatch, Datadog (*https://www.datadoghq.com/*) is a very sophisticated and powerful monitoring and analytics platform. It offers integrations for over 250 platforms and services, including all the cloud services from major providers, and popular software such as Jenkins, Varnish, Puppet, Consul, and MySQL.

Datadog also offers an application performance monitoring (APM) component, designed to help you monitor and analyze how your applications are performing. Whether you use Go, Java, Ruby, or any other software platform, Datadog can gather metrics, logs, and traces from your software, and answer questions for you like:

- What is the user experience like for a specific, individual user of my service?
- Who are the 10 customers who see the slowest responses on a particular endpoint?
- Which of my various distributed services are contributing to the overall latency of requests?

Together with the usual dashboarding (see Figure 16-9) and alerting features (automatable via the Datadog API and client libraries, including Terraform), Datadog also provides features like anomaly detection, powered by machine learning.

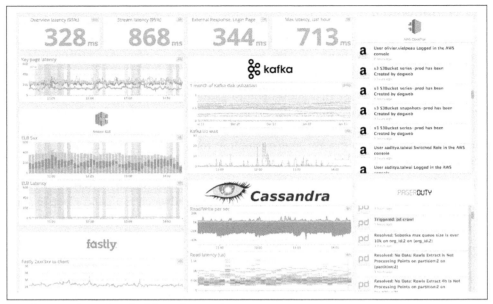

Figure 16-9. Datadog dashboard

As you'd expect, Datadog is also one of the more expensive monitoring services available, but if you're serious about observability and you have a complex infrastructure with performance-critical applications, the cost may well be worth it.

You can read more about Datadog at the website (*https://www.datadoghq.com/*).

New Relic

New Relic is a very well established and widely used metrics platform focused on application performance monitoring (APM). Its chief strength is in diagnosing performance problems and bottlenecks inside applications and distributed systems (see Figure 16-10). However, it also offers infrastructure metrics and monitoring, alerting, software analytics, and everything else you'd expect.

As with any enterprise-grade service, expect to pay a good deal for New Relic monitoring, especially at scale. If you're in the market for a premium corporate metrics platform, you'll probably be looking either at New Relic (slightly more application-focused) or Datadog (slightly more infrastructure focused). Both also offer good infrastructure as code support; for example, you can create monitoring dashboards and alerts for both New Relic and Datadog using official Terraform providers.

Figure 16-10. New Relic APM dashboard

Summary

Measure twice, cut once is a favorite saying of many engineers. In the cloud native world, without proper metrics and observability data it's very difficult to know what's going on. On the other hand, once you open the metrics floodgates, too much information can be just as useless as too little.

The trick is to gather the right data in the first place, process it in the right way, use it to answer the right questions, visualize it in the right way, and use it to alert the right people at the right time about the right things.

If you forget everything else in this chapter, remember this:

- Focus on the key metrics for each service: requests, errors, and duration (RED). For each resource: utilization, saturation, and errors (USE).

- Instrument your apps to expose custom metrics, both for internal observability, and for business KPIs.

- Useful Kubernetes metrics include, at the cluster level, the number of nodes, Pods per node, and resource usage of nodes.

- At the deployment level, track deployments and replicas, especially unavailable replicas, which might indicate a capacity problem.

- At the container level, track resource usage per container, liveness/readiness states, restarts, network traffic, and network errors.

- Build a dashboard for each service, using a standard layout, and a master information radiator that reports the vital signs of the whole system.

- If you alert on metrics, alerts should be urgent, important, and actionable. Alert noise creates fatigue and damages morale.

- Track and review the number of urgent pages your team receives, especially wake-ups and weekends.

- The de facto standard metrics solution in the cloud native world is Prometheus, and almost everything speaks the Prometheus data format.

- Third-party managed metrics services include Google Stackdriver, Amazon Cloudwatch, Datadog, and New Relic.

Afterword

There is nothing more difficult to take in hand, more perilous to conduct, or more uncertain in its success, than to take the lead in the introduction of a new order of things.

—Niccolò Machiavelli

Well, that was quite a ride. We've covered a lot in this book, but everything we've included has been determined by one simple principle: we think you *need to know* it if you're using Kubernetes in production.

They say an expert is just somebody who's one page ahead in the manual. It's quite likely that, if you're reading this book, you will be the Kubernetes expert for your organization, at least at first. We hope you'll find this manual useful, but it's only a starting point.

Where to Go Next

You may find these resources useful, both for learning more about Kubernetes and cloud native, and for keeping up with the latest news and developments:

http://slack.k8s.io/
> The official Kubernetes Slack organization. This is a good place to ask questions, and chat with other users.

https://discuss.kubernetes.io/
> A public forum for discussing all things Kubernetes.

https://kubernetespodcast.com/
> A weekly podcast put together by Google. Episodes usually run about 20 minutes and cover weekly news and usually interview someone involved with Kubernetes.

https://github.com/vmware-tanzu/tgik

TGIK8s is a weekly live video stream, started by Joe Beda at Heptio. The format usually involves about an hour of live demoing something in the Kubernetes ecosystem. All videos are archived and available to watch on-demand.

Not to be left out, we have a blog (*https://cloudnativedevopsblog.com/*) associated with this book that you may like to read. Check in every so often to see the latest news, updates, and blog posts about Cloud Native DevOps.

Here are some email newsletters you might like to subscribe to, covering topics like software development, security, DevOps, and Kubernetes:

- KubeWeekly (*https://twitter.com/kubeweekly*) (curated by the CNCF)
- SRE Weekly (*https://sreweekly.com/*)
- DevOps Weekly (*https://www.devopsweekly.com/*)
- DevOps'ish (*https://devopsish.com/*)
- Security Newsletter (*https://securitynewsletter.co/*)

Welcome Aboard

> We learn nothing from being right.
>
> —Elizabeth Bibesco

Your first priority on your Kubernetes journey should be to spread your expertise as widely as you can—and to learn as much as you can from others. None of us knows everything, but everybody knows something. Together, we just might figure things out.

And don't be afraid to experiment. Make your own demo app, or borrow ours, and try things with it that you're likely to need in production. If everything you do works perfectly, then you're not experimenting enough. Real learning comes from failures, and from trying to figure out what's wrong and fix them. The more you fail, the more you learn.

To the extent that *we've* learned anything about Kubernetes, it's because we've failed a lot. We hope you will too. Have fun!

Index

Jsonnet, 233

K

K8Guard, 105
Kapitan, 234
Keel, 253
KMS (Key Management Service), 196-199
Knative, 240
kompose, 234
kops, 44
KPIs, 284
kube-apiserver, 34
kube-bench, 106
kube-controller-manager, 34
kube-hunter, 207
kube-job-cleaner, 88
kube-lego, 175
kube-monkey, 108
kube-ops-view, 218
kube-proxy, 35
kube-ps1, 129
kube-scheduler, 34
kube-shell, 129
kube-state-metrics, 285
kubeadm, 45
kubectl
    abbreviated flags, 112
    abbreviated resource types, 112
    auto-completion, 113
    automation, 131
    commands
        apply, 60
        attach, 121
        cluster-info, 127
        config, 127
        create, 116, 182
        delete, 57, 116
        delete -f, 62
        describe, 55, 63, 116
        diff, 117, 119
        drain, 101
        edit, 116
        exec, 122
        explain, 114
        get, 30, 55
        get all, 63
        get componentstatuses, 214
        get nodes, 63, 214
        logs, 120

        port-forward, 30, 121
        run, 30, 56
        taint, 164
        top, 215
    contexts, 127
    features, 63
    flags
        --all-namespaces, 215
        --command, 124
        --container, 120, 122
        --follow, 120
        --restart, 124
        --rm, 123
        --selector, 112, 156
        --show-labels, 156
        --tail, 120
        --watch, 115
        -h, 113
        -it, 123
        -o, 118
        -o json, 114
        -o jsonpath, 115
        -o wide, 114
        -o yaml, 118
kubectx, 128
kubed-sh, 130
Kubeformation, 46
kubelet, 35, 58
kubens, 128
Kubernetes
    application deployment, 221-237
    backups and restoration, 208-213
    benefits of, 11-15
    cluster monitoring, 213-220
    cluster operation, 95-109
    configuration, 181-189
    container management, 135-153
    continuous deployment, 249-263
    development workflow, 239-248
    first steps, 21-31
    installation and management, 33-52
    Kubernetes objects, 53-67
    metrics, 279-306
    observability and monitoring, 265-278
    origins of, 11
    Pod management, 155-180
    resource management, 69-94
    Secrets, 189-199
    security, 201-208

tools and utilities, 111-133
Kubernetes Certified Service Provider, 104
Kubernetes The Hard Way (Hightower), 45
Kubespray, 44
kubespy, 121
kubesquash, 126
kubeval, 236, 256
kustomize, 234

L

labels
    Service matching, 62
    working with, 155-159
Lambda, 14
latest tag, 140
LimitRange, 81
limits, resource, 71
liveness probe, 72, 277
load balancer, 176
logs
    audit logging, 106
    information included in, 268
    limitations, 269
    viewing, 120, 130

M

managed services
    Amazon Elastic Container Service for
        Kubernetes, 42
    Azure Kubernetes Service, 42
    benefits of, 41
    cluster autoscaling, 42
    Google Kubernetes Engine, 41
    IBM Cloud Kubernetes Service, 43
    OpenShift, 43
    recommendations for, 47
manifest
    applying, 60
    introduction, 59
    templating, 223
    validating, 236
master nodes, minimum number, 36
maxSurge, 242
maxUnavailable, 76, 242
median, 289
memory utilization, 215
metrics
    alerting, 297
    application, 287

averages, 289
business, 284
cluster health, 286
containers, 286
dashboards, 293
deployments, 286
introduction, 270
percentiles, 290
radiator, 295
RED pattern, 282
runtime, 288
tools and services, 300-304
USE pattern, 283
uses, 279
MicroScanner, 207
microservices, 16
Microsoft Flow, 51
migrations, 245
minAvailable, 76
Minikube, 31
minimal containers, 72
minReadySeconds, 75
monitoring
    black-box, 265, 274
    definition, 265
    internal health checks, 276-277
    limitations, 267

N

namespaces
    default, 78
    kube-system, 78
    tools and utilities for, 127-129
    using, 77
network policies, 79
New Relic, 304
nginx-ingress, 176
nines of uptime, 267
node affinities, 90, 159
node-problem-detector, 218
nodes
    draining, 101
    GPU, 100
    instance types, 88, 99
    sizing, 84, 99
    status, 214
nodeSelectorTerms, 160

W

Weave Scope, 218
weights
    for soft affinities, 160
    helm.sh/hook-weight property, 247

purpose of, 161
    soft anti-affinities, 163
worker nodes
    components, 35
    failure, 36

About the Authors

John Arundel is a consultant with 30 years of experience in the computer industry. He is the author of several technical books, and works with many companies around the world consulting on cloud native infrastructure and Kubernetes. Off the clock, he is a keen surfer, a competitive rifle and pistol shooter, and a decidedly uncompetitive piano player. He lives in a fairytale cottage in Cornwall, England.

Justin Domingus is an operations engineer working in DevOps environments with Kubernetes and cloud technologies. He enjoys the outdoors, learning new things, coffee, crabbing, and computers. He lives in Seattle, Washington, with a wonderful cat and an even more wonderful wife and best friend, Adrienne.

Colophon

The animal on the cover of *Cloud Native DevOps with Kubernetes* is the Ascension frigatebird (*Fregata aquila*), a seabird found only on Ascension Island and nearby Boatswain Bird Island in the South Atlantic Ocean, roughly between Angola and Brazil. The eponymous bird's home island is named after the day it was discovered, Ascension Day on the Christian calendar.

With a wingspan of over 6.5 feet (2 meters) but weighing less than three pounds (1.25 kilograms), the Ascension frigatebird glides effortlessly over the ocean, catching fish that swim near the surface, especially flying fish. It sometimes feeds on squid, baby turtles, and prey stolen from other birds. Its feathers are black and glossy, with hints of green and purple. The male is distinguished by a bright red gular sac, which it inflates when seeking a mate. The female has slightly duller feathers, with patches of brown and sometimes white on the underside. Like other frigatebirds, it has a hooked bill, forked tail, and sharply pointed wings.

The Ascension frigatebird breeds on the rocky outcroppings of its island habitat. Instead of building a nest, it digs a hollow in the ground and protects it with feathers, pebbles, and bones. The female lays a single egg, and both parents care for the chick for six or seven months before it finally learns to fly. Since breeding success is low and habitat is limited, the species is usually classified as Vulnerable.

Ascension Island was first settled by the British for military purposes in the early 19th century. Today the island is home to tracking stations for NASA and the European Space Agency, a relay station for the BBC World Service, and one of the world's four GPS antennas. During most of the 19th and 20th centuries, frigatebirds were limited to breeding on small, rocky Boatswain Bird Island off Ascension's coast, since feral cats were killing their chicks. In 2002, the Royal Society for the Protection of Birds launched a campaign to eliminate the cats from the island, and a few years later, frigatebirds began to nest on Ascension Island once again.

Many of the animals on O'Reilly covers are endangered; all of them are important to the world. To learn more about how you can help, go to *animals.oreilly.com*.

The cover illustration is by Karen Montgomery, based on a black-and-white engraving from Cassel's Natural History. The cover fonts are Gilroy Semibold and Guardian Sans. The text font is Adobe Minion Pro; the heading font is Adobe Myriad Condensed; and the code font is Dalton Maag's Ubuntu Mono.

O'REILLY®

There's much more where this came from.

Experience books, videos, live online training courses, and more from O'Reilly and our 200+ partners—all in one place.

Learn more at oreilly.com/online-learning